CONTESTED TERRITORIES

LOWER GREAT LAKES REGION

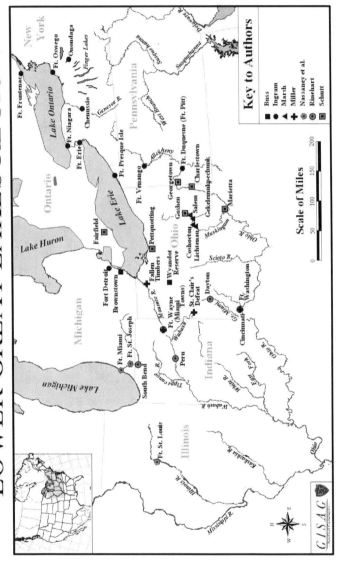

Key to Authors

- ■ Buss
- ● Ingram
- ▲ Marsh
- ✚ Miller
- ◉ Nassaney et al.
- ◉ Rinehart
- ▣ Schutt

Scale of Miles

0   50   100   150   200

New York

- Ft. Frontenac
- Ft. Oswego
- Onondaga
- Finger Lakes
- Ft. Niagara
- Chenussio
- Ft. Erie
- Genesee R.

Pennsylvania

- Ft. Presque Isle
- Ft. Venango
- Allegheny
- Georgetown
- Ft. Duquesne (Ft. Pitt)
- Charlestown
- Gekelemukpechunk
- Salem
- Goshen
- Coshocton
- Lichtenau
- Marietta
- Muskingum
- Ohio R.
- Scioto R.
- Susquehanna R.
- West Branch

Ohio

- Fairfield
- Petquotting
- Wyandot Reserve
- Fallen Timbers
- Ft. Washington
- Dayton
- Cincinnati
- Gt. Miami

Lake Ontario

Lake Erie

Lake Huron

Ontario

Michigan

- Fort Detroit
- Brownstown
- Ft. Miami
- Ft. St. Joseph
- South Bend
- Ft. Wayne (Miami Towns)
- St. Clair's Defeat
- Miami R.
- Wabash R.
- Peru
- Tippecanoe R.

Indiana

- Wabash R.
- White R.
- Ohio R.
- Eagle Fork

Illinois

- Ft. St. Louis
- Ft. St. Louis
- Kaskaskia R.
- Illinois R.
- Ohio
- Mississippi R.

Lake Michigan

N E S W

GISAG

CONTESTED TERRITORIES

Native Americans and Non-Natives in the Lower Great Lakes, 1700–1850

Edited by Charles Beatty-Medina and
Melissa Rinehart

Michigan State University Press
East Lansing, Michigan

♾ The paper used in this publication meets the minimum requirements of ANSI/NISO Z39.48-1992 (R 1997) (Permanence of Paper).

 Michigan State University Press
East Lansing, Michigan 48823-5245

Printed and bound in the United States of America.

18 17 16 15 14 13 12   1 2 3 4 5 6 7 8 9 10

LIBRARY OF CONGRESS CATALOGING-IN-PUBLICATION DATA

Contested territories : native Americans and non-natives in the lower Great Lakes, 1700-1850 / edited by Charles Beatty-Medina and Melissa Rinehart.
     p. cm.
     Includes bibliographical references.
     ISBN 978-1-61186-045-0 (cloth : alk. paper) 1. Indians of North America—Land tenure—Great Lakes Region (North America) 2. Indians of North America—First contact with Europeans—Great Lakes Region (North America) 3. Indians of North America—Great Lakes Region (North America)—History. 4. Great Lakes Region (North America)—History. 5. Great Lakes Region (North America)—Race relations. 6. Great Lakes Region (North America)—Politics and government. I. Beatty Medina, Charles. II. Rinehart, Melissa.
     E78.G7C66 2012
     977.004'97—dc23

Book design by Scribe Inc. (www.scribenet.com)
Cover design by Erin Kirk New
Cover image is *The Signing of the Treaty of Greenville* and is used courtesy of the Capitol Square Review and Advisory Board. Cover map of the United States of North America drawn by William Faden in 1796 is used courtesy of the David Rumsey Historical Map Collection (www.davidrumsey.com).

Frontispiece map created by Peter Lindquist, Ph.D., Director of the Center for Geographic Information Sciences and Applied Geographics (GISAG) of the Department of Geography and Planning at the University of Toledo.

Ⓖ green press INITIATIVE Michigan State University Press is a member of the Green Press Initiative and is committed to developing and encouraging ecologically responsible publishing practices. For more information about the Green Press Initiative and the use of recycled paper in book publishing, please visit www.greenpressinitiative.org.

Visit Michigan State University Press on at www.msupress.org

Contents

Foreword

GREG O'BRIEN

FEW GEOGRAPHICAL AREAS OF NORTH AMERICA EXPERIENCED THE DYNA-
mism of Indian-European interaction that the Ohio Valley and southern
Great Lakes offered prior to the mid-nineteenth century. Here was the land
marked by Native spiritual revitalization movements and prophets such as
Neolin (the Delaware Prophet) and Tenskwatawa (the Shawnee Prophet)
and their nascent pan-Indian movements. Here too were the great conflicts
enacted during the Seven Years' War (French and Indian War); Pontiac's
Rebellion; Lord Dunmore's War, the American Revolution; the multi-
tribal wars against the United States in the 1790s led by chiefs such as Little
Turtle (Miami), Blackhoof and Blue Jacket (Shawnee), and Buckongahelas
(Lenape); and the pan-Indian resistance to American expansion in the Old
Northwest led by Tecumseh and his prophet brother that coincided with
the War of 1812. Trade and interethnic cooperation also characterized the
region from the time when French fur traders first entered the region in the
seventeenth century through to the era of Indian Removal between 1830
and the 1840s. Trade brought material and cultural change to Indian peoples that sometimes worked in their favor and other times contributed to
the many conflicts that characterized the region in the eighteenth and early
nineteenth centuries. Missionaries and Euro-American settlers, especially
prominent in the region after the formation of the United States, further
added to both cultural change and occasional instability as they encouraged
Indian religious and cultural conversion along Christian patriarchal lines.
In this region can be found all of the issues deriving from Indian-European
relations, and as such, the Ohio Valley and southern Great Lakes continues
to offer up new insights into the fundamental frontier experience that characterized the colonial and early national periods of United States history.

The array of peoples in this territory during the era covered in this essay
collection demonstrates the multi-cultural reality of early America. Among
Indian peoples, we find Ottawas, Ojibwas, Potawatomis, Hurons, Miamis,
Weas, Kickapoos, Mascoutens, Piankashaws, Delawares (Lenapes), Shawnees, Wyandots, Mingos, Senecas, and other Iroquoian peoples. Of course,

over the eighteenth century and beyond, many Native villages here counted inhabitants from various different tribes, including French and British citizens. French farmers, fur traders, and missionaries lived in the region from the seventeenth century, and many of them stayed as France lost claims to the area after the Seven Years' War ended in 1763. During and after the Seven Years' War, British soldiers and farmers, as well as those from the German principalities, Scotland, Ireland, Wales, or born in the American colonies, came to live in the area. After the American Revolution, Americans of many stripes and European immigrants sought their future in the Northwest. With them came Quaker, Moravian, Methodist, and Baptist believers and missionaries to join Catholics already there. Native people followed a variety of belief systems too, from primarily traditional cultural outlooks, to the nativist teachings of Neolin and Tenskwatawa, to partial and full conversion to some version of Christianity.

Historians have long focused on this region because of its colorful personalities, and as the place where fundamental questions of colonialism and intercultural relations became and remained sharply focused. For over a hundred years before the 1830s Indian Removal actions, this locale became a border zone between European empires, between opposing Indian groups, and between Indians and Euro-Americans. From the seminal works of Francis Parkman in the mid-nineteenth century to the late twentieth-century studies by Gregory Dowd, Richard White, David Edmunds, and several others who helped establish the New Indian History, the Ohio Valley and southern Great Lakes remains a place that can help those studying Indian-European/American relations to find new perspectives into this formative period of North American history.

This collection makes a significant contribution to literature on Native people in the Ohio Valley and southern Great Lakes. The essays reflect the work of a new generation of historians and anthropologists who fill in some gaps in our understanding of Native–colonist relations in the region. The collection provides a solid ethnohistorical approach by incorporating historical and archaeological approaches and evidence. Most of the essays break new ground by studying this region and its various peoples in a crucial time period of rapid cultural, economic, and political change during the late eighteenth and early nineteenth centuries. As a whole, the essays reflect newer scholarly concerns with gender analysis, religion and prophetic movements, material culture, trade, and the internal political dynamics within Native groups. Especially noteworthy is the collection's effort to connect the colonial era with the early national and Indian Removal periods. Until relatively recently, ethnohistorians have usually limited their studies of Indian peoples or Indian-European/American relations to the colonial, early national, and post-Removal times. The newer approach exhibited by this volume helps to demonstrate the continuity of issues across these time frames, and provides readers a way to understand the long history of Indian-European interaction that is not dependent upon European and American governmental developments for a chronology. By placing Native people at the center of the story rather than on the periphery of Euro-American empires, we can see more clearly how particular geographic regions and particular groups of Native people changed over time and maintained links with more distant pasts. The editors, Charles Beatty-Medina and Melissa Rinehart, are to be commended for putting together a compelling and cohesive collection that helps to fill this and other gaps in the literature.

Contested Territories is an essay collection long in the making. I first encountered this manuscript in early 2010 when the authors submitted it to a series in ethnohistory that I then coedited with James T. Carson of Queens University in Canada. We liked the manuscript from the beginning and planned to see it published in our series. The collection's fundamental ethnohistorical focus, incorporating archival, archaeological, and ethnological research, is a model that we hope to see other volumes follow. Although ethnohistory as an academic field and approach to writing about American Indian history is well established, there are still countless new insights to be gleaned by explicitly combining the techniques and methodologies of history, anthropology, and Native interpretations. Books like this one are needed to display how this interdisciplinary approach yields new understandings of the Indian and American past. Unfortunately, fundamental administrative changes at the press we worked with caused Jamey and I to abandon our series, and we strongly encouraged Charles Beatty-Medina and Melissa Rinehart to pursue publication at another press. I am thrilled to see their efforts come to fruition with Michigan State University Press, and proud to have played a small role in its inception.

Acknowledgments

SCHOLARLY WORK DEPENDS ON THE ASSISTANCE OF MANY PLAYERS for its successful completion. This volume is no different. Its seed was first planted after a 2005 conference called Cultures in Conflict: New Perspectives on Encounters with Native Peoples of the Americas, where many of these essays were first presented. This conference brought together scholars studying all the regions where Europeans and Native peoples interacted in this hemisphere. It was co-organized by Charles Beatty-Medina and Professor Alfred Cave—who, though now retired, continues to benefit us all with his knowledge and expertise in Native American History. Tim Messer-Kruse (then History Department chair) generously agreed to provide funding for the conference—which further insured its success. We are grateful to the University of Toledo for providing the setting for that scholarly encounter.

The running of the conference itself would not have been possible without the organizational acumen of Deborah MacDonald, History Department secretary, and her able assistants (then graduate students, today history professors in their own right) Sarah E. Miller and Deborah R. Marinski. The idea to publish the conference proceedings came afterward. Through several proposals and interactions with publishers, it was decided that the best approach would be to take those presentations that focused on a specific region of the Americas and to collect them into a volume. Authors with scholarly interests in the same region were invited to contribute additional chapters, and the sum of that labor is contained here.

Gathering the authors for this volume was one thing; publishing it was another. We owe a debt of gratitude to Martha Bates at Michigan State University Press, who expertly ushered this book through the acquisition and peer-review process, and we are grateful to the reviewers for the suggestions and comments that we received. Along the way numerous editors and scholars aided our efforts. Since its instigation in 2005, the journey has indeed been an unforeseen odyssey, but one that brought us "home" in the end, and rendered us grateful for having had the experience. We are indebted to Melody Herr, Sarah Hoederman, Gary Dunham, Jamie Carson, and Greg O'Brien, for their input and for helping us develop the volume in the form that it appears here. Michael Nassaney kept us moving forward in spite of the challenges. Special mention needs to be made of the contribution by Professor Peter Lindquist of the Center for Geographic Information Sciences and Applied Geographics of the Department of Geography and Planning at the University of Toledo. His efforts and long hours gave us the wonderful map that opens the volume, thus providing essential points of orientation to the essays herein. The David Rumsey Historical Map Collection and the Capitol Square Review and Advisory Board at the Ohio Statehouse generously allowed us the use of their images for our cover art. We thank Annette Tanner at MSU Press for the beautiful graphics and all the MSU editorial staff: they have treated us professionally and wonderfully throughout the process.

In addition to excellent support from MSU Press we received exceptional assistance from scholars, colleagues, mentors, friends, and family along the way. Special mentions go out to Jeffrey Anderson, the late Susan Applegate Krouse, Lucy Murphy, Margaret Pearce, the Miami Tribe of Oklahoma, the Myaamia Project at Miami University, and the Miami Nation of Indiana. And we especially thank our families—Julian Charles Beatty-Duarte, Eloisa Duarte, Noemi Masters, Robert Masters, Ted and Leola Wilson, Ben Rinehart, Aimee Rinehart, Jim Rinehart, Pat Rinehart, Matt Buchanan, and Sedona Purdy. Thank you all.

Any omissions to this list are by no means intentional and any errors encountered in this volume are the responsibility of its editors and authors.

Introduction

THE LOWER GREAT LAKES REGION OCCUPIES A CRITICAL, IF OFTEN underrecognized, place in the history of America's post-Revolutionary westward expansion. During the eighteenth century and through the first half of the nineteenth century, areas that presently make up the states of Ohio, Indiana, Illinois, and southern Michigan, in addition to parts of Pennsylvania and New York, served numerous Native American communities. Wedged between the western frontier, the Upper Great Lakes, and the Eastern Seaboard of North America, most of this great swath of middle land made up what the U.S. Congress of the Confederation called the "Territory Northwest of the Ohio River." More commonly, it was referred to as the Northwest Territory. In this period, the region encased a Euro-American settlement gradient, a flow from east to west (and from south to north) in which the Great Lakes, and interlinked waterways, including rivers, streams, and swamps, served as important natural resources and highways for residents and travelers. The Great Lakes waterways, as Helen Tanner contends, are critical for understanding the history of the surrounding region.[1] Even a cursory examination of the map at the front of this volume demonstrates the intimate links between waterways, land, and human settlements.

Beginning in the seventeenth century, the different methods by which Native American communities and Europeans regarded and interacted with the land created new ethnogeographies in the Lower Great Lakes. In an age of Atlantic expansionism and competition, the region witnessed stark transitions through the second half of the eighteenth century as settler predominance switched and melded from French, to English, and finally American interests. James Taylor Carson proposes that greater consideration of this nexus between people and land is critical to understanding Indian/non-Indian interactions and resulting periods of mutual accommodation, conflict, and war.[2] Much was evident by the nineteenth century, when these ancestral landscapes of the Seneca, Delaware, Wyandot, Shawnee, Miami, Wea, Kickapoo, Ojibwa, Odawa (Ottawa), and Potawatomi peoples were contested by Europeans who were pushing for continuous expansion for settlement, agricultural production, and other projects—such as canal construction, in order to alter and thus "improve" the landscape.

Over the course of the nineteenth century, the Northwest Territory gained greater importance as settlement corridors traversed Pennsylvania, Ohio, Indiana, and Illinois. Thus, the Lower Great Lakes was the crux of economic and territorial power elsewhere. In the early movement of westward expansion, these lands became attractive to traders and settlers, as did the souls of Native American peoples to missionaries.[3] Euro-American penetration into the region contributed to an already diverse ethnogeography during the eighteenth and nineteenth centuries. Typically, newcomers had both violent interactions and peaceful exchanges with Native American communities through intermarriage, trade, and treaties. Native Americans, by turn, plied the waters between strategies of accommodation and a fierce ideological and physical resistance that often ended in conflict and bloodshed. In addition, the heightened movement and interaction among Indian peoples shifted local indigenous dynamics. In large part it is these various interactions—meetings, encounters, and engagements—that form the record of how Native Americans and Euro-Americans coexisted during the early republican period. Their imprint tells us much about how the new nation would interpret and elaborate its relations with the larger and culturally intensive territories of Indian peoples. A key goal of the essays in this volume is to interrogate these exchanges between Native Americans and Euro-American communities, and examine how they affected human outcomes in the Lower Great Lakes.

Mutual accommodation in the Lower Great Lakes evolved out of necessity. Richard White's seminal work *The Middle Ground* demonstrates how the region formed a space between cultures and peoples that mediated everything from daily interactions to formalized diplomatic relations between Native American and Euro-American communities.[4] Cultural mediation was flexible in the Great Lakes because power was defined and experienced differently within Native American and Euro-American communities. A middle ground made all parties' worlds more comprehensible, thereby lessening the need for bloodshed. This strategy, however, was not new to Native Americans: it already existed between groups like the Hurons and Iroquois prior to Indian-European contact, where mediation and negotiation mitigated unruliness.[5] Individuals like Miami chief Jean Baptiste de Richardville and William Walker Jr. (of Wyandot descent, and described by Rinehart and Buss in their respective essays) were thus products of the middle ground. Well-versed in Euro-American language and culture, yet also faithful (in their own ways) to their Indian languages and upbringings, these men led their communities in the face of persistent Euro-American aggression.

Although White contends that the middle ground faded after the War of 1812, the essays in this volume describe a different reality, particularly for those Indian communities in the Ohio Country in the period leading up to the Removal Era. Indeed, it appears that no single discourse governed cultural mediation during the middle eighteenth and nineteenth centuries. Instead, both Native American and Euro-American communities spoke on their own terms—navigating the best path toward individual and community interests. Indian desires to protect their ancestral landscapes from continued encroachment and exploitation developed, whether through accommodation, negotiation, or conflict, in order to ensure continued survival. Thus, their strategies spoke directly to the regional logic of political and environmental interactions, where Europeans sought ways to commodify land while isolating and removing Native American peoples.

Importantly, land held different meanings for Natives and Euro-Americans. Four biotic provinces linked by the region's waterways produced significant biodiversity throughout the Great Lakes. The Carolinian Biotic Province, also referred to as the Oak-Deer-Maple Biome, dominated much of northern middle North America—including southern Wisconsin, Michigan, Ontario, northern Indiana, Ohio, and Illinois.[6] This extensive area held a rich flora with variegated fauna that eased hunting, fishing, trapping, and gathering practices, but most critically, contained fertile soils ideal for horticulture. Native American exploitation of these natural resources required a sophisticated knowledge of the environment. In addition, the landscape held an ideological value for Native Americans. Carson has proposed a view of the region as a "moral space" and notes that the land steered the course of Native American economies and foodways, and it conditioned kinship and marriage practices, sociopolitical organization, community rituals, and language.[7] Many of these sociocultural constructs underwent alteration as interactions between Native Americans and Euro-Americans intensified. Indian economies and kinship patterns provided the backbone to political organization; however, this changed with intermarriage between Native American women and non-Indian men. The authority of Indian women was often devalued, aside from their assistance in the trade, and their domestic responsibilities shifted. In response to this changing cultural tide, Native American political organization often became centralized and patriarchal. Furthermore, ritual cycles formerly based on these localized environments were altered, especially as Christianity spread in conjunction with western expansion. Finally, Indian teachings based on longstanding oral tradition, rich with stories connected to their traditional landscapes, were usurped following the pressures of religious conversion and formal education. Such separations from their ethnoscapes, whether physical or ideological in nature, proved disruptive to Native American communities.

With the arrival of frontier capitalism through the fur trade, Native Americans focused on commodity production and eschewed earlier reciprocal interactions that existed between peoples and communities.[8] Beginning in the sixteenth century, the fur trade introduced a new exchange economy in Indian communities by commodifying natural resources. Beaver pelts became a key medium of exchange. Native American men and women worked as trappers and served as guides and interpreters for their Euro-American counterparts, with whom they exchanged pelts for goods like clothing, blankets, beads, kettles, and alcohol. Over time, the trade established a mutual reliance between Native Americans and traders. In addition to altering Indian economies, the trade transformed the physical landscape. Commerce complicated the seasonal round, when communities migrated for available natural resources. Increased traffic through Indian territories also led to the disappearance of game species, increased European settlement, land cessions, and intensive agriculture. The creation of Indian reserves and territories further dwindled the Indian land base.

Intermarriage between traders and Native American women has generated considerable scholarly interest over the past two decades. Studies by Sylvia Van Kirk, Susan Sleeper-Smith, and Jennifer Brown examine the social nature of the fur trade and the importance of marriage in strengthening ties between Native and Euro-Americans.[9] Among other things, they conclude that traders married Native American women to gain better access to the backcountry, while Indian women extended their roles as economic providers by working alongside their husbands. Although these marriages tended to be culturally and linguistically accommodative for both parties (in uneven and differentiated ways), from them evolved new concepts regarding gender roles and descent within Native communities. By introducing new familial hierarchies and a shift in domestic responsibilities, descent often shifted away from a unilinear system (matrilineality or patrilineality) toward a pattern of bilateral descent. In addition, missionaries and traders brought Christianity, introducing Catholic, Quaker, Moravian, Methodist, and Baptist teachings. Their preaching moved many women and their extended families to convert. Thus, polygamous marriages declined, family sizes decreased, and rituals and the roles of healers with their extensive ethnobotanical knowledge faded.

The majority of the essays in *Contested Territories* share a common theme of examining competition—typically for key resources in the Lower Great Lakes. From the mid-eighteenth to the mid-nineteenth century, alternating periods of war and peace marked relations among European colonials and their respective Native American allies. A short chronicle of the large-scale conflicts that affected the region provides a clearer image of the tensions that set the stage for localized interactions later. The mid-seventeenth-century Beaver Wars, so named for the quarry sought in the disputed Lower Great Lakes territories, involved the Iroquois and their Dutch and English trading allies desiring to expand their economic domains. After 1680, French-backed Indian communities such as the Miamis fought vigorously to maintain a presence in their ancestral landscapes, though many fled to present-day Wisconsin as refugees. Intercolonial warfare in the Michigan and Ohio Country, so named by Helen Tanner, led to massive displacement of Native peoples.[10]

The French and Indian War pitted the British against the French for imperial control over much of the eastern half of North America. Both countries made extensive use of Native American allies in continuous conflicts from 1754 to 1763. France's defeat brought with it a furthering of Britain's ascendancy. They won significant land cessions, including Louisiana, thus extending Anglo dominance throughout the eastern half of North America. For Native peoples, peace ended with the American Revolutionary War (1775–1783), yet they were divided over the Revolution. Most would defend British interests, as Indians feared losing their land to early American settlement. The Treaty of Paris in 1783, marking the formal beginning of America's independence, not only excluded Native American people, it officially ceded their lands between Appalachia and the Mississippi River. Native Americans, understandably troubled, would have to negotiate with Americans thereafter, and did so through a series of treaties until the Removal Era (circa 1830). However, episodic violence ensued as well.

Violent conflicts from the latter part of the eighteenth century continued into the nineteenth century as the United States established its policy towards Native peoples and lands on the frontier to Britain's reduced North American colonies. The Battle of Fallen Timbers, 1794, involved Native American communities in different ways. Both Americans and the British on the front exploited longstanding factionalism within Indian communities, and antagonisms between them. An Indian Alliance of several native American communities, including the Wyandots, Lenapes (Delawares), Shawnees, Odawas (Ottawas), Ojibwas, Potawatomis, Miamis, Weas, Kickapoos, and Kaskaskias, fought American armies and settlers in the Ohio Country.[11] Warfare continued until 1795 with the Treaty of Greenville, where signatories ceded most of the Ohio Country and areas including Fort Detroit (and present-day Chicago) in exchange for annuities, trade goods, and the maintenance of hunting rights. The treaty served as the catalyst for opening the Old Northwest. The war-torn region left Native American communities vulnerable to ongoing American settlement. From the non-Native perspective, an Indian presence impeded American expansion and even statehood; as a result, after the turn of the nineteenth century, Miami, Wea, Kickapoo, Illinois, Ojibwas, Odawa (Ottawa), Potawatomi, Shawnee, Delaware, and Seneca communities were pushed to sign treaties ceding their land and agreeing to various terms for relocation.

The War of 1812 involved four years of extensive fighting along the American-Canadian borderlands, as well as in the southeastern states. While the British were defeated, they did not retreat from the United States, nor did they cease to support their Native American allies. Still, Native American populations and their land base dwindled due to the cumulative effect of war losses, American settlement, disease, and intermarriage. Statehood was progressive, as Pennsylvania and New York entered the Union in 1787 and 1788, followed by Ohio (1803), Indiana (1816), Illinois (1818), and Michigan (1837). Epidemics, including smallpox, influenza, plague, and pneumonia, devastated Indian communities, while political contestation over the land rarely abated. Native American communities throughout the Lower Great Lakes faced expulsion and exclusion from continued participation in the early American landscape with the passage of Andrew Jackson's Removal Act in 1830, timed to diminishing European demands for beaver pelts, and earnest American settlement.

Native American dispossession continued its methodical march during the first half of the nineteenth century. Although Indian peoples sought ways to accommodate Euro-Americans, the passage of the Removal Act in May 1830 called for their expulsion west. In Indiana alone, five treaties were signed with Miami Indians in the years leading to statehood, and seven thereafter, with the Treaty of 1840 resulting in the removal of nearly half of their community.[12] These contests, therefore, were not only military, but involved the legal, ideological, and cultural outcomes of encounters and interactions. In some cases the outcomes were mixed, and Native American peoples struggled against losing every vestige of their homelands. For the first two decades following the passage of the Removal Act, eighteen tribes were forcibly relocated; however, removal did not equate to the disappearance of Native Americans in the Lower Great Lakes. Various individuals and clans from the Miami and Potawatomi communities, as well as others, successfully petitioned for exemptions from removal, while clans and individuals left only to return after the threat of removal abated. Dispossession and removal from these ethnoscapes impacted Indian communities deeply, "trigger[ing] a crisis of cosmology" that shook them to their cultural core.[13]

Indian accommodation during the post-Revolutionary period was diverse, and no single community defined the strategies employed. As Indian leadership changed, so did the rationale used to chart a course for their respective communities. Progressive and traditional factions led to tribal divisions that compounded the problem associated with their attempts to stave off removal collectively. While it is arguable that this led to an identity crisis for some communities (as Rob Mann asserts for the Miamis), it is less doubtful that intertribal dissent between progressive and conservative factions was, indeed, exploited by colonizers.[14] In this collection, Ingram, Marsh, Schutt, Rinehart, and Buss explore the exploitation of intertribal and intratribal political contestation, and the fallout from such antagonisms. While Native Americans and Euro-Americans accommodated one another, they did so with a keen perception of protecting their interests. Irrespective of the outcomes, these interactions became the root of Indian and Euro-American relations. As Daniel Barr notes, "Together they created a landscape of fluid boundaries and negotiated identities, a rapidly changing world where the possibility for accommodation or conflict ebbed and flowed with the context of local circumstances and individual choices."[15]

Indian villages, typically organized by kinship and status, became markers of clan and community identities, and during the late-eighteenth and early-nineteenth centuries, these villages became symbols of Native American autonomy. When Native land was marked, mapped, ceded, deeded, sold, or stolen, physical boundaries shifted and became subject to interpretation, complicating removal greatly. Native Americans who did not want to leave their homelands had support from non-Indians. Most missionaries wanted to continue their work with Indian communities, and traders wanted Indian communities to remain in order to ensure their exploitative enterprises. However, settlers' desires for agricultural land, and the federal government's collusion, trumped these collective interests, pushing Indians to various forms of resistance, treaty signing, and, ultimately, removal. Although Indian communities shared the ideological goal of remaining on their homelands, the diversity of their cultures, languages, and respective histories drove community autonomy differently. Alliances between Native Americans and others were altered depending on community and individual interests. Along with skillful leadership, Native Americans enabled many communities and individuals to remain in the region well beyond passage of the Removal Act.

In addition, Native peoples responded to change through the self-proclaimed prophets who emerged around the turn of the nineteenth century. These spiritual leaders sought to ensure a peaceful future for their followers. Concurrent revitalization movements, motivated by spiritual and political contingencies, attest to the cultural crises at the time.[16] The Shawnee prophet Tenskwatawa, frustrated by Iroquoian alliances with the British, exploitation by fur traders, increasing Shawnee war losses, land cessions, and alcoholism, motivated his call for a return to tradition.[17] Tenskwatawa's movement spread quickly, gaining acolytes among Indian communities in Michigan, Illinois, Wisconsin, Ohio, and Indiana. By blending spiritual and political ideologies, Tenskwatawa unintentionally created new ways of thinking and acting in the shifting dynamics of colonialism. Many prophets preached for a return to the old ways, while others—such as the Seneca prophet Handsome Lake—combined tradition with accommodation. Native traditionalism was the central tenet of his movement, as with other revitalization movements, but Handsome Lake supplanted it with selective borrowings from Euro-American culture that resonated with his followers. Prophetic teachings often led to community unrest where nativist and accommodationist factions evolved. Witch-hunts ensued in many communities—as described by Marsh, Schutt, and Buss in this volume—but even these failed as prophets became politically weak, and intratribal chaos and resistance ensued even after the Removal Era in some communities.[18]

Most prophetic movements failed to curtail American encroachment because they required absolute allegiance to their teachings (a topic explored in Marsh's chapter). However, their creative methods for fashioning change in order to improve Native lives cannot be discounted. As Gregory Dowd contends, these were not regressive, but innovative movements, which compelled many Native American communities and individuals toward action.[19] Prophetic movements demonstrate that from 1745 to 1815, pan-Indian unification premised upon the creation of common spiritual beliefs evolved into autonomous collectives that resisted colonialism. Native American peoples, prophets, and their followers alike were active agents directly challenging further cultural and political accommodation.

Native American responses to dispossession, factionalism, and removal affected every facet of life in the Lower Great Lakes. The essays in this volume testify to the struggle against Indian disappearance. This multivocal examination of autonomy between Native Americans and Euro-Americans builds upon a growing literature concerning the Northwest Territory and peripheral areas. Michael McConnell's examination of the Ohio frontier in *A Country Between: The Upper Ohio Valley and Its Peoples, 1724–1774* emphasizes autonomy among Delaware, Shawnee, and Ohio Seneca (Mingo) communities.[20] McConnell places Native Americans in the forefront of British and French struggles for the Ohio Country. Although not their ancestral lands, Delawares and Senecas identified the region as their historical homelands, and took defensive steps to maintain a viable presence. Shifting political allegiances with Europeans, and selective accommodation augmented by a larger pan-Indian nativist collective made the Indian presence in Ohio difficult to ignore. Nativist movements served as a further reminder that Indians were not leaving the Ohio Country without a fight. In *Elusive Empires: Constructing Colonialism in the Ohio Valley*, Eric Hinderaker compares Native American, French, British, and American interactions as "negotiated systems" premised more upon intercultural exchange than federal machinations.[21] Hinderaker offers an insider view of Indians, Euro-American settlers, traders, and others, eschewing bureaucratic dictates and focusing on Ohio Country residents. As Hinderaker demonstrates, a micro-analysis of historical events and event makers can provide a deeper understanding of how history was lived. The essays presented here offer similar approaches to McConnell's and Hinderaker's, along with an emphasis on Native American experiences and perspectives for accommodating and resisting Euro-Americans culturally, spiritually, politically, and economically.

The Ohio Country serves as a good example of the myriad of social, economic, and political interests held by Native Americans, the British, French, Americans, and other colonizers in the Old Northwest. Relationships between these groups during this period were litigious at best, and navigating the myriad of alliances, estrangements, and renewed associations became their primary focus toward maintaining or securing a presence on the frontier. Stephen Warren's work *The Shawnees and Their Neighbors, 1795–1870* takes a look at the Ohio Country and how early interactions with missionaries, traders, and bureaucrats led to changes in Shawnee political governance.[22] Through accommodationist strategies, consolidated leadership, and missionary alliances, the Shawnees managed to remain in the Ohio Country until 1832. Dawn Marsh and Amy Schutt explore strategies not so different from the Shawnees' in this volume. James Buss's essay also investigates Wyandot effort to avoid removal from Ohio, and Melissa Rinehart examines how Miami leadership shrewdly straddled accommodation and resistance in the Indiana-Ohio corridor. These essays further support the argument that Native American peoples in the Lower Great Lakes did not acquiesce to Euro-American expansionism quietly, only to become historical anecdotes. Instead, they fervently defended their autonomy in the most unique ways, and it is the goal of this volume to explore these individual stories.

The essays in this volume represent a diversity of perspectives on the Lower Great Lakes region that unpack the issues confronting Native Americans and Euro-Americans as they faced one another along a shifting frontier of culture, economy, diplomacy, and war. Together these chapters argue for a reassessment of Indian-newcomer interactions along the continuum of waterways and territories forming the Lower Great Lakes region. As such, this volume also complements R. David Edmunds's work *Enduring Nations: Native Americans in the Midwest*.[23] Here, Indian identity, agency, gender, and accommodation are thematically explored in order to consider how continuous engagement with Euro-Americans frequently reshaped economic and political orders. Through active participation, Native peoples quickly became influential participants in the greater political landscape. While many of the essays in Edmunds's volume originate from larger works, together they extend the discourse on Native American ethnohistories, revealing long-term Indian endurance in the Old Northwest. Similarly, *The Boundaries Between Us: Natives and Newcomers along the Frontiers of the Old Northwest Territory, 1750–1850*, edited by Daniel Barr, examines the tenuous—or as Barr states, the "porous"—nature of the middle ground in the Old Northwest.[24] Cultural interactions led to mutual accommodation, hostilities, and conflict. These processes are examined by scholars from various disciplines such as Donald Gaff, an archaeologist, who offers a distinctive look into three Miami leaders—Little Turtle, William Wells, and Jean Baptiste Richardville—through material culture. Similarly, in *Contested Territories*, Michael Nassaney, William Cremin, and LisaMarie Malischke look at the material culture of Fort St. Joseph to elucidate Native American and European interactions in southwestern Michigan.

Other works detailing Native American and Euro-American interactions during the Revolutionary period and later include Andrew Cayton and Frederika Teute's *Contact Points: American Frontiers from the Mohawk Valley to the Mississippi, 1750–1830*.[25] Although extending beyond the geography of *Contested Territories*, the essays in *Contact Points* offer a look into ethnic pluralism and the careful balance between accommodation and discord between Native Americans and Euro-Americans. Andrew Cayton and Stuart Hobbs's *The Center of a Great Empire: The Ohio Country in the Early Republic* contends that political and social hostilities and epidemic violence (also examined here in Sarah Miller's essay) dismantled the middle ground, thereby opening the region to settlement, pushing American borders further westward.[26] Similarly, in *The Sixty Years' War for the Great Lakes, 1754–1814*, Skaggs and Nelson investigate the strategic importance of the Ohio Country and how Native Americans and settlers fought for dominion over the land.[27] These works covering topics that include the effects of disease, missionary alliances, violence, and diplomacy support an underlying argument for the political importance of the Old Northwest and peripheral areas—and how contestation over this large corridor shaped the future of American expansionism.[28]

For the essays in *Contested Territories*, ethnohistorical methodologies have been employed to describe and analyze the changing dynamics of interactions between Native American and Euro-American peoples over two centuries during which the dynamics of European relations placed the Lower Great Lakes at the center of competing interests. These scholarly reconstructions depict the landscape, political organization, diplomacy, warfare, economic exchange, subsistence methods, material culture, as well as ritual and kinship practices that are significant in Indian and non-Indian discourse. Importantly, this volume's focus on resistance, changing worldviews, and early forms of self-determination demonstrates that non-Indian authority was never consummate over Native Americans, nor was Indian compliance with their assertions. The original perspectives offered in these essays revise scholarly understandings of the contested terrain of land and sovereignty that proved consequential for Indian and non-Indian communities. They also serve as a map of encounters throughout the Lower Great Lakes, emphasizing the continuous repositioning and interplay of actors and agency as numerous discourses governed eighteenth- and nineteenth-century interactions between Indian and Euro-American communities.

In "A Year at Niagara," Daniel Ingram explores the unique history of a key but lesser-known area in upstate New York—the Niagara River region, a formidable juncture along the Great Lakes passage linking the East Coast colonies to the Northwest Territory. During the eighteenth century, Niagara served as a main supply point for western trade posts, and the Seneca, other Iroquois, and British and French governments recognized its strategic importance. Examining the conflicts that rose in the Niagara region from a Chenussio Seneca perspective, Ingram invites us to strip the colonial narrative, driven by British strategic and material aims, and consider the 1763–1764 conflicts from a Seneca point of view. Seneca autonomy persevered as they astutely allied themselves with whichever colonial regime served their purposes best. They and their Iroquoian kin jockeyed for socioeconomic autonomy from British and French governments, while an Iroquoian dominion in the fur trade spread throughout many regions of New York,

Ontario, and Quebec. The Iroquois, disliking any restrictions placed on the trade, as well as relentless missionary efforts and unremitting European encroachment, were only pushed to compete more fiercely with European traders. As such, travel through the Niagara River region increased, as did the spread of disease, violence, and hostile diplomacy. Tenuous relationships between the Senecas, British, and French were offset by periodic violence and neutrality. Well aware of the true nature of their relationships, Native Americans who attended the British-hosted Niagara Peace Conference in 1764 benefited solely from the gifting and feasting offered them, while providing little war intelligence to their hosts in return.

Although European sources saw the Senecas' concession of the Niagara corridor as a mark of Iroquoian decline, here we see that Seneca policy and diplomacy encouraged favorable relations with non-Indian traders and authorities. This critical reframing helps us to gain insights into Native American motives as European commerce and competition brought conflict to the Lower Great Lakes. However, it was also the very expansion of the Atlantic fur trade that brought Native Americans and Europeans into closer, more intimate, and sometimes violent, contact. Through an analysis of eighteenth-century developments and milestones—the building of fortified posts, the increase in Indian wage laborers along the portage trail, France and Britain's war, and British policy after 1760—Ingram charts how Chenussios' interest remained tied to their land and its use within a context of commerce and settler encroachment. Ingram's close examination of Niagara points to the many ways that common concepts of space, usage, and communication itself, even when extensive, could be lost in translation.

Sarah Miller's chapter takes us to the Ohio Country, where violence became normative during the post-Revolutionary era. She examines the politics and ethics of these encounters, from 1783 to 1795, and considers how violence on the frontier existed in forms both sanctioned and unsanctioned. Violent attacks were not only military acts, but functioned as political chips in the Ohio Valley. Euro-American settlers and Native Americans acted on their own accord. Settlers repeatedly attacked Native Americans, contrary to American political and military desires, and young Indian warriors retaliated in spite of tribal leanings toward accommodation and neutrality. While government reports emphasized Indian atrocities, Indian agents and traders recognized that Americans were just as guilty. Accordingly, Miller demonstrates the limits of local authorities in curtailing violence within both camps, but continued treaty making with select members of those in the Indian Alliance only worsened matters—and many of the treaties were never seen as binding by Indian leaders. Federal treaty obligations were typically stalled or ignored, and Native Americans blamed the confusion and continued violence on the inefficient treaty procedure—the very process the federal government relied upon for peaceful relations with Indian peoples.

The treaty-making process was more efficient in dismantling tribal relations in the Ohio Country, and continued political inconsistencies raised tensions between and within Indian communities. These hostilities were further heightened by intolerance of Indians in the backcountry. As Miller asserts, retaliatory raids by any party typically compounded the problem; therefore, periodic violence continued until the Removal Era. Among other things, this essay reminds us that the process of white settlement and Indian response was not fully under the control of either group, but played out in hundreds, if not thousands, of individual interactions. At the same time, such interactions became an integrated part of the political engagements between United States and Native authorities. Notably, Miller's "foolish young men" illustrates a point made by Colin Calloway: that Indian and non-Indian communities imprinted patterns upon each other that, in certain aspects, made them indistinguishable.[29]

Archaeology and ethnohistory offer "comprehensive re-creations of the past," and Michael Nassaney, William Cremin, and LisaMarie Malischke illustrate this through material culture and historic evidence from the Fort St. Joseph site in southwest Michigan in their chapter. Constructed in 1691, this French mission/garrison/trading-post complex along the banks of the St. Joseph River served as a meeting place where French, Potawatomi, and Miami communities lived and worked together cooperatively until the 1760s, when the fort came under British control. Native American and European artifacts, including plant, animal, and structural remains, demonstrate that Indians and the French mutually accommodated one another in an interdependent society. Historical records also support the authors' thesis that the French relied on Indian knowledge of the region for hunting, gathering, and protection. Reciprocally, Miami and Potawatomi peoples at Fort St. Joseph relied on trade items like guns, brandy, and French expertise in metallurgy and carpentry. All parties were amicable opportunists for different reasons, and Fort St. Joseph exemplifies a middle ground, forged in southwest Michigan, where mutual accommodation strengthened cultural, social, political, and economic relationships.

Nassaney, Cremin, and Malischke's interpretation and analysis of the material remains at Fort St. Joseph provide invaluable insights into a world about to shift from commerce to settlement. The materiality of everyday life unearthed conveys an enhanced understanding of day-to-day interactions than the grand narrative. And, as Nassaney et al. make clear, cooperation typified Native American relations with Europeans when and where common understanding could be built. In addition, they remind us that Indian agency stood at the forefront of specific areas of interaction between Miamis, Potawatomis, and French traders/settlers. Moreover, this essay raises questions, Atlantic in scope, about the comparative methods and strategies of European competition for colonies, and how Native/non-Native interactions shaped relationships in the breach. Variances in colonial methods, and the relationships that grew from them, fomented completely different understandings and colonial realities within the Indian-European middle ground. The view from Fort St. Joseph, not yet dominated by English interests, provides a window into another world of Indians and Europeans, the meeting of cultures, and mutually formed alliances that occurred in the early- and mid-eighteenth century. The material basis of this view, afforded by the fort's archaeological remains, demonstrates a society deeply shared between Native American and European inhabitants.

Dawn Marsh's essay also examines sites of mutual acceptance during the second half of the eighteenth century. Focusing on the Lenapes and their history with missionary movements in Pennsylvania, this essay shows how Indian worlds intersected and were interpreted through contact with religious communities. Both Quakers and Moravians believed Delaware souls were eager for conversion, while the Delawares sought food, trade items, and loyal alliances with their missionary kin. Marsh asserts that missionaries and the Delawares held mutual objectives. Furthermore, complementary worldviews nurtured a lasting alliance with Quakers and Moravians—and, as such, Native American communities found common cause with these new settler groups, and their societies quickly began to shape one another in the late seventeenth century.

Marsh demonstrates that Indian relations with spiritually based groups did not follow a single narrative with a one-to-one history. While Quaker beliefs and policy continued to encourage mutual relations with Native Americans, Delaware Indians had physically and spiritually "moved on." Delaware leadership was divided over Moravian support. Some Delawares were more militant and joined Indian allies like the Shawnees, even allying themselves with the French to wage war in the backcountry. Prophets such as Neolin and Papoonan called for a return to Delaware traditions and the forsaking of all things European, including liquor, while other leaders wanted to strengthen missionary alliances with the Moravians. Although methods varied, all contenders shared an objective to coexist and thwart removal for the Ohio and Indiana Delawares. Tribal factionalism compounded by anti-Indian sentiment and subsequent human loss in the backcountry, as well as years of periodic famine and disease, splintered Indian communities. The experience of settlement, interaction, conflict, and alliance itself formed and reformed each group's ideas and approaches to such trans-ethnic community relationships.

While Marsh considers shifting relations between different missionary groups and the Delawares, Amy Schutt expands on the Delawares at the Moravian mission in Goshen. These essays, both focusing on displaced Lenapes, illustrate how examining the Lower Great Lakes at different levels of magnification and scale brings with it new perspectives. Attuned to the community fractures produced by Indian removals, Schutt picks up where Marsh leaves off, tracing lesser-known communities that remained allied to Moravians yet ambivalent about religious conversion. Although a small settlement, Schutt suggests that regardless of its size and brief tenure, this mission's history is not only worthy of greater examination, but offers additional insight into local responses to missionary agendas and a larger American agenda of Indian dispossession. In addition, this essay considers the network of communities and outposts that inhabited eastern Ohio, where places like Goshen became a temporary refuge to Indian peoples cast out of the eastern United States. Goshen Indians demonstrated their autonomy by traveling to distant stores, seeking temporary employment, and becoming literate.

As a detailed snapshot of a Lenape community aligned to a religious society, this essay examines the limits and opportunities presented by the Moravians' civilizing mission. Goshen offered the Delawares economic, social, and political stability as they went about their own business, whether purchasing trade items or hunting, which allowed them to travel on both sides of the Greenville Treaty line. Goshen, however, also served as a space of spiritual renewal for the Lenape, where Delaware prophets proselytized a message warning against Euro-American lifeways, while more accommodationist Delawares continued to convert to the Moravian faith. By the mid-nineteenth century, Lenapes would be moved once again; yet, as Schutt affirms, "the story of the Goshen mission complicates this familiar narrative of dispossession."

In the last two chapters, Melissa Rinehart and James Buss examine the period between the War of 1812 and passage of the Removal Act in 1830. As Buss observes, historical treatment of this period is typically overlooked. But, if examined closely, a better idea of the backstory to the metanarratives before and during the Removal Era in the Old Northwest comes into view. As these two chapters demonstrate, no two removal stories were alike, and the ways Native American communities responded supports Nassaney, Cremin, and Malischke's argument that interactions "between Natives and newcomers were neither inevitable nor predictable." As Buss asserts, "The end of the War of 1812 did not mark a direct line to removal" for the Wyandots, and this can be applied to the Miami removal story as well. Through strategic leadership, both communities asserted their autonomy, enabling them and their people to remain on the land for as long as possible. These were no small feats.

Melissa Rinehart's chapter charts Miami resistance to removal through the first half of the eighteenth century. The Miamis' long-held ability to ethnically reorganize—whether through intermarriage with French traders, immersing themselves in a market economy, or traditional belief systems such as Catholicism—provided them an advantage in negotiating with American traders, settlers, and bureaucrats. During the early part of the nineteenth century, settlers threatened Miami relationships with the land, pushing them to the treaty table several times, with each treaty diminishing the Miami land base. As Sarah Miller also discusses in chapter 2, selected Miami leaders were invited to the treaty table, inadvertently homogenizing Miami leadership and fracturing the greater community. Inconsistencies in the treaty-making process were clearly evident in pre-Removal diplomacy between the federal government and the Miamis.

Miami chief Jean Baptiste de Richardville, of mixed Miami-French ancestry, was a formidable figure. Recognizing that removal was slowly becoming a reality, he manipulated American bureaucrats in many ways. Until he signed the Removal Treaty of 1840, Richardville carefully excluded specific terms for removal in previous treaties, much to the consternation of Washington bureaucrats. Even though the Miami land base was shrinking, Richardville secured reserve lands for himself and others, and his family's exemption from removal in 1840. While these tactics may have been self-serving in part, through his astute leadership, the greater Miami community successfully thwarted removal sixteen years past the passage of the Removal Act, and several families retained a marginal land base. Other leaders and community members took Richardville's lead and secured land reserves as well as personal exemptions from removal. Trips to Kansas to inspect their new lands and to Washington, D.C., coupled with claims investigations, were also successful tactics for stalling the removal process. Why Richardville changed his mind about removal in 1840 is unclear, and even today, perceptions of his motivations inspire both reverence and odium. Problems within the tribe most likely led him to sign the removal treaty, as tribal debt was exorbitant, and alcohol wreaked havoc in the greater community, even within Richardville's own family. Nonetheless, between those who fled the region prior to removal and those who received official exemption from removal, more Miamis were able to remain in the East than those removed to Kansas. Rinehart reminds us that even through the successful use of tactics and strategies to resist removal, communities like the Miamis faced continuous challenges to their social and cultural structures. Indeed, those structures came under stress as the difficulty of maintaining their homeland east of the Mississippi mounted.

In the final chapter, James Buss examines the roles of mixed-race intermediaries in the Ohio Wyandot community, a group not unlike those referred to by Alida Metcalf in her study of colonial Brazil as "go-betweens."[30] In the fascinating case of William Walker Jr. (not to be confused with the nineteenth-century filibusterer) the go-between plays a role that clearly involves resistance shrouded by accommodationist rhetoric. Ohio Wyandots, like the Miamis, were against removal and struggled to remain in Ohio, and through shrewd leadership and clever alliances, they were successful in delaying their departure for over a decade. Wyandot communities experienced much internal strife concerning factionalism, alcoholism, and an increasingly mixed ancestral population. While nativist leaders refused aid from American missionaries and agents, the revivalist teachings of Tenskwatawa and Handsome Lake brought a renewed sense of community and traditionalism. However, factionalism grew in the Wyandot community between nativist and accommodationist members, and such differences led to conflict, including violence and witch-hunts. It became increasingly difficult for the Wyandots to maintain their autonomy as pressures to assimilate and remove from the Ohio Country mounted.

Like Miami chief Richardville, William Walker Jr., of mixed Wyandot ancestry, consolidated tribal leadership to stare down American encroachment, but in doing so replaced village autonomy. Missionaries attempted to obstruct Wyandot removal, and although contrary to their initial goals, tore the community in two. Infighting between the "Pagan Party" and Christian converts was common, and coupled with unabated American settlement made the Wyandots extremely vulnerable to removal. By 1841, a removal treaty was passed, and two years later, seven hundred Wyandots left the Grand Reserve. For the Wyandots, removal was mediated, not simply dictated, by Native American agency and ingenuity.

Together, the essays in *Contested Territories* provide a compelling portrait of the many groups—Native American, French, English, and American— that, in the eighteenth and nineteenth centuries, came to co-opt, defend, and contest their cultural, economic, and political spaces within the Lower

Great Lakes region. While much of the region's history and the essays in this volume verify Richard White's contention that peoples and their cultures "melted at the edges and merged" along the middle ground, this apparently did not suspend the conflicts that arose with the dust of the settlers' wagon wheels, nor did it end the process of removing Native American cultures of the Lower Great Lakes.[31] As Nassaney et al. offer in this volume, the broad metanarratives of the past do not serve the Lower Great Lakes sufficiently when trying to increase a better understanding of Native American and European-American relations. An attentive examination of the interactions between Native Americans and newcomers at the local level allows a more diligent look into the backstory of larger narratives. As Michel-Rolph Trouillot asserts, power influences history, and different groups often have competing contributions and narratives.[32] Humans retain the knowledge that propels history; therefore, everyone remains an active participant in history as actor, agent, and narrator. Native Americans in the Lower Great Lakes were agents of change and actors within a broader transformation; they propelled History just as non-native colonizers did. The ethnohistorical investigations into Native and non-native relations in *Contested Territories* examine the distinctive ways people enacted and responded to encroachment. In unearthing the complexities of Native/non-Native relations these essays revise what has often been an oversimplified vision of the Native and non-Native past.

NOTES

1. Helen Hornbeck Tanner, *Atlas of Great Lakes Indian History* (Norman: University of Oklahoma Press, 1987), 6. The atlas contains data on more than 1,500 Indian village sites in the region.
2. James Taylor Carson, "Ethnogeography and the Native American Past," *Ethnohistory* 49, no. 4 (2002): 769–88.
3. The most-cited text for missionary relations in Native American communities in the Great Lakes is Ruben Thwaite's edited volume *The Jesuit Relations* (Cleveland: Burrows Brothers Company, 1899).
4. This is the thesis proposed by Richard White in his work *The Middle Ground: Indians, Empires, and Republics in the Great Lakes Region, 1650–1815* (Cambridge: Cambridge University Press, 1991).
5. White, *Middle Ground*, 87.
6. Ronald Mason, *Great Lakes Archaeology* (Caldwell, NJ: Blackburn Press, 2002), 60.

7. Carson, "Ethnogeography," 769.

8. The French dominated the fur trade from the seventeenth to the mid-eighteenth centuries, while the British experienced their peak in the trade from the mid-eighteenth to the early nineteenth centuries. Americans dominated the fur trade from the early nineteenth century until 1850, when demand for pelts plummeted.

9. In *Many Tender Ties: Women in Fur Trade Society, 1679–1870* (Norman: University of Oklahoma Press, 1983), Sylvia Van Kirk explores the social history of the fur trade, where marriages sustained fur-trade society for nearly two centuries. Susan Sleeper-Smith in *Indian Women and French Men: Rethinking Cultural Encounter in the Western Great Lakes* (Amherst: University of Massachusetts Press, 2001) investigates the role Catholicism played in extending kin networks in fur-trade marriages; and Jennifer Brown's *Strangers in Blood: Fur Trade Company Families in Indian Country* (Norman: University of Oklahoma Press, 1996) looks at blood-reckoning as a result of fur-trade marriages, and how it reshaped family dynamics. A special edition of *Frontiers[0]: A Journal of Women's Studies* 29 (2008): 2–3, also examines intermarriage in different Indian communities.

10. Tanner, *Atlas of Great Lakes*, 6.

11. Also referred to as the Miami Confederacy, Indian Confederacy, and the Great Alliance.

12. *Indian Affairs: Laws and Treaties*, vol. 2, *Treaties*, compiled and edited by Charles J. Kappler (Washington, DC: Government Printing Office, 1904), available at http://digital.library.okstate.edu/kappler (accessed January 2011).

13. Carson, "Ethnogeography," 769.

14. Robert Mann, "The Silenced Miami: Archaeological and Ethnohistorical Evidence for Miami-British Relations, 1795–1812," *Ethnohistory* 46, no. 3 (Summer 1999): 399–427. This article examines the period prior to the French and Indian War in relationship to the Miamis' change of allegiance from French to British and back to French. These shifts of allegiance led to political divisions within the tribe that in turn led to geographical separation.

15. Daniel Barr, *The Boundaries Between Us: Natives and Newcomers along the Frontiers of the Old Northwest Territory, 1750–1850* (Kent, OH: Kent State University Press, 2006), xxi.

16. Gregory Dowd, *A Spirited Resistance: The North American Indian Struggle for Unity, 1745–1815* (Baltimore: Johns Hopkins University Press, 1993), 465.

17. R. David Edmunds, *The Shawnee Prophet* (Lincoln: University of Nebraska Press, 1983).

18. Alfred Cave, "The Failure of the Shawnee Prophet's Witch-Hunt," *Ethnohistory* 42, no. 3 (Summer 1995): 445–75.

19. Dowd, *Spirited Resistance*, 19.

20. Michael McConnell, *A Country Between: The Upper Ohio Valley and Its People, 1724–1774*, Lincoln: University of Nebraska Press, 1992.

21. Eric Hinderaker, *Elusive Empires: Constructing Colonialism in the Ohio Valley, 1673–1800* (Cambridge: Cambridge University Press, 1997), xi.

22. Stephen Warren, *The Shawnees and Their Neighbors, 1795–1870* (Urbana: University of Illinois Press, 2005).

23. R. David Edmunds, *Enduring Nations: Native Americans in the Midwest* (Urbana: University of Illinois Press, 2008).

24. Barr, *Boundaries Between Us*, xv.

25. Andrew Cayton and Fredrika Teute, *Contact Points: American Frontiers from the Mohawk Valley to the Mississippi, 1750–1830* (Chapel Hill: University of North Carolina Press, 1998).

26. Andrew Cayton and Stuart Hobbs, *The Center of a Great Empire: The Ohio Country in the Early Republic* (Columbus: Ohio State University Press, 2005).

27. David Curtis Skaggs and Larry Nelson, *The Sixty Years' War for the Great Lakes, 1754–1814* (East Lansing: Michigan State University Press, 2010).

28. For a contemporary look at Great Lakes peoples, see Rita Kohn and W. Lynwood Montell, *Always a People: Oral Histories of Contemporary Woodland Indians* (Bloomington: Indiana University Press, 1997). This anthology of contemporary Indian peoples originally from the Old Northwest includes interviews of eleven tribal members that demonstrate that the Great Lakes region continues to serve "as reservoirs of tribal tradition [1] . . . [that in part foster] a part of a continued Woodland People's consciousness [20]."

29. Colin Calloway, *New Worlds for All: Indians, Europeans, and the Remaking of Early America* (Baltimore: Johns Hopkins University Press, 1998), 1–2.

30. Alida Metcalf, *Go-Betweens and the Colonization of Brazil, 1500–1600* (Austin: University of Texas Press, 2005).

31. White, *The Middle Ground*, 50.

32. Michel-Rolph Trouillot, *Silencing the Past: Power and the Production of History* (Boston: Beacon Press, 1995).

A Year at Niagara: Negotiating Coexistence in the Eastern Great Lakes, 1763–1764

DANIEL INGRAM

IN EARLY SEPTEMBER 1763, THE BRITISH GARRISON OF FORT NIAGARA felt lucky. They had been spared the fates of Fort Michilimackinac and many smaller western forts that had been overtaken or destroyed in the Indian rebellion that would soon be named after the Odawa leader Pontiac. Niagara lay within the nominal country of the Senecas, and some of them had become disaffected with the British regime. Many of the westernmost Senecas living in the Genesee River area, often called Chenussios by their contemporaries,[1] had joined in the rebellion and may have played a role in fomenting the uprising in the first place. They had long been friendlier to the old French regime in Canada than most of their English-allied Iroquois kin, and they saw the uprising as a way to assert their influence in regional affairs. However, except for a few small skirmishes, mainly in Pennsylvania, the rebellious Chenussios had not yet subjected the Niagara region to the kind of violence that had roiled through the Great Lakes region earlier that summer. This was vital to British plans for quelling the uprising because Niagara was the main supply point for all the western posts, and any chance of relieving besieged Fort Detroit and stopping the rebellion would begin there. In the meantime, British representatives continued to parley for peace with western Indian groups. To that end, the sloop *Michigan* had sailed into Lake Erie on August 26, carrying provisions for Detroit's besieged garrison, and an Iroquois delegation to meet with Pontiac. The small delegation included Daniel Oughnour, a Mohawk friend of Sir William Johnson, the British superintendent of Indian Affairs for the Northern Department, and their mission was a routine peace negotiation. But, soon after the ship entered Lake Erie, it was cast ashore. The effort to reclaim its wreckage from the lakefront prompted a series of events that brought the full force of the Indian uprising to the Niagara region.

Niagara's role in the Indian uprising of 1763 has been less prominent in studies of the rebellion than more familiar events at Detroit, Michilimackinac, and Pittsburgh.[2] Pontiac and his allies in the Great Lakes region, the Ohio Valley, and Illinois have garnered more attention than the western Seneca group, despite the Chenussios' roles as early instigators and supporters of the rebellion, and their success in overthrowing Pennsylvania forts Venango, Le Boeuf, and Presque Isle in 1763. The Seneca attack at Devil's Hole on the Niagara portage is usually noted as an important British defeat, but second to the battles of Bushy Run near Fort Pitt, or Bloody Run near Detroit. Johnson's 1764 Niagara peace conference is often depicted as a smashing diplomatic success because it resulted in the supposedly desperate Senecas ceding control of the Niagara corridor to the British.[3] From the British military's point of view, and with the benefit of hindsight, these interpretations seem well founded.

However, studying these events from the Senecas' perspective complicates the picture. The Anglocentric vantage emphasizes Iroquoian social and military decline and economic dependency during the eighteenth century. The Senecas would have understood the events of the 1760s differently. For six decades, Senecas and their Iroquoian kin had worked to establish favorable economic and political relations with both the British and French governments in North America without taking part in European military conflicts. By the 1760s, the Six Nations Iroquois had become vital consumers in the Atlantic fur trade. They desired fair trade, political neutrality in European affairs, and, like nearly all Eastern Woodland peoples of the eighteenth century, restriction of white settlement in their country. But the Iroquois Confederacy was not a monolith; the Mohawk, Oneida, Onondaga, Cayuga, Seneca, and Tuscarora nations that made up the confederacy, and indeed each town within those nations, exercised significant autonomy in managing their own affairs. The Chenussios held long-established relations with French traders at Niagara, and viewed French defeat in the Seven Years' War and the new British military hegemony in the Great Lakes with trepidation. Restrictions on trade, rising prices of English goods, and the threat of English civilian settlement near Niagara gave the Chenussios common cause with Odawas, Shawnees, Ojibwas, and other groups in open rebellion against the British Great Lakes military regime of the early 1760s. There is little evidence of desperation or decline in this initiative; indeed, the Chenussios used time-tested military and diplomatic techniques to strengthen their position.[4] The Seneca attack at Devil's Hole made strategic sense, given the ever-increasing British presence at the Niagara Strait and the portage's vital importance for supplying Great Lakes outposts. The Senecas' subsequent cession of the Niagara corridor to the British in 1764 continued a diplomatic strategy employed by the Iroquois twice before in the eighteenth century, and the Chenussios had no reason to think that the cession would exclude them from the region or eventually reduce their influence over Niagara's affairs. From the summer of 1763 to the summer of 1764, Senecas and their allies operating near Niagara used the best methods available to them, both violent and diplomatic, to maintain the use of their territory and as much of their traditional lifeways as possible in the face of British economic and military expansion. They understood from long practice that maintaining cooperative relationships often involved both intimidation and acquiescence. Therefore, they sought a negotiated coexistence with British military neighbors who had clearly come to stay.

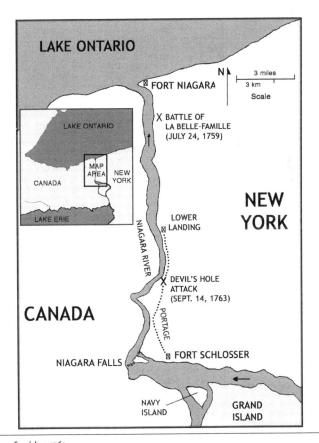

Niagara River Corridor, 1764

For centuries, Indian groups had traveled through the Niagara Strait, following a well-defined portage route around Niagara Falls. Archaeologists studying the Lower Landing site, near present-day Lewiston, New York, have found evidence of Native use from the Archaic stage (at least 3,300 years ago) through the French and British occupations of the region in the seventeenth and eighteenth centuries.[5] The Portage Site, located at the top of the steep Niagara escarpment where the portage path around Niagara Falls begins its decline to the Lower Landing, has produced artifacts that reveal continuous portaging since at least 1,000 C.E.[6] Substantial Indian portage around Niagara Falls is not surprising, considering the passage's strategic and practical importance. As French explorers realized by the 1670s, the portage was the only land carriage in a continuous waterway stretching between Lake Ontario and the Gulf of Mexico, and therefore represented an important key to the western fur trade.[7]

The seventeenth century was a period of upheaval for people living in the Niagara region. By the 1630s and 1640s, the peoples of the Iroquois League had become enmeshed as suppliers and consumers in the growing Atlantic fur trade. The five nations that made up the Iroquois League each played vital roles in supplying furs for European markets. The easternmost nation, the Mohawks, lived closest to Dutch traders in Fort Orange (later Albany) and French traders in Montreal and Quebec, and thus became involved deeply in the trade. The Oneidas, Onondagas, and Cayugas, who occupied the middle territories of Iroquoia in the Finger Lakes region of what is now upstate New York, hunted and hauled furs to Dutch or French traders, sometimes using the Mohawks as middlemen. The most populous nation of the league, the Senecas, occupied the western end of Iroquoia. Their territory extended from just west of the Genesee River Valley eastward to the Finger Lakes. When overhunting reduced the numbers of beaver and other fur-bearing animals by the 1630s, Iroquoians began to seek new hunting grounds to their west, north, and east. Mohawks began this expansion in the 1630s by attacking and dispersing some Algonquian groups in the Great Lakes region. Senecas followed by expanding into the Niagara River corridor. From 1638 through the 1640s, the inhabitants of this region, the Iroquoian-speaking Eries, Neutrals, and Wenros, vacated their territories in western New York and southern Ontario. An Iroquoian invasion of the Lower Great Lakes region followed. Senecas and other Iroquois attacked Eries, Neutrals, Petuns, Hurons, Odawas, Ojibwas, and Susquehannocks from the late 1640s through the 1670s, dispersing several towns throughout the Great Lakes region. By at least 1669, when French priest René de Bréhant de Galinée described the existence of a Seneca hunting village near the western end of Lake Ontario, the Niagara region had become a nominal Seneca domain. Historians have disagreed over the reasons for Iroquois expansion and its effect on Great Lakes peoples, but Seneca influence in the Niagara region of the late seventeenth century is not disputed.[8] However, Senecas and other Indians used the Niagara corridor as a highway and a place for hunting and fishing, not for permanent settlement; there is no record of a Seneca post on the Niagara River itself until 1707.[9] Niagara's strategic importance and lack of a large, permanent Native population therefore made it a natural target for French expansion by the end of the seventeenth century.

The French had begun the North American fur trade in the sixteenth century as an extension of their successful fisheries in the St. Lawrence Valley. By the early seventeenth century, they had established an advantageous alliance with the Hurons and had turned the fur trade into a truly transatlantic enterprise. This attracted competition, and by the years 1610–1620, Dutch traders had established themselves in the trade, especially with the Iroquois living closest to their Fort Orange entrepôt. Dutch-allied Five Nations Iroquois vied with French-allied Hurons and others for fertile hunting grounds, and to pillage furs and goods. Population losses from European-borne diseases led Indian groups increasingly to take captives as replacements for lost kin. By the middle of the seventeenth century, these escalating Beaver Wars, deadly cycles of violence, mourning, captive-taking (to replace lost kin), and revenge led to further population losses among many northeastern Indian groups. In the 1650s and 1660s, Dutch-allied Iroquoians sought peace with French officials in Montreal, but these truces never lasted long. However, French traders made the most of these brief periods of peace by exploring and expanding their fur trade into the Great Lakes region. In the 1670s English traders replaced the Dutch at Albany following British victory in the Anglo-Dutch wars. This severed the Five Nations' trade lifeline with the Dutch at the very time that Iroquoian animosities with other Indian groups, especially Susquehannocks in Pennsylvania, demanded a continuous supply of European arms and ammunition. The Iroquois made peace with the French in the 1660s and 1670s, but worked to maintain their trade with Albany under its new British proprietors. Senecas found keeping peace with the French especially difficult; they resented the efforts of French missionaries to spread European religion and culture in Seneca towns, and sought to limit the efforts of French fur trappers and traders in the west. By the 1680s, English-allied Iroquois began to intensify their efforts to restrict the French fur trade, leading to open warfare throughout New France from Illinois to the St. Lawrence. The French response would have long-lasting effects for Senecas and the Niagara region.[10]

In 1687 two thousand French troops under the command of New France's governor-general, the Marquis de Denonville, invaded the Senecas' territory in the Finger Lakes region. Denonville's invasion was destructive but short-lived. After burning the Senecas' corn crops, Denonville retreated to the Niagara frontier. There he built a small fort at the outlet of the Niagara River into Lake Ontario, believing that the outpost would keep the Senecas "in check and in fear" if properly garrisoned. Eight years earlier, explorer and trader René-Robert de la Salle had tried unsuccessfully to establish a trading post at Niagara. Denonville hoped his fort, along with Fort Cataraqui (later called Fort Frontenac) at the eastern end of Lake Ontario, would establish French dominance over the lake and its trade. He correctly guessed the Senecas would rebuff his attempt to control the Niagara passage and would seek to prevent French hegemony by enlisting the aid of the Iroquois' British allies in New York. The Five Nations had already met the year before with New York's governor Thomas Dongan, agreeing to tear down any forts the French might build south of Lake Ontario. In return, Dongan promised to assist the Iroquois against any French threats. He gave no credence to Denonville's argument claiming the region for France based on the small house La Salle built on the fort's site in 1676. Dongan demanded that Denonville abandon the fort and remove the four hundred men garrisoned there. Denonville relented in 1688, citing "the bad air, and the difficulty of revictualling that post," while noting that he had always meant the fort to be a place of refuge for threatened Indians, though none had used it for that purpose.[11] But, Denonville's abandonment of Niagara represented only a temporary pause in French plans to fortify the strait and the constant violence between the Iroquois and French-allied Indians in Canada, which continued through the following decade.

By the end of the seventeenth century, warfare and disease had depleted Iroquois ranks, and they began disentangling themselves from European conflicts. In 1700 Iroquois delegations visited Montreal and Albany to conduct peace negotiations that established the Five Nations as neutral middlemen in the economic and political struggles between New France and New York. British-allied Iroquois, led by Onondaga speaker and diplomat Sadekanaktie, knew that the French retained their designs to fortify the Niagara Strait and had already begun establishing a western post at Detroit, in what many Iroquois considered part of their territory. In July 1701, Sadekanaktie and other Iroquois leaders representing all of the five Iroquois nations met with

New York's lieutenant governor John Nanfan in Albany to establish Iroquoian neutrality and to ensure a peaceful continuance of Iroquois-English trade.[12] To counter French expansion, twenty Iroquois town leaders and chiefs granted the king of England a deed to their professed beaver-hunting grounds, which encompassed most of Michigan and Upper Canada between Lakes Michigan and Erie. The land cession included "the great falls Oakinagaro," or Niagara, and gave the British "power to erect Forts and castles" in any part of the ceded territory. In return, the British were required to protect Iroquois rights to hunt in the region forever, "free of all disturbances expecting to be protected therein by the Crown of England."[13] Of course, this "deed" was not a genuine land cession in either a legal or practical sense; western Native groups, many of them allied to the French, dominated much of the ceded territory. The French government in Montreal did not recognize the deed at all. Any British forts built in the land cession would still cause conflict between the European powers, with or without Iroquois permission. From the Iroquois viewpoint, however, the treaty was a bond of friendship and mutual protection with powerful allies that could be used to prevent destructive wars with both European and Indian enemies, and to continue a steady trade lifeline. Unlike the neutrality provisions of the 1701 settlement treaties, carefully negotiated and signed by Anglophilic, Francophilic, and neutral representatives of the Five Nations; French-allied western Indian groups; and the governments in Albany and Montreal, the Beaver Hunting Ground deed was a marginal factor in subsequent French-Anglo diplomacy. However, it demonstrated the Iroquois' hopes that maintaining amity with the British in Albany would give them leverage in their dealings with French authorities. As for the Niagara Strait, the Iroquois diplomats' insistence upon retaining perpetual hunting rights in the ceded region made it clear that Iroquois hunters and travelers intended to continue using the passage as they always had.[14]

The Iroquois did not undertake diplomacy of this kind lightly. The Iroquois League (separate from the Five Nations Iroquois Confederacy, the political-diplomatic body that formed in the late seventeenth century) existed specifically to ensure that peaceful relations and friendship could exist between its five member nations. The league was not an authoritative body; rather, Iroquois townsfolk, chiefs, leading men and women, and any men old enough to gain respect made the most fundamental decisions in Iroquois life. The fifty sacred sachems of the Grand Council of the league met at Onondaga once per year to renew their friendship, condole with each other for deaths, settle minor disputes, and seek continued peace. Because Iroquois peoples viewed interpersonal relationships through the lens of kinship, diplomatic alliances were truly friendships based on love and mutual responsibility. Reciprocity formed the fabric of these friendships; hospitality, gift-giving, and condolence rituals were more than exercises in expedient pragmatism. Reciprocal exchange, especially of material goods, represented the love and mutual kinship obligations that ensured peace and prosperity in the face of changing sociopolitical conditions and the constant pressures of the natural world. However, friendships, either between Iroquois kin or between Indians and Europeans, needed constant maintenance to ensure fidelity. Council fires, whether in individual Iroquois and colonial towns or at the Grand Council in Onondaga, were occasions where friendships, treaties and other agreements, and individual authority could be renewed, moderated, or rejected. By the beginning of the eighteenth century, the work of Iroquois-European diplomacy had been taken over by the Five Nations Confederacy, a more political body in which the authority of powerful village leading men took precedence over war chiefs, peace chiefs, and other sachems. Even with Europeans, the Iroquois configured relationships as fictive kinships, referring to European equals as "brothers" or "cousins," and European kings as "fathers." The texture of diplomacy remained the same in Indian-European relationships: the constant and careful maintenance of friendship through reciprocal exchanges. During the period of Iroquois neutrality, from 1701 to 1759, diplomacy would continually define and refine friendships among Iroquois nations and individuals, and between Indians and Europeans. In such a diplomatic atmosphere, where local autonomy was retained within the loose framework of the larger Iroquois Confederacy, it is not surprising that Chenussios might diverge in some ways from their Iroquois, and even their Seneca, kin.

Over the next twenty years, hundreds of French traders, settlers, and soldiers traveled over the Niagara portage, and Indian carriers, now wage earners, helped move the baggage. Exactly when Senecas began to work for wages on the portage is unknown. By 1707 Senecas had established a fortified post on the river, encouraged by Chabert de Joncaire the Elder, a French interpreter and adopted Seneca whose family would later establish a permanent trading post at the Lower Landing. It was largely through Joncaire's efforts, and those of his son Daniel, that Francophilic sentiment increased among the western Senecas during the early eighteenth century. By 1715, Senecas regularly worked with Joncaire as porters on the passage (and may have begun much earlier).[15] A 1718 memoir by an unknown writer includes a description of the porters' town: "Above the first hill [south of the Lower Landing] there is a Seneca village of about ten cabins, where Indian corn, beans, peas, water-melons, and pumpkins are raised, all of which are very fine. These Senecas are employed by the French, from whom they earn money by carrying the goods of those who are going to the Upper Country." When French *coureurs de bois* returned from the beaver grounds, the Senecas would accept peltry in lieu of currency for carrying their huge packs of furs around the falls. Some Native carriers were also said to "pilfer" to augment their pay. Of course, Indian wage laborers were also consumers. Seneca porters used their pay to buy *mitasses* (leggings), shirts, guns, ammunition, and other manufactured trade goods, including liquor.[16] Alcohol consumption was always controversial in the eastern woodlands of the seventeenth and eighteenth centuries. Wages spent on alcohol could not be used for basic necessities like clothing, food, or ammunition, and drinking introduced the same social and health problems into Indian culture that already existed for Europeans. Still, Senecas chose to act as consumers with the same degree of freedom enjoyed by their European counterparts. They enjoyed alcohol's intoxicating effect for both recreational and ritual purposes, and resisted efforts by both European and Indian authorities to restrict its sale. Seneca sachems oversaw the portage operation, possibly at the behest of the French portage operators, to prevent alcohol-fueled problems.[17]

Wage labor presented both pitfalls and benefits for Eastern Great Lakes Natives. Permanent Indian wage labor at Niagara and other locations, such as the Oneida portage in the Mohawk Valley, demonstrates the extent to which Iroquoian groups had become dependent on European trade goods and business. It also shows how some Indians living near Europeans found ways to coexist with the newcomers while retaining as much of their independence and way of life as possible in the face of these changes. By the early eighteenth century, hunting had long since moved from a subsistence activity to a way to procure consumer goods. Wage labor served the same purpose, and there is no evidence that Indian laborers gave up their cultural lifeways or identities any more than did hunters.

While some Senecas and Onondagas began migrating to portage locations to find paid employment in the early eighteenth century, France and England worked to position their eastern Great Lakes trading posts advantageously in the increasingly competitive fur trade. French posts erected at Detroit (1701) and Michilimackinac (1715) helped capture a good deal of the Great Lakes business, but French authorities never gave up on the idea of maintaining a substantial post at the outlet of the Niagara River, to grab the Upper Canadian trade before it could move into Lake Ontario and on to Albany. By 1720, Joncaire's diplomatic efforts paid off when some of the Chenussios allowed him to establish a small trading house at the Lower Landing site, about eight miles below the falls. Since 1701, the Iroquois had tried to establish themselves as neutral middlemen in the trade between western Great Lakes Indians and Albany traders, and prohibiting the construction of both French and British forts on Lake Ontario was essential in keeping trade flowing through Iroquoia.[18] Joncaire's new post represented a step backward for Iroquois middlemen, and a British post built in 1721 at Irondequoit—on Lake Ontario near modern-day Rochester, New York—eroded their policy further. In 1726, Joncaire circumvented the Senecas and appealed to a small group of Onondagas eager to prevent war between France and England. These Onondaga chiefs granted the French permission to build a new trading house at the site of Denonville's old fort. This fortified "house of peace," so called because the Iroquois disallowed new "forts" in their territory, formed the center of French and British occupation of the Niagara River for the next seventy years. With Joncaire's trading house at the portage and this new fort at the outlet of the Niagara, the French now exercised considerable control over trade passing in and out of Lake Ontario. Albany traders would have to offer substantially better prices to induce Indian consumers to bypass the new posts.

Over the subsequent years, Senecas would establish an even closer relationship with French traders and military men at the "house of peace," later called Fort Niagara. Though they resented the building of an armed French post, they determined to make the best of the situation by learning to coexist with its occupants. Senecas could continue to hunt and trade with both French and British traders as they had during the previous century. The building of Fort Niagara and the advent of Indian wage labor opened a new era of Seneca-European coexistence near the strategic river corridor. However, though this neutral coexistence worked reasonably well for Senecas, it angered New York officials and tested the Iroquois' ability to retain their neutrality.

Senecas and other Iroquois groups eagerly aimed to minimize the diplomatic damage caused by this new French incursion. At an Albany council in September 1726, New York governor William Burnet suggested to a small delegation of Onondaga, Cayuga, and Seneca sachems that they might show their friendship by reaffirming the little-enforced 1701 Niagara deed. This suited the Iroquois representatives, who hoped that the British king "would be pleased to defend them from the Incroachments of the French."[19] This new deed of "Surrender and Submission," signed by seven Iroquois sachems from three nations, once again gave Britain mastery "all along the river of Oniagara."[20] But, as with the earlier deed, the British role would be that of protectors rather than landlords, defending the ceded territory for the perpetual use of both Natives and the English military.

This new deed would have no greater impact on diplomatic efforts between Indians and Europeans than the 1701 cession. The French completed their fortified post at Niagara, and New York traders based in Albany built a new post at Oswego in 1727 to counter the French expansion and grab some of the Lake Ontario commerce. Furthermore, most Iroquois groups did not recognize the authority of the small negotiating team to represent the entire Iroquois Confederacy in ceding so much of their hunting land to the British. The fractious nature of Iroquois diplomacy, based less on the confederacy's unity than on village leadership and kinship ties, demanded that such agreements be constantly reviewed over subsequent council fires.[21] But, the deed exemplified the willingness of some Iroquois to play European diplomatic games for their own benefit. For example, a Seneca speaker, Kanakarighton, insisted that the Senecas had not given permission for the building of Fort Niagara. He promised to rebuke the Onondagas for allowing it, to resist further French encroachment, and to desist from listening to anti-British rumors (though he reminded Burnet that the English also spread rumors of "the Evil of the French, that they have from time to time deceived us"). But Kanakarighton made it clear that the Iroquois also had interests that needed to be maintained. He asked Burnet to restrict alcohol sales in Iroquois towns, to keep other colonial governors from breaching the peace (specifically the lieutenant governor of Virginia, Robert Carter), and, most importantly, to keep trade plentiful and prices low. "We must acquaint you how our fraternity came anciently, it came by the Trade," Kanakarighton reminded him. "We received the Goods in former times cheap, and we were convinced of Your goodness, but now the goods are sold to us dearer and dearer." He requested that prices be dropped, especially on gunpowder. "But do not lay powder on one side of the scale and Beavers on the other, that is too little powder," he stipulated. Finally, Kanakarighton asked for the return of a smith and armorer to service the Senecas, reminding Burnet to have these tradesmen "bring all their tools with them."[22] Burnet may have been angry about the construction of Fort Niagara, but this deed was not a forced Iroquois capitulation. Iroquois interests were at the heart of the negotiations. They could still use the Niagara corridor as they always had, and their increasingly powerful British allies would protect them. Iroquois diplomats understood that transference of land titles held great significance in European affairs, and they hoped that British negotiators might enforce the deed by discouraging further French incursions into Iroquois territory. In ceding these lands, Iroquois representatives gave away nothing, and expected to accrue diplomatic and material advantages they would need to negotiate their way through the complex economic and political climate of the eighteenth century.

Even with French Fort Niagara guarding the northern end of the strait and Little Niagara, a new fort commanding the portage's southern landing after 1751, France required the consent and cooperation of the Iroquois to maintain its control of the Lake Ontario trade. This was especially true regarding the Chenussios, who held significant power in the region. To maintain the Chenussios' approbation and contentment, French authorities at Niagara kept Seneca and Onondaga carriers employed at the waterfall portage and other land carriages in the region. By 1750, this had become an extensive operation. That year, Swedish traveler Peter Kalm reported seeing "above 200 Indians, most of them belonging to the Six Nations, busy in carrying packs of furs, chiefly of deer and bear, over the carrying-place" at Niagara, and noted that they received 20 pence for each pack they carried around the falls.[23] By mid-century, wage labor had become a viable alternative to hunting for some Chenussios and other Iroquois living near land portages.

In 1757, French officer Louis-Antoine de Bougainville confirmed the scope and importance of Indian carriers at Niagara and Fort Presque Isle (near modern-day Erie, Pennsylvania) and encouraged their increase. He noted that at Presque Isle, Indian carriers earned six francs per sack. This was twice the rate paid to French porters, but the Indians' superior abilities were worth the expense. Furthermore, Bougainville insisted that using Native carriers was both functionally and strategically necessary. "Policy demands that they be employed, especially in times of war," Bougainville reported. "When they are employed in portaging they hinder the tribes that might be badly intentioned from troubling our transportation." In addition, the wages they made allowed them to purchase necessities. "Without this resource they would turn to the English who deal with them much better than we do, and it is essential that they should not perceive this difference." Bougainville noted that it was just as "essential" to employ Indians at Niagara, where 250 to 300 trips traversed the portage each year.[24]

Despite their profitable relationship with Niagara traders, the Chenussios maintained some of their old antagonisms against the French portage operators. Their main complaint with French conduct of the portage was the increased use of horses and wagons, a military necessity for the French after the onset of the Seven Years' War, which threatened the Seneca carriers' wages. Onondaga chief Chinoniata spoke for the whole Iroquois Confederacy when he complained about the threat to Native livelihoods in a 1756 congress with New France's governor-general, the Marquis de Vaudreuil.

"Formerly when we were coming from war we had the Niagara portage; 'twas promised us that we would always possess it," Chinoniata reminded the governor. But lately, horses had been hauling more goods, and the Onondaga chief wanted the French regime to preserve the Seneca carrying concession on the portage.[25] These complaints may indicate a change in French policy at Niagara during the middle of the Seven Years' War, which Senecas would interpret as a breach of friendship and a threat to their livelihoods. A Seneca delegation visited Montreal in April 1757 and complained directly to Vaudreuil about the increased use of carts on the portage, arguing that Senecas had "formerly" handled all the portaging themselves. This implies that Indian porters may have been excluded from the Niagara carrying trade two years before the British took over Fort Niagara.[26]

Iroquoian nervousness may have been exacerbated by the expanded French military presence at Niagara since the outbreak of the Seven Years' War. The fort's garrison increased from about thirty soldiers and officers in 1754 to a defensive force of over six hundred in 1756. The fort itself was renovated and enlarged in 1756 to include expanded earthen breastworks and several new buildings. Throughout this period, western Indians continued to throng to the fort to trade—as many as two thousand at a time during the summer seasons. By the eve of British occupation, Fort Niagara and the Niagara portage had become major centers of cultural confluence. But the onset of French-British hostilities threatened Iroquoian neutrality as well. Chennusios and other Iroquois living close to Fort Niagara would be forced to take sides if the war spread to the Niagara region.

On July 6, 1759, the Niagara-based Senecas' lives changed abruptly. A few miles from Fort Niagara, a British force of 1,500 regular soldiers and 1,000 Indians from all six Iroquois nations, including some Chenussios, landed on the Lake Ontario shore to begin the siege and eventual conquest of the fort. Sir William Johnson had convinced several Iroquois groups to suspend their long-held neutrality and assist in the British reduction of Niagara and Montreal. Within the fort, five hundred French troops and about one hundred Indians, many of them Niagara residents, lay in wait. The presence of so many hitherto neutral Iroquois fighting men allied with the British created a dilemma for Niagara-based Senecas. Working at the portage had helped them maintain friendly relations with the fort's garrison and its commandant, Captain Pierre Pouchot. However, this new military alliance between the British and the rest of the Iroquois Confederacy placed Niagara Senecas in the middle of a conflict between their French friends and their own Iroquoian confederates. Pouchot's Seneca ally Kaendaé left the fort and negotiated a general Iroquoian withdrawal from the siege, a dubious achievement since siege work was largely the domain of engineers and artillerymen. Kaendaé then turned to Pouchot and negotiated an exit from the fort for his people. On July 26, two miles south of the fort at La Belle Famille, Johnson's British-Iroquois force defeated a relief army of over 1,500 French soldiers and Ohio-based Indians, probably Odawas, Potawatomies, Eries, Shawnees, Ojibwas, Wyandots, Miamis, and possibly Delawares. Without hope of relief, Pouchot surrendered. Fort Niagara and the portage passed into British control, and local Natives had to find ways to continue their European-Indian coexistence under a new regime.[27]

After the reduction of Fort Niagara, Indian superintendent Johnson was left with a problem concerning Senecas living nearby. Though their first allegiance was clearly with Pouchot and his garrison, they had remained neutral during the siege, and could hardly be barred from the Niagara region when they had not joined the French in arms against British forces. Johnson chose conciliation, telling Fort Niagara's new commandant, Hugh Farquhar, that local Senecas would be friendly "at least in appearance," and to "receive them with civility; give them provisions, and assure them that traders will soon arrive to buy their skins more to their advantage than ever the French did." But Johnson also warned Farquhar not to admit more than twenty Senecas into the fort at a time, even if they arrived in large groups.[28] Having given his orders to the fort garrison, Johnson turned to regional diplomacy. He made it clear to Chenussio leaders that he expected them to protect Fort Niagara and its new British garrison. To ensure their cooperation, Johnson sought to drive a wedge between the Chenussios and other Iroquoian groups. For example, Johnson heaped profuse thanks upon most of his Iroquois allies for their assistance at Niagara, giving them wampum belts and other gifts. However, he rebuked the Chenussios for their French sympathies, giving them only a thin black string of wampum and warning them to ensure the safety of the Niagara garrison lest the North American commander in chief, Jeffrey Amherst, "be obliged to take proper measures" to punish them. The initial returns of Johnson's diplomacy were not encouraging. Several Iroquois leaders promised that they would encourage the Chenussios to watch over Niagara, but made no guarantees for the garrison's safety. They then made it clear they expected more smiths, traders, and goods at posts throughout Iroquoia. The Iroquois Confederacy would help keep the Chenussios in line, but not for free.[29]

During the first year of British occupation, Fort Niagara's garrison helped prepare the portage trail for resumption of trade and, of more immediate importance during wartime, military traffic. Amherst planned an attack on Montreal and the rebuilding of Fort Presque Isle on Lake Erie, destroyed during the war; thus, constant traffic rolled through the portage.[30] Years of war and the siege left much damage at the strait. Fort Niagara required extensive rebuilding, Joncaire's trading post had been abandoned, and Fort Little Niagara had been burned down by a group of Indians from Johnson's detachment soon after the end of the siege. By the end of 1760, Fort Niagara's garrison had restored Little Niagara and improved the portage road enough to allow soldiers, wagons, oxen, and carts to transport military and trade goods previously carried by Indian porters.[31] Whether local Senecas approved or disapproved of the increased employment of wagons and animals is unclear. Neither Johnson nor Amherst mentioned any Indian complaints about lost portage jobs. But, as Amherst's subsequent activities demonstrated, the Chenussios still recognized the Niagara region as part of their country and hunting grounds, with or without Indians working at the portage.

Amherst felt that the best way to secure the portage would be to populate the area with British traders and families, to ensure friendly control of the portage and reduce the presence of Indians in the region. In May 1761, he licensed a group of former army officers to monopolize trade at Fort Little Niagara and to operate on the portage. The traders began building a settlement and raising corn, which Johnson feared would confirm the Chenussios' long-held suspicions that the British planned "rooting them out of their Country."[32] Johnson warned Amherst that such settlements would violate the 1726 agreement with the Iroquois, which restricted European settlement and reserved the Niagara portage area for the Crown's military use. The commander in chief refused initially to remove the traders, despite Johnson's urgent pleas that the Senecas would see the settlement as an attempted land grab. "It was never my design to take an inch from them," Amherst insisted, and he assured Johnson that the settlements were military necessities and not permanent.[33] Amherst's plans also upset Albany merchants based at Fort Niagara, who worried that traders at Little Niagara would scoop up all the Great Lakes trade for themselves. Under emphatic pressure from traders, Senecas, and Johnson, Amherst withdrew his permit, though he maintained his belief that civilian settlement was the best way to secure the Niagara region for Britain.[34]

Amherst's attempt to populate the Niagara region with settlers exacerbated existing Seneca tensions, and over the next two years Seneca-British relations deteriorated rapidly. In July 1761, Johnson heard rumors that some Chenussios disapproved of British efforts to garrison former French posts in the West and had sent two Seneca agents to Detroit to foment a general rebellion against British occupation of the Great Lakes posts. When

Johnson stopped at Niagara on his way to a Detroit conference, local Senecas stonewalled his attempts to ascertain the depth of imminent danger, despite dire Mohawk warnings that Senecas must give up their troublemaking or face the wrath of Iroquoian kin.[35]

Available alcohol helped fuel Indian animosities throughout the region. Indians expected gifts of alcohol upon visiting forts, and traders made rum easily available throughout the Great Lakes region. However, many Indians in the region disliked the social and economic effects alcohol and drunkenness brought to their towns and families, and petitioned for its restriction. For example, Mahicans led by Pápehánoak and Chickságan asked Johnson to restrict rum sales. "In case we have no redress therein we shall in a little time become naked," Chickságan told Johnson. "We therefore wish you'll prevent it being sold us hereafter, that we, and our Wives & Children, may be enabled to earn their bread." Johnson told them that Amherst had already ordered the restriction to prevent further "pernicious Consequences."[36] Johnson and Amherst hoped that restricting alcohol sales would prevent drunkenness and, more importantly, force Indians to trade furs for necessities. This would help make them less dependent upon gifts, which encouraged Indians to become "Slothfull and Indolent," according to Amherst. In early 1762, in response to urgent requests from the British commandants of Forts Pitt, Detroit, and Niagara, and from some Indians in the region, Amherst ordered alcohol sales suspended at all the western posts, including Niagara.[37] These new restrictions on alcohol sales and gift-giving in general only made a bad situation worse. Despite the inclinations of Amherst, Johnson, and some Native leaders, alcohol was an important and much-desired trade commodity and gift that many expected to be available. Consequently, by 1763, Fort Niagara's garrison found itself frequently beset upon by Senecas increasingly dissatisfied with the new British regime.[38] The situation worsened with the onset of the 1763 Indian uprising. Among the posts to fall that summer were Venango, Le Boeuf, and Presque Isle, a chain of forts between Lake Erie and Fort Pitt. Amherst and Johnson became convinced that Senecas were involved in those raids, and feared an imminent attack on or near Fort Niagara.

Senecas had reasons for rebelling against British hegemony that differed from the reasons of others involved in the uprising. Odawa war chief Pontiac and some of his followers desired a return to traditional lifeways and less dependence upon European trade. He and his fellow rebels, such as the Shawnee leader Charlot Kaské, cared about fair prices and honest trade practices, but they also interpreted British victory in the Seven Years' War as a social and cultural nightmare for all peoples of the eastern woodlands.

French traders had certainly disrupted Native lives with their goods, diseases, and European conflicts. However, they had kept their garrisons small, and limited white farming in most parts of New France to moderate levels. Settlers in British colonies sought to extend their agriculture-based economies into Indian country, which would wreak havoc on hunting, fishing, and other staples of traditional Native life. Pontiac used the theme of cultural renewal to attract participants to his cause. Only by rejecting European culture and returning to their old ways, argued Pontiac, could Native Americans maintain their independence. This message played upon pervasive Indian fears of losing their spiritual and cultural power. Though Pontiac's direct influence was mainly felt in the southeastern Michigan region, where he and his followers laid siege to Fort Detroit, he sent his message of cultural revitalization, along with wampum belts, throughout the Great Lakes basin and attracted many allies.[39]

Senecas cared more about preventing British settlement and preserving fair and plentiful trade than about Pontiac and his message of cultural renewal. For example, the Senecas who attacked Fort Venango and killed its garrison and commandant stated (in a letter signed by the fort's commandant just before they executed him) that inflated costs of powder and goods and lack of sufficient means to redress unfair trade practices motivated their assault. These factors, along with the establishment and maintenance of new British posts, convinced them that the British intended "to possess all their Country."[40] Johnson blamed the Senecas' disaffection on their proximity to Niagara, and feared that their exposure to "assiduous Missionaries" and "zealous Partizans" in Canada would ensure their continued loyalty to France.[41] By late July, small attacks near the Niagara portage threatened the safety of that vital British supply line, and Johnson feared for Detroit and the other upcountry posts if provisions could not be brought over the land carriage.[42]

Unlike other major Great Lakes forts, Fort Niagara did not face attack or siege during the Indian uprising, because an easier and more valuable target lay only six miles to the south. Fort Niagara had proven to be a poor guard over commerce traveling between Lakes Erie and Ontario because Indians could easily bypass the fort by land or water at night, trading their goods at Little Niagara or other posts on the lakes. Fort Niagara was in a strategic position for defense and refuge for soldiers, and for local Indians still friendly to the British. However, the crux of the region's defense was not Fort Niagara, but the portage itself. Most European goods moving into America's interior passed over the six-mile land carriage. Though the strategic importance of the portage was well known, the British conquerors of Fort Niagara had never fortified the portage path; only Little Niagara—which had been strengthened in June 1763 and renamed Fort Schlosser—and the small post at the Lower Landing protected the portage. With Chenussios now in open rebellion in Pennsylvania, traversing the Niagara portage through the Seneca rebels' own territory must have been terrifying for the civilian teamsters, with their slow ox carts and small military escorts. But, only small skirmishes troubled the land carriage until August 1763, when the loss of the *Michigan* prompted a chain of events that brought the full force of the Native uprising to Niagara.

Two days after the *Michigan* left Buffalo Creek, New York, bound for besieged Fort Detroit, leaks and bad weather cast the ship onto the south shore of Lake Erie about fourteen miles from the Niagara River, near the site of present-day Highland-on-the-Lake. With the help of army engineer John Montresor, a passenger on the *Michigan*, the shipwrecked crew erected a small defensive log breastwork and waited for help to arrive from Fort Niagara. Two companies of Major John Wilkins's regiment, encamped at Fort Niagara, arrived at the wreck site on September 2 in time to fight off a small Seneca attack. Mohawk diplomat Daniel Oughnour's presence prevented further Seneca attacks, giving Wilkins and his regiment time to organize a salvage operation. This was done with some trepidation because on September 7, Colonel Henry Bouquet reported rumors from Fort Pitt that a force of "800 Western Indians in 80 Canoes were gone towards Niagara to take Post at the carrying Place and cut off all communication with ye Detroit."[43] For days, wagons and oxen rolled back and forth across the portage with no sign of trouble. Couagne wrote that from the time of the attack on the wreck through September 13, the Senecas who had attacked the shipwreck allowed the wagon trains to "pass, and repass under an escort of 20, or 30 at most, with an Officer."[44]

On September 14, a large Native band, probably numbering just over three hundred men, attacked one of the convoys and its military guard. Two companies of British regular troops waiting at the Lower Landing hurried up the escarpment to aid the convoy and stumbled into a well-laid trap. Several soldiers were killed on the portage; others were forced over the steep cliff, where they plunged into the raging Niagara whirlpool called Devil's Hole. By the time relief arrived from Fort Niagara the following day, eighty men lay dead. The attackers escaped without suffering any serious casualties. To make matters worse, the attackers had slaughtered or stolen all the draft animals and hurled wagons and harnesses into the swirling rapids. Without the draft teams and wagons, the portage was cut off, as were all of the posts on the Great Lakes, including besieged Fort Detroit.[45]

Amherst and Johnson immediately set about repairing the damage and placing blame for the attack, and both found the latter easier than the former. Initially, they supposed that the attacking force was the same one Bouquet had reported the previous month, meaning that some of the Indians had come from western Great Lakes communities. But, all reports of the ambush identified Senecas among the attackers, and this was confirmed by the discovery of tracks leading toward Chenussio. With the onset of Seneca attacks on the portage, fear set in at Niagara and throughout the West. Amherst warned Bouquet to watch out for deception because the attackers had taken the uniforms of the dead soldiers.[46] Wilkins's relief expedition, bound for Detroit, was delayed for the year by devastating storms on Lake Erie, which wrecked several boats and killed even more British soldiers than the portage attackers. Provisions for Wilkins's winter camp at Fort Erie had to cross the portage on foot until fresh oxen and wagons arrived on September 25. Johnson warned of worse tidings to come. Knowing that the Chenussios were involved, he feared that "The Success which they met with, may perhaps Encourage all the Senecas to Joyn them, and . . . that Nation consists in the Whole of near *1000* Fighting Men."[47] Continued attacks on the portage, Fort Schlosser, and the Lower Landing throughout the fall of 1763 only exacerbated fears of greater violence in the Niagara corridor.[48]

Amherst believed that dealing quickly and harshly with the Chenussios was the answer to Niagara's problems. In November, he ordered Niagara's commandant William Browning to plan the destruction of Chenussio itself. "It will Ensure an Uninterrupted Communication from Oswego to Niagara," he promised, "And probably hinder any further Attacks on the Carrying Place." Amherst remained convinced that his plan to reduce the number of gifts given to Indians at the posts was sensible and just, despite growing suspicions that his restrictions were a major source of animosity among rebel Indians.[49]

In November, Amherst was recalled to London, and the new British commander in chief, General Thomas Gage, took over resolving the Indian uprising. He gave Johnson greater latitude to formulate Indian policy. Johnson sought to convince the new commander to deal leniently with the Chenussios. He argued that the Senecas were probably not instigators, but had been "drawn in as Auxilliaries" by other rebellious groups. He guessed that part of the Senecas' disaffection stemmed from the difference between "the present & former possessors of Niagara" and "the loss [the Senecas] sustained at the carrying place where they used to earn a good deal by transporting the Traders & Western Inds goods." Johnson asked Gage for permission to negotiate separately with the Chenussios and the rest of the Six Nations. He also suggested that the threat of British vengeance might be enough to induce the Senecas to make another cession of the portage to Britain for military use. Gage deferred to Johnson's deeper understanding of Indian affairs and allowed him to begin parleying with the Chenussios.[50]

Johnson's case for leniency was helped when Chenussio representatives took it upon themselves to begin peace overtures. The rebellion was slowing in the West, and France showed no signs of entering the conflict and retaking its lost North American territories. On December 15, three Chenussio deputies and more than two hundred delegates from other Iroquois nations met with Johnson at his new home in the Mohawk Valley. The Chenussios agreed to end hostilities against the British, blaming their involvement in the uprising on Delaware and Odawa instigation. Johnson dismissed their arguments as "insignificant & dissatisfactory" and warned that Gage would be unlikely to accept their offers of peace. Johnson left it to the Senecas' Iroquois brethren to remind them that if Gage sent a punitive force against Chenussio, the Iroquois Confederacy would not defend rabble-rousers who had endangered Iroquois-British amity. Conoquieson, an Oneida leader, scolded the Chenussios for endangering the "Covenant Chain" of peace between the Iroquois and the British. "Take Pity of your Children, and Families—consider also your Country, if you have any Regard for the same, and leave of[f] your silly Pride," he urged. "I speak only to you of *Chenussio*, as the rest of the Confederacy have nothing else in View but to keep up that Friendship with the English which has so long subsisted—do you the same, and perhaps you may live to have *white Heads*." The Chenussio deputies thanked the Oneida speaker for the advice. "You have really *shook* us by the *Head* so often, that we have not a Hair left on it," a Chenussio speaker joked. With most of the Iroquois Confederacy eager for peace, and Gage ready to send a punitive force against them in the spring, the Chenussios knew they had played out violence as a negotiating tactic. At the end of the conference, Johnson rewarded all the participants with currency except the Chenussio deputies, telling them that their returning home empty-handed "was owing to their own Folly, and Wickedness."[51]

In March 1764, Chenussio leaders traveled to Johnson Hall and gave Johnson exactly what he wanted, much to his surprise and delight. A delegation of British-allied Senecas from Kanadasego had subsequently visited the Chenussios and elicited their agreement to cease hostilities and to reaffirm their adherence to the Covenant Chain. The Seneca Nation agreed to deliver up two Indians accused of killing a trading party in 1762, along with all "Prisoners, Deserters, French men, and Negroes" who had taken refuge among them. They agreed to give free passage and assistance through their country to any British traders or military personnel, and promised not to communicate with any Indians warring against the British. As for the portage, the Senecas ceded to the king full rights to a strip of land fourteen miles long and four miles wide on both sides of the river, from Fort Niagara running south to Fort Schlosser. The Senecas agreed "never to obstruct the passage of the carrying place, or the free use of any part of the said tract," on the condition that the ceded tract "be always appropriated to H. M's sole use," and subject to boundary lines drawn with Seneca witnesses present to avoid disputes. In return, Chenussios who had participated in the uprising would receive full pardons and be restored to full membership in the Iroquois-British Covenant Chain alliance.[52] "The Chenussios & Enemy Senecas have been here several days," Johnson reported to Gage, "And after due consideration on the Articles of peace, have at length agreed to them beyond my Expectations."[53]

Johnson had wrested title to the portage from the Senecas, but as he prepared for a major peace conference to be held at Niagara in June, rumors and doubts still plagued the garrisons there. In April, a soldier was killed near the Lower Landing, and unidentified Indians still threatened the portage, harassing express riders and convoys.[54] Rumors flew through the region that a 2,000-man "western" Indian force, possibly composed of Odawas, Shawnees, Potawatomis, Ojibwas, or any number of other Great Lakes groups, had assembled and intended to attack either Detroit or Niagara. Though neither Johnson nor Gage believed the rumors, Johnson thought it prudent to send a body of Senecas and "a few Whites" to guard the portage. Meanwhile, Colonel John Bradstreet began organizing an expedition at Niagara to relieve the upcountry posts and to punish warring Indians, for which fortifying the portage became a vital priority.[55]

John Montresor and a detachment of 550 men arrived at Fort Niagara on May 19 to begin building a series of redoubts along the portage road, and to improve the defenses of smaller posts along the Niagara River. The engineer spent most of his time surveying the entire route of the portage, and the system of "cradles": rope-drawn winches and platforms installed to haul goods and bateaux up the escarpment above the Lower Landing. Reinforced by 110 soldiers from the 46th Regiment, Montresor's total command consisted of 656 men comprised of "Regulars, Canadians, Provincials, Indian Teamsters & Artificers." Their task was to guard the portage, build the redoubts along the portage road, and keep the wagon trains moving. With this large force in place, traffic on the portage began to increase; by June 4, provisions moved through the passage without armed escorts. A few days later, Montresor's men had finished their ten redoubts and began palisading and arming the small posts, improving the portage road, and cutting back the woods 150 yards on both sides of the path. By the end of the month, oxen and wagons carried hundred of barrels of goods per day across the route.[56]

Indians sent to guard the portage maintained a constant presence there during Montresor's efforts, though not always to the engineer's benefit or satisfaction. Indian disinterest in their mission, or outright hostility to the fortification effort diminished their effectiveness as protectors. On June 8, Native guards pursued three "enemy Indians" sighted near the portage, but were unable or unwilling to catch them. The nervous Fort Schlosser garrison mistakenly fired at thirty friendly Indians the following day, wounding three of them and angering the entire Native force. The Seneca guards' subsequent efforts to chase down "enemy" Indians were half-hearted at best. Even after the redoubts were finished, the Indian guards hesitated to disperse, remaining "as indolent and inactive as ever," according to Montresor.[57] Johnson's Seneca protectors probably provided an important deterrent to attacks by virtue of their presence alone, but they cannot have been happy to see the portage fortified. The new redoubts made the Carrying Place a vital, armed British outpost in the heart of Indian country, and represented a step backward for Seneca coexistence efforts.

While Montresor and his men labored to secure and improve the portage, and Bradstreet planned his expedition to retake and relieve the Great Lakes posts, Johnson prepared for a summer Niagara peace conference. Johnson chose Niagara because it was centrally located for Six Nations, Huron, Odawa, Ojibwa, and other groups participating in the rebellion, and because it lay outside the territory of the most belligerent groups in Illinois and the western Great Lakes. Of course, Niagara sat within the country of the Crown's other enemies in the uprising, the Chenussios, but this also served Johnson's plan to treat with the Senecas and the Great Lakes groups separately in order to drive a wedge between them and to prevent further collusion between rebellious Indians of the two regions.[58]

Indians throughout the Great Lakes had suffered for want of essential trade goods after the siege of Detroit and the fall of Michilimackinac and other trading posts the previous year. Johnson hoped to elicit promises of friendship from western Indians already well-disposed toward the British and eager for a renewal of trade. He planned to quell hostile groups through the threat of military force and the inducement of trade renewal. Finally, he desired Indian assistance for the punitive and relief expeditions to be led by Bradstreet and Bouquet later that summer. Johnson was optimistic about the diplomatic possibilities for the conference, but others remained skeptical. Bradstreet thought that Indians would come to Niagara "more for the sake of the goods they are to receive and to watch our Motions than any real service they intend us."[59] Indeed, Johnson intended to reward Indian attendees handsomely; £25,000 New York currency would be budgeted for Indian provisions at the conference.[60] News of the general conference must have seemed a blessing to Indians eager for trade and gifts and exhausted by war.

Johnson arrived at Niagara on June 9 to find that several groups of friendly Ojibwas, Odawas, and others from the western Great Lakes had been filtering in since May. These delegates quickly reminded Johnson of their friendship and promised the aid of their young men in Bradstreet's military mission. Most attendees denied any knowledge or participation in the uprising. Several professed great poverty and requested provisions, ammunition, trade goods, and especially rum, either through trade or as gifts. Johnson had expected to reward rebels who agreed to give up the hatchet, and was even happier to supply staunch friends who could be used to encourage peace in the embattled Lakes region. But, Johnson elicited little useful intelligence and met with few combatants early on; not until July 17 would Johnson meet with actual participants in the rebellion, a group of Hurons from the Detroit area who claimed that the Odawas forced them to aid Pontiac in his siege. So far, Bradstreet's suspicions had been partially justified: most visiting Natives saw the Niagara Conference as a trading rendezvous and an opportunity to receive gifts. Once there, they reaffirmed their attachment to British interests and friendship to Johnson and, either through actual ignorance or willful dissemblance, gave the superintendent little useful war intelligence.[61]

Indians at the conference took full advantage of opportunities for trade and recreation, and an abundant supply of rum helped lubricate the latter. Johnson had hesitated to allow rum sales at the conference, but after conferring with Gage, he conceded to the inescapable reality of Native consumerist demand. Conference visitors could purchase a gallon of rum for one beaver skin, half the price of a stroud blanket or a calico-lined bed gown.[62] Montresor complained of several episodes of Indian drunkenness during his tenure at the portage, from his arrival in May, when a group of Ojibwas and Mohawks left Fort Niagara for the portage "almost all Drunk," to June 13, when intoxicated Indians in the portage encampment threatened to kill army captain Andrew Montour. On July 17, Montresor reported that the 1,200 Indians attending the conference were being given "Rum and Oxen" to "regale with."[63] Trader Alexander Henry also ran into problems with frolicking delegates. He arrived on July 10 in command of a 96-man "Indian battalion" from the Lake Erie region, which he ordered to Fort Schlosser to join Bradstreet's expedition. After visiting Fort Niagara and receiving provisions and gifts, most of them left immediately for home. The fourteen who stayed went on to Fort Erie and drank until Bradstreet cut off their liquor. Then they went home, too, leaving an embarrassed Henry without his battalion.[64] In addition to any serious diplomatic motives, and to the occasional detriment of British military plans, war-weary Indians intended to enjoy themselves at Niagara.

Although most attendees were already friendly to the British and treated the conference as a trade jamboree, Johnson was still determined to convey his main diplomatic message: that resumption of trade in the Great Lakes region depended on the cessation of violence. "What you suffer by this pro-hibition," Johnson told a group of friendly Odawas from Michilimackinac, "Should convince you of the ill consequences of Quarreling with the Eng-lish who Command all the Doors into your Country & without whose Consent you can receive no Supplys." Johnson made it clear that those loyal to the British must make every effort to curtail other Indians' belligerence. "Soon as that is done," he told the Odawa leader Bildanowan, "Trade will immediately flourish, & not before."[65] Native attendees seemed amenable to Johnson's argument, professing their noninvolvement, blaming the uprising on "those Indians who became drunk [lost their good sense]," and asking for Johnson to "Indulge them with a fair Trade."[66] Johnson felt that his efforts at marshaling friendly Indians to discourage Great Lakes combatants were successful. But, Pontiac and other enemy leaders did not show up at Johnson's conference, and by July 23 neither had any Chenussios. A peace arrangement with at least one of the major hostile groups was needed for the conference to be called a success.

Amid the general commotion caused by a major Indian conference and the muster and organization of Bradstreet's large invasion force, the absence of the region's masters, the Chenussios, must have added great tension for soldiers and Indians alike. They had not yet complied with their treaty obligations; nor had they delivered all the prisoners, British deserters, and slaves demanded by Johnson. To make matters worse for the British, a band of unfriendly Delawares had taken refuge near Chenussio, despite Seneca promises to join the British in opposing rebellious Delaware and Shawnee groups.[67] Johnson began to spread dire warnings among conference attend-ees about the terrible consequences that would ensue if the Chenussios did not arrive and fulfill their treaty requirements.[68] But the Chenussios had a perfectly good reason to delay their arrival, though Johnson did not know it at the time: a rumor had spread in the Genesee region that the Brit-ish could never forgive the Devil's Hole attack, and that Johnson would order the Chenussios' destruction as soon as he had the chance.[69] Without a conclusion to the Seneca peace treaty, the portage would not be secure, and Bradstreet's military expedition would leave behind a threatened Niagara.

Much to Johnson's (and everyone's) relief, the Chenussio messengers arrived on July 23 and agreed to hold a general meeting the next day. Johnson rebuked them for breaching their treaty obligations and for keeping him waiting so long at the conference. At the meeting the following day, Johnson lost no time in bringing up his latest sore point. "I little expected you would have been capable of Acting so bad a Part," he scolded the Seneca delegation, "As to give shelter to the Enemy Delawares, after the Promises made by your People last Spring." He also noted that they had brought only four prisoners from Chenussio. Johnson told them that they must deliver up the Delaware ringleaders within thirty days and leave two of their chiefs as hostages, or Gage would cut off their trade indefinitely. A Chenussio chief, Tohaditkarawa, answered that their whole party had not yet arrived with the rest of the prisoners, and they were prepared to comply fully with the April treaty. "We Chenussios acknowledge ourselves to be great Transgressors," the chief admitted. He promised to provide young men to fight in the West and to finalize their cession of the land around the Niagara portage. However, they regretted not being able to supply the two "murderers" of the trading party as stipulated in the treaty; one of the assailants had died recently, and the other fled upon hearing he was to be given up. The Chenussios hoped their failure to deliver the suspects would not be considered a breach of the treaty. "We are not Masters over the Lives of our People," the Seneca chief glumly reminded Johnson, who knew well how Iroquois community politics worked.[70]

On August 5, the Chenussio delegates agreed to deliver the Delaware leaders Squash Cutter and Attyatawitsera to Johnson, and they handed over a total of thirteen prisoners and one British deserter. They also provided Bradstreet with twenty-three young men for his expedition. "The most of our People being drunk ever since they came here, we are not yet able to collect any more," the Chenussio speaker apologized, but promised to supply more fighting men as soon as his people finished celebrating.[71] Johnson's only alteration of the original deal, aside from the requirement to deliver over the Delaware leaders, was an augmentation to the land cession. "I would further recommend it to you to give a higher Proof of your friendship," Johnson insisted, "that you should cede to his Majesty the Lands from above your late Gift, to the *Rapids* at Lake Erie on both sides of the Straights, in Breadth as the former, and to include all the Islands."[72] With this new cession, England would have the entire Niagara Strait from Fort Niagara to Fort Erie, four miles in breadth on both sides, "for (the King's) sole use, and that of his Garrisons, but not as private property."[73] The Senecas agreed to the augmentation of the land cession, though they insisted on designating the islands in the Niagara River as a present for Johnson. "We have for some time had it in view to give them to you as a small Reward for your great trouble, and Care of us," the Senecas told Johnson, eager to prevent further British-Seneca hostilities. Johnson accepted the islands for diplomatic reasons, but never intended to keep them for himself. He later turned them over to the Crown along with the other ceded territory.[74] The final treaty, signed by seven Chenussio sachems, gave Johnson assurance of a safe British portage protected by Seneca neighbors. In turn, Johnson's stipulation that the cession would be for military use and not for civilian settlement gave the Chenussios assurance that the sociopolitical status quo would be protected, albeit at the cost of an increased British military presence. Chenussios had escaped punishment, and remained free to use the Niagara River region as they had previously. From their point of view, coexistence had been maintained.

Despite his lofty goals of western pacification, Johnson's main accomplishment at the Niagara Conference was in laying groundwork for the British subjugation of Niagara itself. He did not know the Chenussios' intentions toward the British until the very end, and Bradstreet's expedition to the western Great Lakes was held hostage to this uncertainty.[75] For their part, the more than two thousand western Indians who attended the conference did well for themselves. They were rewarded for their past friendship, allowed to trade at Fort Niagara, and charged only with encouraging warring Indians to put down the hatchet. In the end, the conference was more about the security of the Niagara passage and resumption of trade in the West than it was a harsh subjugation of Indians participating in Pontiac's Rebellion. Pressured by Johnson's economic coaxing and the warnings of other Six Nations groups, the Chenussios seemed to have given up control of the most strategically important land carriage on the Great Lakes to the sole remaining European power in eastern North America. However, they suffered no punishment and paid little for their attack on the portage, and maintained the right to hunt, fish, and travel through the Niagara corridor. But, at the end of this turbulent year at Niagara, much remained unresolved.

Johnson was optimistic about the future of the portage when he wrote the Lords of Trade on August 30 to boast of his success at Niagara. "The cession made by the Senecas is very considerable, and will, I hope, put a stop to all future disputes about the carrying place," he wrote, noting that the Senecas "have been great loosers [*sic*] by us concerning it." Johnson explained that when the French possessed Niagara, the Senecas enjoyed the sole carrying concession on the portage, but under the English regime, oxen and wagons had replaced the Indian carriers.[76] Gage and Johnson briefly discussed returning this concession to the Chenussios to retain their cooperation. As long as goods kept moving through the Niagara corridor to support the fur trade and provision the forts, it would not matter to the king or the Lords of Trade who carried them; however, it might mean much to the Senecas because of their former employment there.[77] But, keeping local Senecas happy was not the only rationale for renewing their carrying concession. British carriers had been a source of frustration for the army and traders throughout 1765. John Stedman, the civilian portage master who had survived the Devil's Hole attack, was not in the army's good graces that year; in fact, Bradstreet caught him overcharging the Crown and replaced him briefly.[78] Gage did not trust any of the "waggon men," insisting that they would leave military stores to rot if a fur trader paid them more to bring his trade goods across.[79] At the end of 1765, Gage still considered the possibility of a Seneca carrying concession at Niagara.[80] But, economic and military necessity had come to dictate events at the portage, and keeping wagons and goods moving edged out Indian diplomacy.

Senecas would never work at the portage again. While Gage and Johnson considered restoring Indian carriers, Stedman and his military partner, Lieutenant Francis Pfister, had already established themselves among traders as the sole portage masters. Rather than shake up the system, Gage awarded Pfister and Stedman the concession in March 1766, and allowed Pfister to set up shop at Fort Schlosser. This would entail Pfister's planting corn and keeping cattle at the fort, which worried Johnson just as much as when Amherst had proposed the same arrangement four years earlier.[81] Indians always objected to "the Establishment of familys, which they know will encrease (when once a beginning is made)," he wrote to Gage, and he agreed to talk to the Senecas before they interpreted the expanded settlement as an insult. But, the portage trade had become lucrative for Gage's British contractors, and their successful enterprise at the portage ensured that Senecas would never again work as carriers at Niagara, and that ever more Europeans would begin to move into the region to stay.[82]

With their role as masters of the Niagara region diminishing each year, Senecas began to act out their frustrations. Local Senecas began stealing animals, harassing portagers, and making incessant demands on Fort Niagara's garrison for gifts. In coexistence as in diplomacy, Senecas based their relationships on reciprocity. If their roles were to be diminished at Niagara, they would take whatever compensation they could find.[83]

As British-Seneca animosities increased over the ensuing years, Indian agents such as Daniel Claus blamed the frustrations on the Chenussios' loss of the portage carrying trade, which he claimed had greatly "enriched" the Seneca nation.[84] This began a persistent tradition of overstating the importance of the Chenussio carrying trade at Niagara. The myth that the Devil's Hole attack was a Native labor uprising, and that wage labor at the portage constituted a major source of overall Seneca revenue, endures to the present day. But, there is scant evidence of any Indians working as carriers at Niagara under the British regime, except during Montresor's fortifying mission from May to August 1764, and every reason to think that Native portaging ended during the French tenure. Neither is there any evidence that the Devil's Hole attackers had any connection with Native portage workers. Johnson himself noted that the Chenussios never stipulated any interest in the carrying concession during their 1764 talks.[85] Wage labor at the portage was undoubtedly important to those Indians who performed the work under the French regime, and it established visibly the Senecas' influence at Niagara while it lasted; but it was not the cause of the Senecas' rebelliousness toward the British.

From the summer of 1763 to the fall of 1764, Chenussios used familiar methods to preserve a solid footing in the face of increasing European expansion. They had always occupied a middle position between the French in Canada and the English in New York. But, after the British triumph in the Seven Years' War, they foresaw a new economic and political climate where the price of goods could rise without possibility of redress, and their hunting lands might be subject to white settlement. Some of them took action immediately after the British victory in 1761 by unsuccessfully trying to stir up rebellion in the West, while more turned to actual violence to achieve their ends during the Indian uprising of 1763. When the Devil's Hole attack worsened their negotiating position by ensuring the fortification of the important Niagara portage, Chenussios turned away from violence and returned to the tactics of the early eighteenth century. They gave away a strip of land that had already been given away in 1701 and 1726, and with almost the same terms as before. As long as they could pass freely through the lands to hunt and fish, they risked nothing. Agreeing to Johnson's terms ensured that none of their people would be punished for the Devil's Hole attack, one of the worst losses to British arms in the entire Indian uprising. But, the situation had changed in the thirty-eight years since their last cession of the Niagara corridor. In 1764, British military authorities and traders had the economic and demographic means to begin settling the Niagara region. Contrary to Seneca expectations, and unlike their two earlier deeds, the Treaty of 1764 would eventually turn out to be a true land cession.

Fort Niagara, the Carrying Place, and Indian wage labor were all manifestations of the European fur trade, and they all worked toward the same ultimate, if sometimes unconscious, goal: remaking Indian country for the Europeans' benefit. Indians operating as suppliers and consumers in the fur-trade economy made the best of it, and that sometimes included performing manual labor for wages, a livelihood that seldom "enriched" anyone, despite what Daniel Claus and others may have thought. But, Chenussios and other Native participants in the rebellion of 1763–64 did not fight against European encroachment and change to preserve wage labor. They fought to protect their customary use of Indian country, where they had hunted, lit council fires, and buried ancestors for generations. The year that stretched from the summer of 1763 to the summer of 1764 showed Chenussios attempting to maintain more than a few jobs carrying packs around a waterfall. They joined the rebellion and attacked at Niagara to establish their power and defend their territory. When the rebellion ceased, they agreed to a treaty that they thought would preserve their rights to live and hunt on their traditional lands at the cost of a negotiated coexistence with familiar British military personnel. Neither the Chenussios nor their new British landlord-tenants understood the full extent to which events were already moving out of their control.

NOTES

A version of this essay was published previously in *Indians and British Outposts in Eighteenth-Century America* by Daniel Ingram (2012). It appears here with the permission of University Press of Florida, Gainesville.

1. Chenussio is an orthographic variation of "Genesee" or "Geneseo" commonly used in eighteenth-century English and French documents. It refers to the western Seneca group, its people, and their primary town on the Genesee River in northwestern New York. This Seneca group is sometimes called the western Senecas, Genesees, or Geneseos in ethnohistorical studies. This essay uses the term Chenussios to avoid confusion with material quoted from the primary documents.

2. Francis Parkman, *The Conspiracy of Pontiac and the Indian War after the Conquest of Canada*, 2 vols. (Lincoln: University of Nebraska Press, 1994);

Howard H. Peckham, *Pontiac and the Indian Uprising* (Detroit: Wayne State University Press, 1994); William R. Nester, *"Haughty Conquerors": Amherst and the Great Indian Uprising of 1763* (Westport, CT: Praeger, 2000); Gregory Evans Dowd, *War under Heaven: Pontiac, the Indian Nations, and the British Empire* (Baltimore: Johns Hopkins University Press, 2002); David Dixon, *Never Come to Peace Again: Pontiac's Uprising and the Fate of the British Empire in North America* (Norman: University of Oklahoma Press, 2005); Richard Middleton, *Pontiac's War: Its Causes, Course, and Consequences* (New York: Routledge, 2007). An exception is William Parmenter, "Pontiac's War: Forging New Links in the Anglo-Iroquois Covenant Chain, 1758–1766," *Ethnohistory* 44, no. 4 (Autumn 1997): 617–54.

3. Nester, *Haughty Conquerors*, 191, 193, 208. Dixon, *Never Come to Peace Again*, 228.

4. J. A. Brandão and William A. Starna, "The Treaties of 1701: A Triumph of Iroquois Diplomacy," *Ethnohistory* 43, no. 2 (Spring 1996): 209–44; Kurt A. Jordan, *The Seneca Restoration, 1715–1754: An Iroquois Local Political Economy* (Gainesville: University Press of Florida, 2008), 1–25.

5. Stuart D. Scott, *An Archaeological Survey of Artpark and the Lower Landing, Lewiston, New York* (Lewiston, NY: Edwin Mellen Press, 1993), 7–17.

6. Marian E. White, "Late Woodland Archaeology in the Niagara Frontier of New York and Ontario," in *The Late Prehistory of the Lake Erie Drainage Basin: A 1972 Symposium Revised*, ed. David S. Brose (Cleveland: Cleveland Museum of Natural History, 1976), 115–16.

7. Frontenac to Colbert, November 14, 1674, in *Documents Relative to the Colonial History of the State of New York*, ed. E. B. O'Callaghan and Berthold Fernow (Albany, NY: Weed, Parsons, 1853–1887) [hereafter *NYCD*], 9:116–21; Marian E. White, *Iroquois Culture History in the Niagara Frontier Area of New York State* (Ann Arbor: University of Michigan, 1961), 50; Frank H. Severance, *Studies of the Niagara Frontier* (Buffalo, NY: Buffalo Historical Society, 1911), 315, and *An Old Frontier of France: The Niagara Region and Adjacent Lakes under French Control* (New York: Dodd, Mead, 1917), 1:35.

8. Daniel K. Richter, *The Ordeal of the Longhouse: The Peoples of the Iroquois League in the Era of European Colonization* (Chapel Hill: University of North Carolina Press, 1992), 50–104; Richard White, *The Middle Ground: Indians, Empires, and Republics in the Great Lakes Region, 1650–1815* (New York: Cambridge University Press, 1991), 1–49; Heidi Bohaker, "'Nindoodemag': The Significance of Algonquian Kinship Networks in the Eastern Great Lakes Region, 1600–1701," *William and Mary Quarterly*, 3rd series, 63, no. 1 (January 2006) [hereafter *WMQ*]: 23–52; Thomas S. Abler and Elizabeth Tooker, "Seneca," and Marian E. White, "Neutral and Wenro" and

"Erie," in *Handbook of North American Indians*, vol. 15, *Northeast*, ed. Bruce G. Trigger (Washington, DC: Smithsonian Institution, 1978), 409–10, 415–16, 506–7; F. Dollier de Casson and R. B. Galinée, *Exploration of the Great Lakes, 1669–1670*, trans. and ed. J. H. Coyne (Toronto: Ontario Historical Society Papers and Records 6:1, 1917), 176.

9. *NYCD*, 9:805.

10. Richter, *Ordeal of the Longhouse*, 1–161.

11. Denonville to Seignelay, May 8, 1686, *NYCD*, 9:287–92; Lawrence H. Leder, ed., *The Livingston Indian Records* (Gettysburg: Pennsylvania Historical Association, 1956), 101; "Establishment of the French at Niagara," *NYCD*, 9:335–36; "Examination of Adandidaghko," *NYCD*, 9:435; Dongan to Palmer, *NYCD*, 9:476; "Dongan's First Demand of French Agents," *NYCD*, 9:520–21; "Journal of Denonville and Champigny," *NYCD*, 9:393–98.

12. "Conference of Lieutenant Governor Nanfan with the Indians," *NYCD*, 4:896–908.

13. "Deed from the Five Nations to the King of Their Beaver Hunting Ground," *NYCD*, 4:908–11.

14. *NYCD*, 4:909–10.

15. *NYCD*, 9:805–8; Severance, *An Old Frontier of France*, 1:163.

16. "Memoir on the Indians between Lake Erie and the Mississippi, 1718," *NYCD*, 9:885; "Enumeration of the Indian Tribes Connected with the Government of Canada, 1736," *NYCD*, 9:1057; Beauharnois to Maurapas, November 7, 1744, *NYCD*, 9:1111–12.

17. Peter C. Mancall, *Deadly Medicine: Indians and Alcohol in Early America* (Ithaca, NY: Cornell University Press, 1995); Beauharnois to Maurapas, November 7, 1744, *NYCD*, 9:1112.

18. "Proposal to Take Possession of Niagara in Canada, 1706," *NYCD*, 9:773–75; Journal of Schuyler and Livingston," *NYCD*, 5:542–45; "Journal of Lawrence Clawsen's Visit to Niagara," *NYCD*, 5:550–51; Robert Livingston to Peter Schuyler, August 23, 1723, *NYCD*, 5:559–60; Cadwallader Colden, "Colden's Account of the Conference between Governor Burnet and the Five Nations, 1721," in *Collections of the New York Historical Society* (New York: New York Historical Society, 1868–1975), 50:128–34; Burnet to Lords of Trade, June 25, 1723, *NYCD*, 5:684–85.

19. "A Conference Held at Albany," *NYCD*, 5:799.

20. "Deed in Trust from Three of the Five Nations of Indians to the King," *NYCD*, 5:800–801.

21. Mary A. Druke, "Linking Arms: The Structure of Iroquois Intertribal Diplomacy," and Richard L. Haan, "Covenant and Consensus: Iroquois and English, 1676–1760," in *Beyond the Covenant Chain: The Iroquois and Their*

Neighbors in Indian North America, 1600–1800, ed. Daniel K. Richter and James H. Merrell (Syracuse, NY: Syracuse University Press, 1987), 29–57.

22. "Conference between Governor Burnet and the Indians," *NYCD*, 5:795–97.

23. Severance, *Studies of the Niagara Frontier*, 326.

24. Louis-Antoine Bougainville, "Memoir of Bougainville," in *Collections of the State Historical Society of Wisconsin* (Madison, WI: State Historical Society of Wisconsin, 1854–1931), 18:180–83.

25. "Indian Conference," *NYCD*, 10:503.

26. "Account of the Embassy of the Five Nations," *NYCD*, 10:559.

27. M. (Pierre) Pouchot, *Memoir upon the Late War in North America between the French and the English, 1755–60*, ed. and trans. Franklin B. Hough (Roxbury, MA: W. Elliot Woodward, 1866), 1:165–206; "The Prideaux and Johnson Orderly Book," in *Papers of Sir William Johnson*, 14 vols., ed. James Sullivan et al. (Albany: University of the State of New York, 1921–65) [hereafter *WJP*], 3:48–105.

28. "Orders for William Farquhar et al.," *WJP*, 13:156–59.

29. "Journal of the Niagara Campaign," *WJP*, 13:120, 149, 156.

30. Brian Leigh Dunnigan, "Portaging Niagara," *Inland Seas* 42, no. 3 (Spring 1986): 181–82.

31. Johnson to Amherst, July 31, 1759, *WJP*, 3:115–16; Michael N. McConnell, *Army and Empire: British Soldiers on the American Frontier, 1758–1775* (Lincoln: University of Nebraska Press, 2005), 16–17.

32. Johnson to Daniel Claus, May 20, 1761, *WJP*, 10:270.

33. Johnson to Amherst, July 29, 1761, *WJP*, 10:322; Amherst to Johnson, August 9, 1761, *WJP*, 3:515.

34. "Petition of Merchants of Albany to the Lords of Trade," *NYCD*, 7:488–89; Johnson to Amherst, February 6, 1762, *WJP*, 3:620, 623; Amherst to Johnson, February 14, 1762, *WJP*, 10:382–83; Amherst to William Sharpe, October 20, 1762, *NYCD*, 7:509.

35. Johnson to George Croghan, July 26, 1761, *WJP*, 10:319–20; Johnson to Daniel Claus, August 9, 1761, *WJP*, 10:323–25; "Niagara and Detroit Proceedings," *WJP*, 3:463–67; "Journal to Detroit," *WJP*, 13:227, 236.

36. "Journal of Indian Affairs," *WJP*, 10:387.

37. Amherst to Johnson, January 16 and February 14, 1762, *WJP*, 10:354, 382–83; "Journal of Indian Affairs," *WJP*, 10:386–88.

38. William Walters to Johnson, April 5 and 27, 1762, *WJP*, 3:721–23, 10:426–28; Couagne to Johnson, June 5, 1763, *WJP*, 4:134–35.

39. Clarence Monroe Burton and M. Agnes Burton, eds., *Journal of Pontiac's Conspiracy, 1763*, trans. R. Clyde Ford (Detroit: Speaker-Hines Printing Company, 1912).

40. Johnson to Amherst, July 11, 1763, *NYCD*, 7:533.

41. Johnson to Lords of Trade, July 1, 1763, *NYCD*, 7:525–27.

42. Johnson to Lords of Trade, July 26, 1763, *NYCD*, 7:559–62.

43. J. C. Webster, "Life of John Montresor," *Transactions of the Royal Society of Canada*, 3rd series, 22 (May 1928): 14–18; Couagne to Johnson, September 8, 1763, *WJP*, 10:812; Collin Andrews to Johnson, September 9, 1763, *WJP*, 10:812–13; Bouquet to Amherst, September 7, 1763, in *Michigan Pioneer and Historical Society, Collections and Researches* (Lansing, MI: Michigan Pioneer and Historical Society, 1877–1929) [hereafter *MPHC*], 19:230–31.

44. John Stoughton to Johnson, September 16, 1763, *WJP*, 10:814; Couagne to Johnson, September 16, 1763, *WJP*, 10:815.

45. William Browning to Johnson, September 17, 1763, *WJP*, 10:816; George Etherington to Johnson, September 17, 1763, *WJP*, 10:817–18; Johnson to Lords of Trade, September 25, 1763, *NYCD*, 7:559–62; Johnson to Amherst, October 6, 1763, *WJP*, 10:866–70.

46. Amherst to Johnson, October 1, 1763, *WJP*, 10:860–61; Amherst to Bouquet, October 3, 1763, *MPHC* 19:237–38.

47. Thomas Moncrieffe to Johnson, October 4, 1763, *WJP*, 4:212–13; Johnson to Amherst, September 30, 1763, *WJP*, 4:209–11.

48. Browning to Johnson, October 22, 1763, *WJP*, 10:906–7; Couagne to Johnson, October 17 and November 11, 1763, *WJP*, 10:884, 921–22.

49. Amherst to Browning, November 11, 1763, in Sir Frederick Haldimand: Unpublished Papers and Correspondence, 1758–84, microfilm (London: World Microfilm Publications, 1977) [hereafter Haldimand Papers], reel 8, section 21678, 29; Amherst to Johnson, September 30, 1763, *NYCD*, 7:568–69.

50. Johnson to Gage, January 27, 1764, *WJP*, 4:308–10; Gage to Johnson, January 12 and 31, 1764, *WJP*, 4:290–93, 314–15; Johnson to Lords of Trade, January 20, 1764, *NYCD*, 7:599–602.

51. "Journal of Indian Congress," *WJP*, 10:968–71.

52. "An Indian Conference," *WJP*, 11:139–40; "Articles of Peace Concluded with the Seneca Indians," *NYCD*, 7:621–23.

53. Johnson to Gage, April 6, 1764, *WJP*, 4:389.

54. Browning to Johnson, April 10, 1764, *WJP*, 11:124–25.

55. Johnson to Gage, April 27, 1764, *WJP*, 11:162–63; Johnson to Gage, April 27, 1764, *WJP*, 11:163; Johnson to Colden, April 28, 1764, in *The Letters and Papers of Cadwallader Colden* (New York: New York Historical Society, 1918–1937), 6:304–5; Gage to Johnson, April 25, 1764, *WJP*, 4:408–9.

56. "The Journals of Captain John Montresor," ed. G. D. Scull, in *Collections of the New York Historical Society* [hereafter "Montresor's Journals"], 14:258–62; Dunnigan, "Portaging Niagara," 217–18; McConnell, *Army and Empire*, 16–17.

57. "Montresor's Journals," 14:261–68; Johnson to Gage, June 29, 1764, *WJP*, 11:245–46.

58. Johnson to Gage, January 27, 1764, *WJP*, 4:308–10; Johnson to Lords of Trade, May 11, 1764, *NYCD*, 7:624–26.

59. Bradstreet to Gage, June 4, 1764, Thomas Gage Papers, American Series, William L. Clements Library, University of Michigan, Ann Arbor [hereafter Gage Papers AS], vol. 19.

60. "Montresor's Journals," 14:275.

61. "Conference with Indians," *WJP*, 11:262–73; "An Indian Congress," *WJP*, 11:273–89.

62. Johnson to Gage, May 11, 1764, *WJP*, 11:189–90; Gage to Johnson, May 28, 1764, *WJP*, 4:432–33; "Equivalents in Barter," *WJP*, 4:490–91.

63. "Montresor's Journals," 14:259, 263, 272.

64. Alexander Henry, *Travels and Adventures in Canada in the Years 1760–1776* (1809; reprint, Chicago: R. R. Donnelly and Sons, 1921), 182–84.

65. "Conference with Indians," *WJP*, 11:266–69.

66. "An Indian Congress," *WJP*, 11:284–86.

67. Browning to Johnson, May 23, 1764, *WJP*, 11:196; "Journal of Indian Affairs," *WJP*, 11:236.

68. "An Indian Congress," *WJP*, 11:288.

69. Johnson to Gage, August 5, 1764, *WJP*, 11:325.

70. "An Indian Congress," *WJP*, 11:290–97.

71. Ibid., 316.

72. Ibid., 319.

73. "Articles of Peace between Sir William Johnson and the Genesee Indians," *NYCD*, 7:652–53.

74. "An Indian Congress," *WJP*, 11:321–22.

75. Johnson to Gage, August 5, 1764, *WJP*, 11:324–25.

76. Johnson to the Lords of Trade, August 30, 1764, *NYCD*, 7:647–48.

77. Gage to Johnson, September 25, 1764, Gage Papers AS, vol. 24; Johnson to Gage, September 30, 1764, *WJP*, 11:365.

78. Bradstreet to Gage, April 7, 1765, Gage Papers AS, vol. 33; Gage to Bradstreet, April 15, 1765, Gage Papers AS, vol. 34.

79. Gage to Vaughan, April 18, 1765, Gage Papers AS, vol. 34.

80. Gage to Johnson, November 24, 1765, *WJP*, 4:878–79; Johnson to Gage, December 21, 1765, *WJP*, 11:983.

81. Gage to Johnson, March 17, 1766, *WJP*, 12:44.

82. Dunnigan, "Portaging Niagara," 219–21.

83. Gage to John Brown, July 28, 1764, Haldimand Papers, reel 8, section 21678, 89; "Journal of Indian Transactions at Niagara in the Year 1767," in *The Documentary History of the State of New York*, ed. E. B. O'Callaghan (Albany, NY: Weed, Parsons, 1849–1851), 2:871–80; Brown to Johnson, October 26, 1767, *WJP*, 5:759.

84. Daniel Claus to Alexander Knox, March 1, 1777, *NYCD*, 7:702–3.

85. Johnson to Gage, December 21, 1765, *WJP*, 11:983.

"Foolish Young Men" and the Contested Ohio Country, 1783–1795

SARAH E. MILLER

IN THE YEARS FOLLOWING THE AMERICAN REVOLUTION, VIOLENCE BETWEEN Native Americans and frontier settlers spiraled into reciprocal and uncontained depredations. Although many Native American leaders and the government of the United States strove for peace, uncontrolled and unsanctioned men, both Indian and American, committed serious depredations against each other. My work builds on studies by scholars such as Richard Slotkin, Richard Drinnon, James Merrell, and Colin Calloway, as well as the recent scholarship presented in Daniel P. Barr's edited work *The Boundaries Between Us: Natives and Newcomers along the Frontier of the Old Northwest Territory* (2006), Patrick Griffin's *American Leviathan: Empire, Nation, and Revolutionary Frontier* (2007), and Peter Silver's *Our Savage Neighbors: How Indian War Transformed Early America* (2008). This chapter expands the study of violence on the frontier past the American Revolution as it examines the coveted Ohio Territory during the first years of the United States.

The Ohio Country included much of modern day Ohio, but stretched east towards Pittsburgh and west to the Wabash River. This area, most Native Americans felt, had not been ceded to the United States. It was generally, but not unanimously, accepted by the Natives that land south of the Ohio River, referred to as Kentucky even before statehood, belonged to the United States. The Treaty of Fort Stanwix (1768) had established the Ohio River as a boundary between Great Britain's American colonies and Indian Territory.

Within the Ohio Country, and the larger Northwest Territory that encompassed it, lived a variety of Native American tribes. For example, the

Wyandots and Delawares inhabited the eastern part of the region and were generally more responsive to governmental overtures. The Shawnees and Miamis lived in the western sections that were eventually settled by polyglot communities along the Wabash River, resistant to Americans infringing on Indian Territory.

Indian leadership lacked coercive powers over their warriors, thus creating the complicated dynamic that is displayed in this study. Indian chiefs, while greatly respected, could not compel all young men to follow their wishes, and sometimes dissident groups acted contrary to council decisions. Although some leaders of tribes were friendly with the United States, or at least condemned violence against settlers, they were unable to demand obedience. These "foolish young men" were often warriors from different tribes, although living in the same or nearby villages. Warriors sometimes initiated violence and sometimes sought revenge against frontier settlers for depredations. Conversely, Americans on the frontier, despite government discouragement, attacked Indian settlements. Neither side was interested in distinguishing between friend and foe, thus establishing an escalating spiral of violence on both sides of the Ohio River.

In 1794, Secretary of State Henry Knox wrote his final report evaluating the continuing violence between Native Americans and frontier settlers in the Ohio Country. To President George Washington, he noted:

> The encroachment of white people is incessantly watched, and in unguarded moments, they are murdered by the Indians. Revenge [from previous depredations] is sought, and the innocent frontier people are too frequently involved as victims in the cruel contest.[1]

This followed up on a report written five years earlier in which Knox told Washington:

> Hostilities have almost constantly existed between the people of Kentucky and the . . . Indians. The injuries and murders have been so reciprocal, that it would be a point of critical investigation to know on which side they have been the greatest.[2]

Despite efforts by both the United States government and Indian councils and chiefs, the frontier between Indian lands and American settlement was filled with acts of hostility. This violence could be seen as the continuation of a larger pattern of American frontier violence, with the origins impossible to sort out. Ultimately, the origins of the violence became less important than the fact that cycles of violence developed on the borders and made things difficult for political leaders who were broadly committed to some form of peace, however tenuous. It is clear that the men who perpetrated frontier violence acted on their own, without official sanction from their governments or councils. And the "foolish young men," as the Indian councils referred to their unruly warriors, had equally vicious counterparts among frontier settlers.

When the Treaty of Paris ended the American Revolution in 1783, it did not mention the Native Americans. However, the United States considered the Ohio Country conquered territory according to the British capitulation. Indian agents for the Crown, aware of the terms of the treaty, tried to keep peace because they recognized that the Indians would be unhappy and might erupt in violence against the American settlers. In councils, they urged the tribes not to offensively attack the Americans south of the Ohio River, the line that had been established by the Treaty of Fort Stanwix in 1768. But in one council, a Lake Indian named T'Shindatton, representing the various communities along Lake Erie, asserted that while the Indian confederacy hoped to restrain any aggression, peace could not be guaranteed. He explained, "Our Tomahawks are now laid close to our sides, but there are yet many of our young men who have their eyes fixed upon it, and they might steal it from our sides to make use of it unknown to us." Although chiefs were respected, they did not have coercive powers over their warriors and could not always stop them from committing depredations. T'Shindatton expressed his desire to restrain the warriors by metaphorically throwing "rubbish over [the tomahawk] that they may not find it," but he could make no promises.[3]

Outbreaks of violence between Americans and Indians were not curtailed by the announcement of the Treaty of Paris (1783). Within the year, warriors attacked several travelers en route to Detroit. News reached American commissioners during the negotiations of the second Treaty of Fort Stanwix (1784), who demanded an explanation. In response, the Iroquois, answering for the Delawares and Wyandots, replied, "We have enquired into it, and suppose it to have been only the act of a few bad people, and not authorized by the voices of any particular tribe." The chiefs hoped that the action would not "interrupt the important business" of the treaty. The men who perpetrated the attack—or as the council referred to them, the "foolish young men"—were not under direct control of tribal or confederacy leaders, and yet they, and others like them, continued to disrupt the peace process between the United States and Native Americans in the Ohio Country.[4]

Often, attacks revolved around American encroachment (legal and illegal) on lands claimed by the Indians. In May 1785, Captain Johnny, a Shawnee chief, expressed his dismay about Virginians moving into the Ohio Country. He complained that they were "so near our bedsides that we can almost hear the noise of [their] axes felling our Trees and settling our Country." The Shawnees, and their allies, were "strong, unanimous, and determined to act as one man in Defence of" their land, and if the Americans continued to encroach across the Ohio River, they would "take up a Rod and whip them back to [the other] side of the Ohio." The encroachment of American settlers on the lands claimed by the Indians, whether Shawnees, Miamis, Delawares, or others, incited warriors to violence.[5]

Shortly after the 1785 signing of the Treaty of Fort McIntosh, an American trader was killed along the Tuscarawas River. Accusations that Wyandot and Delaware warriors were involved prompted Major John Doughty to question Chief Captain Pipe. Denying any allegation that the murder had been sanctioned by the tribes, Captain Pipe explained, "Wise men endeavor by every means to prevent such practices," but "the young the ignorant and the lazy who are naked and wretched and too idle to hunt support themselves by robbing occasionally." These rogues were, as Captain Pipe characterized them, "bad men [who] stole away without leave of their chiefs."[6]

Official government documents and personal papers elaborate almost exclusively on Indian atrocities, when in fact American settlers perpetrated many atrocities of their own. Eastern conservatives, such as Senator Rufus King of New York, even blamed settlers for much of the violence. King believed that bloodshed on the frontier was based on "the lawless, and probably unjust, conduct of the inhabitants of Kentucky towards the Indians bordering on the Western side of the Ohio."[7] These infringements and hostilities led to retaliation that was reported and documented in ways that often blamed the Indians. When reporting depredations, either officially or privately, frontier settlers expanded on Indian hostilities, but rarely connected them to the atrocities enacted by Americans. For example, Kentuckian Samuel McDowell reported to Patrick Henry, governor of Virginia, in April 1786 that the area around Louisville incurred daily depredations; fearing that the settlers would all abandon the town, he claimed that without military help Jefferson County "will soon break up." Major Ebenezer Denny visited Louisville for four days in May, and "every day there were accounts of men being scalped." During his visit, Denny also heard "very alarming accounts of depredations [by] Indians in neighborhood of Vincennes." These reports, usually based in fact but often exaggerated, spurred the people of Kentucky to plan an offensive expedition against the Native settlements along the Wabash River, focusing on Shawnee and Miami villages supposed to have initiated attacks in Kentucky. Many Kentuckians, including George Rogers Clark, began preparations believing that the continued violence meant that war was imminent.[8]

Indeed, accounts of atrocities reported by white captives who escaped from Indian communities caused anxiety and anger among settlers. Hence, many settlers in the backcountry resorted to their own brutality, condoning their attacks and killings as protection for their settlements regardless of whether Indians were friendly or not. Punishment for killing an Indian seldom occurred.[9]

Eager Kentuckians craved the opportunity to invade Indian Territory and attack Native American villages. In June 1786, George Rogers Clark informed Major John P. Wyllys at the Falls of the Ohio (Louisville) that Kentuckians were primed to assault the Indians because "they are daily doing us mischief in different parts of the country." The Indian attacks disrupting frontier life made Kentuckians feel that "the fate of this country depends on the intended enterprise." Despite no official government support for the attack, Clark and his men raided several Indian villages along the Wabash River—specifically the Miami villages, because Kentuckians blamed, correctly or incorrectly, the Miamis for raids against their settlements.[10]

In July, these same Miamis threatened to attack the town of Vincennes (Indiana) in retaliation for Clark's raids. Here again, the attacks did not target the aggressors who lived in Kentucky. Distressed Americans at Vincennes appealed to Kentuckians, still led by Clark, for relief. They wrote, "We are dayly alarmed by the Hostile Savages." Without help from Kentucky, the town claimed it would "Inavitably Perish." Every night they expected an attack on their understaffed garrison. Several settlers, including John Filson, wrote personally to Clark for aid, fearing the possibility of "total depopulation" of the Americans' settlement by "imperious savages." Even within a town protected by a military fort, the citizens keenly felt the possibility of violence against them. Fear of Indian attacks permeated the frontier, and a military presence did not diminish this trepidation.[11]

Meanwhile, continued depredations plagued Kentucky in the summer of 1786. Joseph Saunders told Major Finney that one hundred horses had been stolen and two men killed at Limestone (Kentucky) by the Shawnees and Potawatomis. Robert Patterson reported twenty-two persons killed and seven hundred horses stolen in Fayette and Jefferson Counties. In response, Kentuckians posted a proclamation to rally support for an attack against the Indians in the Ohio Country, declaring an "implied contract between settlers . . . to support and defend each other against our relentless and common

enemies." An offensive attack was needed or the country would "most probably fall prey to savage barbarity." The Americans once again continued the
cycle of violence with an offensive strike north of the Ohio River.[12]

Much of the incessant violence along the frontier resulted from unful-
filled Indian treaties. Despite documents signed at Fort Stanwix (1784),
Fort McIntosh (1785), and Fort Finney (1786), the Indian Confederacy
Council, consisting of many of the Indian tribes of the Northwest Territory, had not ratified these agreements. The confederacy asked, in 1783,
for a meeting with representation from all the tribes of the Northwest, but
none of the treaties signed in the following years accomplished this. By
the spring of 1787, the lack of a representative treaty persuaded many of
the warriors that no treaty was in place, therefore giving them free rein to
hassle the settlers. General Harmar reported to Knox that "several parties
of the Wabash Indians[13] [were] in the Kentucky country plundering the
inhabitants of their horses, and occasionally murdering them." The Indian
confederacy explained to Congress that "when a division of territory is
agreed to by some particular nations without the concurrence of the whole
of our confederacy, we look upon it as illegal and of no effect." In short, the
Indians blamed the unsettled situation on the American treaty process. If
the commissioners had abided by Indian wishes for a treaty involving the
entire Indian confederacy, the council asserted, "we are almost certain that
you and we, would now have been on the most amicable footing." Treaties
made with selected representation, in the minds of many, were not binding
and therefore could not stop warriors from venting their frustration against
Americans with violence. Much of this violence resulted from American
settlers claiming Indian lands and/or occupying lands that the Indians still
felt were theirs. For example, boats carrying settlers down the Ohio River
passed Fort Harmar, at the mouth of the Muskingum, bound allegedly for
established communities in Kentucky; however, some settlers undoubtedly
squatted illegally in Indian Territory. In the last six months of 1787, Ebenezer Denny recorded "146 boats, 3,196 souls, 1,371 horses, 165 wagons,
191 cattle, 245 sheep and 24 hogs" passing the post. These encroachments
heightened the resentment of the Native Americans. Warriors, therefore,
often gathered to exact vengeance on the uninvited settlers.[14]

Indian leaders were well aware of the problems on the frontier, but
had little ability to control them. During a prisoner exchange between the
Shawnees and the United States at Limestone (Kentucky), General Harmar took the opportunity to speak to the Shawnee leader named Wolf.
After admonishing the Indians, although not able to specifically condemn
one tribe or group for the "frequent murders" of Kentuckians, Harmar

threatened the wrath of the "Thirteen Great Fires" to "destroy all their nations." Wolf responded "that none of his Shawanese committed these murders, but that they were done by a banditti countenanced by none of the regular tribes." Although this behavior was unacceptable to the Indian leaders and council, these warriors acted on their own accord to seek revenge or show their displeasure.[15]

As depredations continued on the frontier into 1788, John Francis Hamtramck sent a warning to the Wabash Indians that Congress "would not suffer its subjects to be killed every day." The Indian confederacy, having little control over their young men, claimed in response that they "cannot prevent it." In May 1788, word reached Vincennes that scalps from Kentucky came into the Wabash villages "daily." To curtail the situation, Hamtramck wrote to General Harmar that he would give the Indians one month to cease depredations. If violence continued, he would prohibit all Wabash Indians from entering the village of Vincennes. Harmar approved.[16]

Indian attacks fell upon the isolated frontier settlements as well as along the waterways, especially the Ohio, Miami and Wabash Rivers. Both civilian and military vessels were subjected to occasional attacks. A letter written by Harmar to Knox was delayed going up the Ohio River from Louisville when "the boat returned having been fired on by Indians." When troops asked for the best route to Fort Vincennes, they were informed that it would be "most advantageous to continue your march by water though it will not ward off danger of savage parties." They were urged to use "every precaution in order to avoid surprise."[17]

The Ohio River was a main thoroughfare into the Northwest Territory, but could be very dangerous. In April 1788, five men were captured by one hundred Shawnee, Mingo, and Cherokee warriors between the Little and Great Miami Rivers. The ambush involved a flat boat holding about forty Indians with others attacking from shore. After being captured and marched to the Shawnee village, two of the men, James Gray and William Griffin Garland, escaped to Vincennes. Before their escape, they learned that another boat carrying five men and a "considerable quantity of merchandize" was captured in a similar manner. An attack on a third boat at the Great Miami River, by the same Indians, yielded as many goods, and of the six men aboard, "five . . . they killed, the other made his escape."[18]

With "mortification," Harmar reported another river attack to Secretary Knox in July 1788. Thirty-six men under the command of Lieutenant Peters were attacked near the mouth of the Wabash River. About fifty Indians lining both sides of the Wabash attacked the convoy as it escorted provisions to Vincennes. Ten soldiers were killed and eight wounded. Colonel

Hamtramck blamed a group of thirty unidentified Indians, probably from the Wabash area, who left Vincennes when the mission departed and had not been seen since. The necessity of sending a large number of soldiers to protect provisions weakened the garrison at the fort. Hamtramck reported that he had "but 12 or 14 [men] fit for duty."[19]

Just as the Indian confederacy could not control their "foolish young men," neither could the United States control Kentuckians who overstepped federal laws when striking against the various Indian communities. In August 1788, "one Patrick Brown who call[ed] himself a major and from Nelson County in Kentucky" arrived at Vincennes with about sixty men. They had killed nine friendly Indians in a hunting camp. Hamtramck reported that Brown claimed to have authority from the governor of Kentucky to pursue the Indians, but could not produce any orders to do so. After declaring that only the federal government could declare war on the Indians, Hamtramck "ordered him in the name of *the United States* to depart immediately."

Brown then asked for assistance in crossing the Wabash River, but Hamtramck declined and further insisted that Brown return the horses he had taken from Vincennes. Brown refused and stole canoes to cross the river. Hamtramck considered firing the cannon at the renegades, "but did not think the affair of sufficient consequence to spill blood," and, as he explained, the action would allow little chance of getting the horses back.[20]

Captain Ferguson was sent twice to recover the horses, particularly the ones belonging to Pacan, a Miami Indian in the service of the United States. Ferguson tried to explain to Brown that Pacan, although an Indian, acted as an informant for the United States government at the Indian council at Roche Du Bout. Brown refused to listen, and Hamtramck "was forced to the humiliating necessity of leting him keep the horses." Hamtramck lamented to Harmar, "Never was my feeling so much wonded [wounded] before. But what could I do? I had but nine men fit for duty." The Indians killed by Brown had been part of the Miami bands led by the friendly chiefs Pacan and la Demoisel. When news reached Pacan, he returned to Vincennes without visiting the fort. His departure before the council had started prevented the United States from hearing his intelligence report. Unsanctioned incidents such as those by Brown continued to provoke the heated violence of the frontier and disrupt government business.[21]

Indian leaders complained to American officials of the continuous encroachment of settlers onto Indian lands. In a letter to Richard Butler, Half King and Captain Pipe begged the United States "to be Strong, and Correct your Young men" who were assaulting the Indian villages. Even George Washington recognized the lawlessness of the frontier, arguing that the "spirit of land jobbing" destroyed relationships with the Native Americans, and perhaps more importantly, peace could not prevail when "frontier Settlers entertain the opinion that there is not the same crime (or indeed no crime at all) in killing an Indian as in killing a white man." Government officials clearly recognized that laws could not contain the violent actions of the frontier settlers against Native Americans.[22]

In the summer of 1788, a group of friendly Seneca Indians traveled from Fort Pitt to Fort Harmar and expected safe passage and security provided by the American army, but Arthur St. Clair worried about their safety. Frontier settlers rarely recognized the differences between friendly and hostile Indians, and St. Clair observed, "God knows how the people of the Virginia side [of the Ohio River] may behave." Ten days later St. Clair anxiously wrote, "I do hope the people along the river will not be mad enough to molest them on their passage; at the same time, . . . I fear they will." Even with an army escort, St. Clair could not guarantee the safety of friendly Indians against the wrath of frontier settlers. In this case, St. Clair's fears were not realized. The presence of the United States officials, however, did not always deter violence by the frontier settlers against Native Americans.[23]

Life on the frontier was ever dangerous, and settlers knew that precautions—whether a military presence, scouts, or a constant awareness with weapons at the ready—were necessary for their own protection. So, when violence occurred because of lack of precautions, such as when a Captain King was murdered by Indians at a newly developed settlement near Marietta, there was little sympathy. The difference between this murder and others was that King had been foolish in neglecting to take safety measures. Despite an expectation of Indians "lurking for mischief," King and his associates became lax in their precautions. "Captain King went from day to day, near a mile from other people to work, alone, without his arms, and in this situation he was when he was shot and scalped, by whom is unknown." In conveying news of this death, Rufus Putnam, Revolutionary War general and early Ohio settler, showed little empathy.[24]

Anticipation of frontier attacks played into every aspect of daily life, but most settlers expected to be safe if they took proper precautions, according to Putnam's letter. However, when a group of settlers opted to move from Northbend in the Symmes Purchase to Southbend, seven miles up the Ohio River, the army accompanied them but could not keep them secure. On one of several trips, an attack by Indians[25] severely wounded four of the twelve soldiers. Frightened by the violence, a majority of Northbend settlers moved to Louisville. In this case, even the United States Army could not protect settlers against the Indians.[26]

In his official government report, presented June 15, 1789, Knox informed the President that the Treaty of Fort Harmar (1789) had not ended hostilities. He stated that several murders had been "perpetrated on the South side of the Ohio, [and] the inhabitants on the waters of that river are exceedingly alarmed." These depredations, Knox contended, were committed by the Western Indians,[27] who had rejected all invitations to treat. The violence on the frontier had existed for so long, Knox acknowledged, that blame could not be attributed to one group or the other; instead, hostility was generally understood to be the constant condition of the frontier.[28]

The small United States army at Vincennes was virtually powerless to stop groups of warriors from frequently crossing the Ohio and attacking frontier settlements. In June, Hamtramck threatened harsh punishment if the polyglot Wabash Indians did not "cease their depredations." Despite his tough talk, he had "neither means or power" to effectively attack the Indians. Instead, despite official regulations to prevent such actions, Kentuckians, led by John Hardin, reacted to the aggression with an attack on a Shawnee village along the Wabash, killing twelve Indians. Overall, then, the force commanded by Hamtramck proved ineffective not only in stopping raiding Indians, but also in stopping vigilante Kentuckians from crossing the Ohio north into Indian country.[29]

In September, St. Clair complained to President Washington about the lack of control in the Northwest Territory. But St. Clair did not know how to proceed, because

> It is not to be expected, sir, that the Kentucky people will or can submit patiently to the cruelties and depredations of those savages; they are in the habit of retaliation, or they will apply to the Governor of the Western Country (through which the Indians must pass to attack them) for redress. If he can not redress them (and in present circumstances he can not), they also will march through the country to redress themselves, and the government will be laid prostrate. The United States, on the other hand, are at peace with several of the nations, and should the resentment of those people fall upon any of them, which is likely enough may happen, very bad consequences will follow; for it must appear to them that the United States either pay no regard to their treaties or that they are unable or unwilling to carry their engagements into effect. Remonstrances will probably be made by them also to the governor, and he will be found in a situation from which he can neither redress the one nor protect the other. They will unite with the hostile nations, prudently preferring open war to a delusive and uncertain peace.[30]

Henry Knox was also understandably unhappy about the attacks made on the frontier, because "irregular, and unauthorized, expeditions involve the innocent and guilty in equal calamity, make enemies of those disposed to be friends, disgrace government, and defeat its designs." Yet, despite the concerns of the authorities, the Kentuckians continued their attacks in retaliation for Indian offenses, perpetuating the cycle of violence that incorporated even those blameless in the action.[31]

St. Clair informed Knox in late January 1790 of the murder of three men at Carpenter's Station, and another three on Russell's Creek. Not far from that location, hunters had been fired upon and one man killed. Nearby soldiers attempted pursuit, but were unsuccessful. Writing in March, Judge Harry Innes reported that in February, nine people were found dead on a boat on the Ohio and one woman was missing. He detailed other depredations:

> Three men were killed about the same time in the wilderness, between Rickland creek and Stinking creek; on the road two escaped. Old John Slone and his son, were killed on the head of the Rolling fork; one man killed on Holin. A station on Russell's creek was attacked about the 25th of the month; Isaac and Nathan Farris, a son of Isaac Farris, John Painter, and one other man, killed; a Negro woman, and a white woman wounded, and a number of horses have been taken, but I can't enumerate them. One Harper was killed on State creek.[32]

Furthermore, the station at Mudlick in Kentucky was evacuated out of fear in February, and in March a man was killed and one wounded. Judge Innes gathered "from various reports, there is too much reason to fear they [the Indians] will be hostile this spring."[33]

In April, the lieutenants of Fayette, Woodford, and Mercer Counties in Kentucky wrote to Secretary Knox, "We almost every day receive accounts of their horrid murders on our defenceless frontiers (which entirely surround us) and the taking of horses and other property, to the ruin of a number of families." No single tribe perpetrated the attacks, but rather a combination of warriors from many different nations, unsanctioned by an Indian council—many originating from the Miami villages at Kekionga and the polyglot community it encompassed.[34]

An example of such attacks may be seen in Samuel Stephenson's declaration that he had been called to recover the bodies of two men and return them to Elkhorn: "He assisted to bring two men which were both scalped; one was much cut with his tomahawk, and the other was shot through the hips, and he believe[d] them to be said McBride and McConnel." David

Rankin and James Hays testified that on the 12th of May, "they saw Lewis Parker lying dead: he had received several wounds, with balls, tomahawks, and knives; (he was scalped) [and] that they found him, . . . about one hour after he was killed" and believed Indians had killed him. Benjamin Harrison confirmed this report in a certificate, asserting, "Although I did not see the Indians kill Parker, I do verily believe they did do it."[35]

In a deposition, Joseph Barnett of Nelson County swore, "On the eighteenth of April last past, (being Lord's day) about the hour of five in the evening, a party of Indians fell upon a few defenceless people" on the road returning from church. The Indians killed two children, age eight and twelve, and mutilated "an ancient lady of both respectable family and character" who survived the attack despite being scalped. The daughter of Barnett was taken in this episode, and the Indians escaped with her.[36]

These reports highlight the threat daily felt by the Americans. General Harmar forwarded this information from Kentucky to Secretary Knox in June 1790. In the settlers' view, the Indians were to blame for all violence; they failed to see that retaliatory raids compounded the problem.

Judge Harry Innes declared that since his arrival in Kentucky in 1783, "any incursions made into [Indian] country have been from reiterated injuries committed by them." This assertion was contradicted by some territorial officials who believed that the frontier settlers often initiated attacks. As Knox asserted, it is impossible to tell where the blame lay. And even Innes himself inadvertently admitted to some fault by the militia, claiming that the raids "[render] it difficult, and almost impossible to discriminate what tribes are the offended."[37]

The Kentuckians felt they had organized expeditions "into the Indian countries, upon the principle of *revenge, protection, and self-preservation*." But, considering all Indians enemies, these frontier militia antagonized friendly, nonbelligerent, and hostile tribes alike, creating resentment and provoking retaliation that continued the cycle of violence. Blame could not rest squarely on the Native Americans for frontier violence, as Innes alleged; culpability also rested with the Kentuckians.[38]

Depredation near the settlement of Marietta in the summer of 1790 could also be blamed on a combination of Indians and settlers. Rufus Putnam reported a man killed and horses stolen near the Hockhocking. He called this incident "a Misschief altogather unprovoaked." But, when reporting a woman taken at the end of June, he admits, "This business was prefaced by the White people Stealing a number of horses from the Indians and refusing to deliver them up." Obviously, in many different areas, unauthorized aggression on the part of the "foolish young men" from both the American settlements and Indian villages propagated continued hostility.[39]

The Ohio Company officials warned the citizens of the Muskingum River settlements of an Indian attack spurred by aggressive settlers. After Harmar's campaign against Kekionga, several Indians, mostly Shawnees, made an unusual winter attack on the new settlement of Big Bottom near Marietta. In it, fourteen people were killed.[40] These citizens had settled north of the Ohio River on lands still claimed by some of the Indians of the Northwest Territory. The unusual winter attack caused the Ohio Country inhabitants to brace for a full-scale Indian assault as summer approached. Winthrop Sargent warned the citizens of Gallipolis to be wary. Although French heritage had protected Gallipolis from Indian attacks in the past, Sargent warned that the eager warriors "have made observations, and [were] endeavoring to lull [them] into a false and fatal idea of security." Many officials and residents of the Northwest Territory shared Sargent's view of the Indians as he warned, "They are a subtle and designing enemy, and can bring upon you, in an unexpected moment, a force sufficient to annihilate an unguarded multitude."[41] This attitude contributed to the steady fear that caused many settlers to strike out at any and all Indians.

Settlers continued to spread stories of Indian atrocities. In late November 1791, John P. Duvall, lieutenant of Harrison County, Virginia, reported an attack on cattle drivers from the Muskingum. Four were killed and one was taken prisoner. Bullets riddled the clothing of the only escaping member of the party. A servant boy captured in a previous attack escaped when the cattle drivers were killed.[42] On December 10, a war party killed two men fishing at Floyd's fork of the Salt River in Kentucky. Three boys with them were captured, one of whom was released to carry a tomahawk home and report the incident.[43]

The following summer, four days after an assault on a mowing party in which four soldiers were killed and eight captured, Indians attacked a cattle guard at Fort Jefferson. About twenty Indians, unidentified by the Americans at the fort, killed and scalped two men and took six cattle. The cattle returned, unaccompanied, to the garrison three days later. A group of friendly Indians from the Wabash villages informed Rufus Putnam that a war club left at the site of the attack belonged to the Cherokee "out Casts that live on the [Maumee] River but not admited into the National Council."[44] These Indians were not under the influence of the confederacy chiefs, and therefore their actions were unsanctioned. The mention that they were "outcasts" shows that the Native Americans separated the Indians who followed the council and those who acted against it.

Although many official attempts for peace were made on the frontier in the spring and summer of 1792, depredations carried on by Indian warriors and frontier settlers persisted. Kentuckians still daily expected attacks on their stations and feared a devastating summer. Many inhabitants along the Muskingum River moved into fortified blockhouses for protection, and settlers built homes suitable to sustain an Indian attack.[45] Oliver Spencer described his first house in the Symmes Purchase as having "narrow doors of thick oak plank, [which] turning on stout wooden hinges and secured with strong bars braced with timber from the floor, formed a safe barrier." The upper level had "portholes or small embrasures . . . [to] fire upon the enemy."[46]

At Columbia, the adjoined blockhouses and cabins were attached to the stockades for protection against the Indians. Additionally, "The wooden hinges of the massive doors or gates of these enclosures were so made that they could not be opened without a grating that would awaken the inmates of the cabin." The surrounding trees that could provide cover for attacking Indians were cut down. But these precautions could not stop all raids. John Reily recalled, "It was almost impossible to keep an horse-creature at Columbia." And, after St. Clair's defeat, more blockhouses were built outside of Columbia and manned by local militia to serve as lookouts and add protection.[47]

Furthermore, settlements in the Symmes Purchase organized and hired a group of rangers for the protection of people working in the field. Church services, which often involved the inhabitants of several stations, were held in blockhouses. The men were expected to carry their guns to church and keep them in a corner, where they could be accessed easily. In 1792, John Wallace, a member of Kemper's Cincinnati Congregation, was fined 75 cents for attending a service unarmed.[48] In September of that same year, the city of Cincinnati passed a law that all churchgoers must carry weapons to repel an Indian attack.[49]

Being away from the fortifications was dangerous. While hunting on Mill Creek, about five miles north of Columbia, William Moore killed a doe and "lashed it on his shoulders." A group of Indians observed his actions and waited "until he should be encumbered with his load" before firing. Bullets hit his right shoulder and wrist. Attempting to outrun his attackers with a useless left hand, he dumped the deer. But, after failing to jump clear across a creek, he slid into the water and was captured.[50]

In the summer of 1792, Oliver Spencer, a teenage boy, returned from Fort Washington to Columbia with three others in a canoe. An Indian attack killed one man instantly. Shot through the shoulder, another man survived, but was scalped and "wretchedly mutilated." A woman "frightened, fell into the water, floated down the stream quite a distance, and came safely to the shore and brought the news" to Cincinnati. Spencer was taken captive by the Shawnees.[51]

Tasks closer to home could be equally dangerous. Along the Kenhawa River, in Virginia, a Captain Vonbever and a servant built a camp to make sugar. Surprised one day by an Indian warrior, the servant raised the alarm, and both men reached the cabin safely at the same time. The servant then shot the Indian, and when patrols arrived, they threw his body into the river, where it washed up at Gallipolis the next day. This episode was yet another reminder to the citizens of the Ohio Country to be ever vigilant while performing everyday tasks.[52]

Enoch Buckingham, an inhabitant of a station near Cincinnati, described the death of three men who had "by a strange fatality . . . forgot that there was no moment when they were not watched by their forest bred foe." The five men working in the field had moved away from their weapons when an attack instantly killed two of them and mortally wounded a third. The other two men were captured.[53]

However, frontier setters fueled much of the Indian depredations with unofficial violence of their own. A blatant disregard for Indians, whether peaceful or hostile, was characteristic of many settlers on the frontier. For example, in July 1791, a friendly Indian chief, Wawiachteno,[54] died while in Cincinnati and was buried with military honors. The burial parade included the gentlemen of the town, military officers, and almost all the Indian population. Officers placed a pole with a white flag at the head of the grave, but "Malicious people . . . dug out the body in the night, tore down the flag and dragged the body to the street, where they placed it upright against a fence." The army had the body reburied the next morning and replaced the flag. Secretary of the Territory Winthrop Sargent attached a proclamation to the pole offering one hundred dollars for the identification of the culprits. The criminals destroyed the flag and the proclamation the next night. Sargent responded by replacing the pole and stationing guards to protect the site until the vandalism finally ceased. Actions such as this undoubtedly would have infuriated Indians. They exemplified the disrespect heaped upon Native Americans by the frontier settlers and demonstrated the challenge to well-intentioned authorities.[55]

In late August 1792, Rufus Putnam informed Knox that "a person by the name of Harden" from Kentucky intended to organize a strike against the Indians. Harden, who had allegedly killed some friendly Indians years before, had publicly called for volunteers. Putnam urged punishment for any and all individuals who disregarded the authority of the United States. However, Harden had little trouble organizing a group of men willing to defy the federal government as a means to protect their families from the perceived Indian threat.[56]

The next year, Putnam observed that the Indian councils were also unable to contain the whims of their exuberant warriors. At Vincennes in 1793, Putnam met with several tribes of Wabashes. A "queen" of the Wea tribe "apologized for her Sons' not being [there]; saying: They are wicked when they are drunk—They have done a great deal of Mischief." She felt compelled to explain the reasons why: "Their Older Brothers spurr'd them to do mischief—They were not therefore altogether to blame." Clearly, the Indian confederacy was divided. Although the Indian council strove to make peace with the Americans, factions within the confederacy, and indeed within each tribe, opted for retaliation through violence.[57]

In a letter to President Washington, the Indian leaders of the Northwest Territory directly referred to the vexing problem of controlling both Native and white aggressors. They argued, "You desire us to call in our young men, we desire you also to call in yours." The violence on the frontier could not be curtailed until the Indian warriors believed that the Americans would no longer encroach on Indian lands.[58] These Native American leaders understood that both sides perpetuated the violence as acts of self-defense in a continuous cycle of offensive aggression.

In his final report to President Washington in December 1794, Henry Knox acknowledged that depredations originated from the American settlers as often as from the Indian warriors. He asserted:

> The desires of too many frontier white people, to seize, by force or fraud, upon the neighborhood Indian lands, has been, and still continues to be, an unceasing cause of jealousy and hatred on the part of the Indians; and it would appear, upon a calm investigation, that, until the Indians can be quieted upon this point, and rely with confidence upon the protection of their lands by the United States, no well grounded hope of tranquility can be entertained.[59]

Knox understood that frontier violence and the subsequent Indian wars initiated by unsanctioned actions could not be curtailed without a respectful and authoritative treaty between the United States and the Indian confederacy.

After an attack upon an Indian hunting party along Paint Creek, which was followed by retaliatory violence, Anthony Wayne wrote to St. Clair in July 1795 that the aggression of the "evil-disposed people" of Kentucky could prevent the upcoming peace treaty. Despite preliminary peace agreements, the Indians of the Ohio Country refused to succumb to the aggression of the unruly settlers. Wayne urged St. Clair to act more vigilantly in restraining the "nefarious conduct" of the frontier settlers.[60]

As the United States attempted to gain governmental control over the Northwest Territory, the Indians of the area refused to accept that the Treaty of Paris (1783) had transferred their land to the United States. The Americans arranged several treaty negotiations, but all lacked the participation of the entire Indian confederacy. Without full involvement, the confederacy did not view the treaties as binding, but it continued to try to make satisfactory agreements with the United States. While official negotiations continued, frontier settlers moved onto Indian lands. These uninvited settlers clashed with the Indians of the area, which resulted in bloodshed and hostility on the frontier. Henry Knox expressed the situation as a "confused state" of violence along the frontier. This made it "extremely difficult, nay impossible for an impartial mind to decide which party is right, or which is wrong."[61] These "foolish young men," settlers and Indians alike, acted against the official wishes of the United States government and the Indian confederacy, producing an unstable and violent existence on the Ohio frontier.

NOTES

1. *American State Papers: Indian Affairs* [hereafter *ASPIA*], vol. 1 (Washington, 1832), 544.

2. *ASPIA*, 1:13.

3. Michigan Pioneer and Historical Society, *Collections and Researches*, 40 vols. (Lansing: Michigan Pioneer and Historical Society, 1874–1915) [hereafter *MPHS*], 20:181.

4. Neville B. Craig, *The Olden Time; A monthly publication devoted to the Preservation of Documents and other Authentic Information in relation to the Early Explorations and the Settlement and Improvement of the Country around the Head of the Ohio* (Pittsburgh: Wright & Charlton, 1848; reprint, New York: Kraus Reprint Co., 1976), 2:417, 414, 422.

5. *MPHS*, 25:692.

6. Ms. 248, Northwest Territory Collection, Copy Book: Ohio Historical Society (Columbus, Ohio), 27–33.

7. Quoted in Paul W. Wehr, "The Treaty of Fort Finney, 1786: Prelude to the Indian Wars" (master's thesis, Miami University, 1958), 126, 118.

8. Quoted in Wehr, "The Treaty of Fort Finney," 106; Ebenezer Denny, *Military Journal of Major Ebenezer Denny: An Officer in the Revolutionary and Indian Wars, with an Introductory Memoir* (Philadelphia: J. B. Lippincott & Co, 1859; reprint, New York: Arno, 1971), 85.

9. There are very few references to attempts to apprehend and punish Indian killers. The most famous was Lewis Wetzel, who killed a Delaware Indian named George Washington. After escaping from army custody, Wetzel returned to Kentucky, where the settlers did not turn him in. Upon recapture by the army, prominent Kentucky citizens arranged for his release and even celebrated his return to Kentucky.

10. Ms. 248, Northwest Territory Collection, Copy Book: Ohio Historical Society (Columbus, Ohio), 39–40.

11. Joyce G. Williams and Jill E. Farrelly, *Diplomacy on the Indiana-Ohio Frontier, 1783–1791* (Bloomington: Indiana University Press Bicentennial Committee, 1976), 45, quoted in James Alton James, *The Life of George Rogers Clark* (New York: Greenwood Press, 1928), 351; John D. Barnhart and Dorothy L. Riker, *Indiana to 1816: The Colonial Period* (Indianapolis: Indiana Historical Bureau and Indiana Historical Society, 1971), 256.

12. Quoted in Wiley Sword, *President Washington's Indian War: The Struggle for the Old Northwest, 1790–1795* (Norman: University of Oklahoma Press, 1985), 31.

13. Here the Wabash Indians refer to the Indians living in or near the Miami villages along the Wabash River. By the mid-1780s, these villages consisted of Indians from many different tribes, predominantly Miamis, Shawnees, and Delawares, although some Ottawas, Iroquois, Potawatomis, Cherokees, and others could be found in the villages or nearby. The polyglot communities along the river are often simply referred to as the Wabash Indians rather than identified as a particular group. There are both friendly and unfriendly Indians who fall into this category.

14. William Henry Smith, ed., *The St. Clair Papers: The Life and Public Service of Arthur St. Clair: Soldier of the Revolutionary War, President of the Continental Congress, and Governor of the North-Western Territory* (New York: Da Capo Press, 1971), 2:21–22; *MPHS* 9:468; *ASPIA* 1:8–9; Denny, *Military Journal*, 221.

15. Smith, *St. Clair Papers*, 2:21–22.

16. Gayle Thornbrough, ed. *Outpost on the Wabash, 1787–1791: Letters of Brigadier General Josiah Harmar and Major John Francis Hamtramck* (Indianapolis: Indiana Historical Society, 1957), 108, 76–77.

17. Ibid., 22, 25, 42.

18. Ibid., 80–81.

19. Ibid., 106; Smith, *St. Clair Papers*, 1:87.

20. Thornbrough, *Outpost*, 114–16.

21. Ibid., 123–24.

22. Luke Justin Kiefer, *Gentlemen, Rogues, and Savages: United States–Native American Relations in the Old Northwest Territory, 1783–1812* (master's thesis, Ohio State University, 1996), 49, 38.

23. Smith, *St. Clair Papers*, 2:80, 83.

24. William Parker Cutler and Julia Perkins Cutler, *Life, Journals and Correspondence of Rev. Manasseh Cutler, LL.D.* (Cincinnati, OH: R. Clarke & Co., 1888), 447–48.

25. John Cleves Symmes and others rarely make a distinction between Indian groups in their correspondence; little attempt is made to identify the Indian tribes unless an individual Indian was known to them—at least in documentation.

26. Beverly W. Bond Jr., ed. *The Correspondence of John Cleves Symmes, Founder of the Miami Purchase* (New York: The Macmillan Company, 1926), 96–98.

27. "Western Indians" was a generic term that grouped the Indians living west and north of the Little Miami River, without distinguishing specific associations.

28. *ASPIA*, 1:13.

29. Thornbrough, *Outpost*, 176–85.

30. Smith, *St. Clair Papers*, 2:123.

31. Thornbrough, *Outpost*, 211.

32. *ASPIA*, 1:86.

33. Smith, *St. Clair Papers*, 2:133; *ASPIA*, 1:86.

34. *ASPIA*, 1:87.

35. Ibid., 1:89–90.

36. Ibid., 1:90.

37. Thornbrough, *Outpost*, 211; *ASPIA*, 1:88.

38. *ASPIA*, 1:88.

39. Rowena Buell, ed., *The Memoirs of Rufus Putnam and Certain Official Papers and Correspondence* (Boston: Houghton, Mifflin and Co., 1903), 233.

40. Smith, *St. Clair Papers*, 1:201n.

41. Ibid., 2:206.

42. *ASPIA*, 1:223.

43. Samuel L. Metcalf, *A Collection of Some of the Most Interesting Narratives of Indian Warfare in the West, containing an Account of the Adventures of Daniel Boone, One of the First Settlers of Kentucky, comprehending the most important occurrences relative to its early history—Also, an account of the Manners, and Customs of the Indians, their Traditions and Religious Sentiments, their Police or Civil Government, their Discipline and method of War: To which is added, An*

Account of the Expeditions of Genl's Harmer, Scott, Wilkinson, St. Clair & Wayne (Lexington, KY: William G. Hunt Co., 1821), 131–43.

44. Frazer E. Williams, ed., *Journal of Capt. Daniel Bradley: An Epic of the Ohio Frontier* (Greenville, OH: Frank H. Jobes and Son, 1935), 44–45; Buell, *Memoirs*, 292.

45. Eric Hinderaker, *Elusive Empires: Constructing Colonialism in the Ohio Valley, 1673–1800* (Cambridge: Cambridge University Press, 1997), 243; Don Henrich Tolzmann, ed., *The First Description of Cincinnati and Other Ohio Settlements: The Travel Report of Johann Heckewelder (1792)*, introduction by H. A. Rattermann (New York: University Press of America, 1988), 29–30.

46. O. M. Spencer, *The Indian Captivity of O.M. Spencer*, ed. Milo Milton Quaife (Chicago: Lakeside Press, 1917; reprint, New York: Dover Publications, 1995), 6–7.

47. Quoted in Richard Scamyhorn and John Steinle, *Stockades in the Wilderness: The Frontier Settlements of Southwestern Ohio, 1788–1795* (Dayton, OH: Landfall Press, 1986), 49, 50, 52.

48. Scamyhorn and Steinle, *Stockades*, 23, 39, 103.

49. Smith, *St. Clair Papers*, 2:309.

50. Spencer, *Indian Captivity*, 50–51.

51. Tolzmann, *First Description*, 47.

52. *The American Pioneer* 2, no. 4 (Ohio Historical Society, Columbus, Ohio), 185.

53. Charles Whittlesey, *Historical, Topographical and Geological Notices of Hamilton County, Ohio* (Cincinnati, OH: Cincinnati Historical Society), 14.

54. There is some discussion as to whether Wawiachteno was the chief's name, his title, or his tribe—or perhaps all of the above.

55. Tolzmann, *First Description*, 49–50.

56. *ASPIA*, 1:241.

57. Buell, *Memoirs*, 339, 340, 342–43.

58. *MPHS*, 20:314–15.

59. *ASPIA*, 1:544.

60. Smith, *St. Clair Papers*, 2:374.

61. Thornbrough, *Outpost*, 211.

Native American–French Interactions in Eighteenth-Century Southwest Michigan: The View from Fort St. Joseph

MICHAEL S. NASSANEY,
WILLIAM M. CREMIN, AND
LISAMARIE MALISCHKE

A PERVASIVE TREND IN HISTORICAL SCHOLARSHIP HAS BEEN A MOVE AWAY from broad metanarratives to more detailed examinations of concrete historical moments and contexts to better understand the nuances of events and processes at the local scale.[1] In the Americas, empirical studies have shown that historical outcomes were predicated upon the nature of empire, and the groups encountered in the changing circumstances of colonialism.[2] Considerable attention has been paid to the consequences of colonial encounters, particularly for indigenous groups who were often decimated by disease and warfare and subjugated politically, economically, and socially. While Europeans undeniably had a deleterious impact on Native peoples, the variable encounters and interactions between Natives and newcomers were neither inevitable nor predictable over the past five centuries. It behooves us to examine the conditions that engendered conflict, contestation, and cooperation. Furthermore, our understandings of colonialism are a product of the changing social and political conditions in which we live.[3] Suffice it to say that in a post-NAGPRA world,[4] in which Native peoples rightfully and increasingly insert themselves into popular and academic dialogues about Native histories, interpretations of the past are no longer seen as politically neutral. Yet, even as conflict and struggle have long been recognized as recurrent processes associated with New World encounters, academic and public imaginings acknowledge important variation in the ways in which different European powers interacted with Native hosts.[5]

In a popular treatment on this subject, James Volo and Dorothy Denneen Volo distinguished the French from their English and Spanish counterparts, noting that "the most enduring and harmonious relationships with the Native American population were formed with the French, who attempted with some success to peacefully coexist with the Indians, living with them, marrying into their families, and converting them to Christianity."[6] The intimate relations established between the French and their Native allies in the western Great Lakes, or the *pays d'en haut*, are seen as essential to the concept of the "middle ground" that was introduced and argued persuasively by the ethnohistorian Richard White.[7] The middle ground is a metaphorical space for accommodation in which Natives *and* newcomers were fundamentally transformed. In the middle ground, White sees an eighteenth-century world in which it was in the interests of both the French and Algonquians to form alliances and provide mutual aid to check the expansion of the English and the Iroquois.[8] From their interactions grew a number of practices and material objects that symbolize their political reconciliation. A poignant example is the calumet pipe and associated greeting ceremony that spread throughout the Mississippi Valley in conjunction with French exploration.[9] Originally developed to assuage differences among refugee groups in the mid- to late seventeenth century, the calumet became emblematic of the bonds created between strangers—a hallmark of mediation.

The purpose of this chapter is to examine the nature of relationships between the French and their Algonquian neighbors in southwest Michigan. Archaeological investigations conducted under the auspices of the Fort St. Joseph Archaeological Project since 1998 have led to the discovery and investigation of Fort St. Joseph, an important but heretofore poorly documented French mission/garrison/trading-post complex along the banks of the St. Joseph River.[10] Material and documentary evidence regarding the fort afford us the opportunity to reassess an important chapter in American history and evaluate the appropriateness of White's characterization for this particular historical place. We understand that White's model can be criticized on empirical grounds and may not be applicable to colonial relations throughout eastern North America. Yet investigations thus far suggest that interactions between the French occupants of Fort St. Joseph and the local Potawatomi and Miami populations of the area were generally cooperative and amicable until the 1760s, when the fort fell under British control. In the remainder of the chapter, we discuss the sources of evidence that lead us to this conclusion, and posit some explanations for these cultural patterns and processes. We begin by describing the historical and cultural context of the region immediately prior to European contact.

The site of Fort St. Joseph is located on the east bank of the St. Joseph River at Niles in southeastern Berrien County, Michigan (figure 1). The regional landscape is glacial in origin and consists of gently sloping moraines and till plains with flat, nearly level lake and outwash plains. After entering the county (and state) from Indiana, the river flows in a north-northwesterly direction before emptying into Lake Michigan at the City of St. Joseph. While the valley features extensive floodplains along the river's lower course, in the Niles area the St. Joseph is confined by moraines, and floodplain development is minimal.

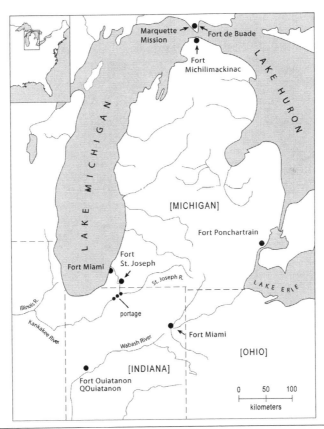

Figure 1. Map of southwest Michigan and adjacent regions showing the locations of Fort St. Joseph and other French settlements. Map drawn by Pamela Rups and used courtesy of the Fort St. Joseph Archaeological Project.

Clearing the land for agriculture beginning in the Pioneer period (ca. 1830–1860) has undoubtedly impacted the landscape of the valley. Immediately before these changes, the vegetation was a rich mosaic of oak-hickory and beech-maple woodlands, prairies or oak openings, swamps, and marshes. These plant associations provided spring sap, greens, tubers, and rhizomes; summer-ripening fruits and berries; and the autumn nut mast. A broad range of animals was of economic importance to both Native and early Euro-American populations. Elk frequented the nutrient-rich grass-lands, whereas white-tailed deer were attracted to the abundant browse found along the many edges created by this vegetative mosaic. Waterfowl and upland birds such as the turkey and ruffed grouse were plentiful, as were turtles, fish, and shellfish in streams, lakes, and marshes. Spawning lake sturgeon, which sought out "shallows" in the St. Joseph River in late spring/early summer, constituted an important seasonal food resource.[11]

Thus, the lower St. Joseph River valley has attracted human occupation for thousands of years, though the settlement patterns and scheduling of activities to exploit these resources remain poorly understood.[12] The archaeological remains of the area's occupants from immediately prior to European contact are identified as the Berrien Phase (ca. A.D. 1400–1600), a cultural manifestation marked by both shell-tempered and grit-tempered pottery associated with seasonally occupied sites, including the Moccasin Bluff site some twelve miles north of the fort.[13] Berrien Phase components have been identified in the lower Kalamazoo River valley at the Schwerdt and Elam sturgeon fisheries,[14] and on the lower Galien River.[15] Evidence obtained from several small seasonal encampments on the Galien, including radiocarbon dates and a piece of European trade brass, may extend this phase to ca. 1640.[16]

Oral tradition and early French documents suggest that the Potawatomis had earlier moved into western Lower Michigan following their separation from their Ojibwa and Ottawa kin at the Straits of Mackinac.[17] Once established in their new homeland, they adopted a mixed economic strategy that included maize agriculture, though its contribution to the diet remains unknown. There is good reason to believe that the Berrien Phase represents the Potawatomis before their relocation to the Green Bay area of Wisconsin in the mid-seventeenth century.[18] However, the ethnic identification of pre-contact groups in the Great Lakes region is fraught with difficulties.[19]

Evidence of Potawatomi settlement on Rock Island (identified by the French as the "Island of the Potawatomis") in the mouth of Green Bay comes from five seasons of excavation, during which Ronald Mason identified pottery with strong similarities to ceramic assemblages only occurring earlier on the eastern side of Lake Michigan.[20] In other words, when the Potawatomis abandoned their homeland under Iroquoian pressure and moved to northeastern Wisconsin, they brought their ceramic traditions with them.[21] Rock Island appears to represent one of several refugee centers brought about by the domino effect of Iroquoian incursions or perceived threats, which led to regional migrations and the abandonment of former homelands. It was in multiethnic communities such as the village on Rock Island that the underlying premise of alliance—mediation as a source of influence—emerged, perhaps accompanied by the spread of the calumet. The Potawatomis perfected this essentially Algonquian practice and showed the French how their "role as mediators has made them the most influential group at Green Bay."[22] According to James Clifton, this environment offered the Potawatomis social and strategic advantages by providing temporary security from Iroquois raids, direct access to French trade goods, and a political climate offering opportunities for expansion and cultural growth.[23]

In 1679, the French explorer LaSalle visited this settlement on Rock Island. He then proceeded south to the mouth of the St. Joseph River, which he called "the River of the Miamis." There he built Fort Miami, the first European settlement in the region. After a month's stay at Fort Miami, LaSalle ascended the river in search of a portage near South Bend, Indiana, by which to reach the Kankakee River, a tributary of the Illinois. While traveling up the St. Joseph, LaSalle did not observe, or at least mention, any Native settlements along the river until he found a mixed community of Miami-Mascouten-Wea Indians located at the southwestern end of the portage near the headwaters of the Kankakee.[24] Given the time of year that LaSalle arrived among this group, together with the reported presence of bison carcasses in the vicinity, this community was almost certainly a temporary winter hunting encampment. Native groups did not permanently reoccupy the area until the 1680s, when some Miamis—possibly at the insistence of the Jesuit missionary Father Claude Allouez—relocated to the St. Joseph River from LaSalle's Fort St. Louis on the Illinois River. There, in proximity to the portage and the old Sauk trail that connected Lakes Erie and Michigan, a mission was established to serve them.[25]

Various documents place the earliest Miami village(s) resulting from this relocation on the east side of the river just north of the Michigan-Indiana line. However, shortly after the construction of Fort St. Joseph near the Jesuit mission at Niles in 1691, the Miamis moved downriver and may have taken up residence along Brandywine Creek, a tributary stream that enters the St. Joseph from the east only a short distance south of the fort.[26] Later, the Miamis relocated once again to the west bank of the river directly opposite the fort.[27] Their decision to move closer to Fort St. Joseph suggests that they and the French residents of the fort were forging mutually beneficial relations.

Occupation of the lower St. Joseph River valley by the Miamis alone proved to be short-lived. In 1695, the vanguard of a Potawatomi expansion from their refuge in northeastern Wisconsin, numbering two hundred strong, took up residence on the river. By 1718, the Potawatomis were numerous enough to replace the Miamis as the dominant force in the valley.[28] Although small communities of Miamis continued to coexist with Potawatomi villages in the vicinity of Fort St. Joseph until the mid-eighteenth century, thereafter only the latter remained.[29]

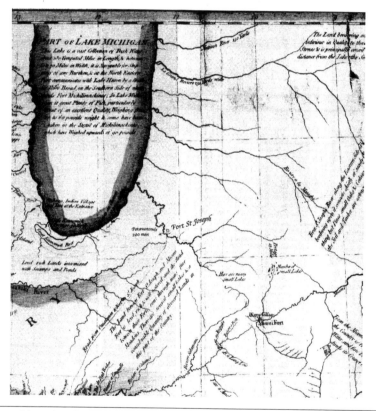

Figure 2. Adaptation of the Hutchins map of 1778 showing Fort St. Joseph and the presence of two hundred Potawatomi men across the river from the fort. Courtesy of the Fort St. Joseph Archaeological Project.

Thomas Hutchins noted the presence of the Potawatomis when he surveyed Fort St. Joseph on behalf of the British Crown in 1762. On his very detailed map of the region, published in 1778, Hutchins marked the Potawatomi village across the river from the fort and indicated that this settlement included 200 men (figure 2).[30] During the next eighty years, the frequently shifting Potawatomi villages would come to occupy the entire lower valley, from the river's mouth to just above South Bend, Indiana.[31] Although we cannot be certain of the size of the resident Potawatomi population during their period of ascendancy, some numbers, certainly to be judged as minimal estimates, are available for the period just prior to American settlement. A 1757 report by Bougainville, who was charged with determining the condition of French posts and the number of Indians associated with them as potential allies, puts the number of Potawatomi men of Fort St. Joseph at 400.[32] This would indicate a local population of approximately 2,000. In 1819, General Jacob Brown reported 790 Potawatomis in six semipermanent villages along the river. A decade later, in 1828, a Mr. E. Reed of Carey Mission near Niles was commissioned by Governor Lewis Cass to conduct a census of the Native population residing on the river between its mouth and the Michigan-Indiana line. Conducted in July, Reed found only 175 Potawatomis residing in eight villages, but assured Cass that 400–500 people regarded these villages where they planted their corn as home.[33] Suffice it to say that there was a significant Native presence in the lower St. Joseph River valley in the late seventeenth and eighteenth centuries, and their population size certainly exceeded that of the French.

Sites associated with Native occupation immediately prior to contact and into the seventeenth and eighteenth centuries have been identified and documented in the state site files, although only limited archaeological investigations have been conducted. Some of these consist of no more than isolated finds, whereas others are based on documentary sources and have not been verified in the field. While most sites cannot be assigned to specific ethnic groups, the presence of low-fired earthenware ceramics, triangular projectile points, chipped stone debris, human remains, and associated imported European artifacts testify to a significant Native presence in the vicinity of the fort.

Archaeological evidence of eighteenth-century Native activity has been documented across the river from the fort, where the Potawatomis settled after the departure of the Miamis. Salvage excavations conducted there in 2000 identified the burials of an adolescent and an adult female associated with an eighteenth-century brass kettle.[34] Another Indian burial was exhumed in the 1950s,[35] and many of the French artifacts in the Fort St. Joseph Museum collected from the vicinity of the fort may come from eighteenth-century Native sites. The nearby Brandywine Creek 2 site south of the fort has yielded Indian pottery that may tie it to "the Miami Village of 1693."[36]

Excavations conducted under the auspices of the Fort St. Joseph Archaeological Project since 2000 have led to the recovery of a mixed assemblage of Native and European artifacts from the terrace immediately above the fort site. First identified in the 1930s and designated the Lyne site (20BE10), materials from the terrace include triangular stone projectile points of the Madison variety, shell-tempered pottery, copious amounts of fire-cracked rock, several stone smoking pipes, and a range of European imports— including gunflints, flintlock hardware such as a trigger and a sideplate, a pewter brooch, numerous copper-alloy scraps, a cut fragment of trade silver perforated for use as an ornament (figure 3), and a copper-alloy hair pipe, among other probable eighteenth-century artifacts.

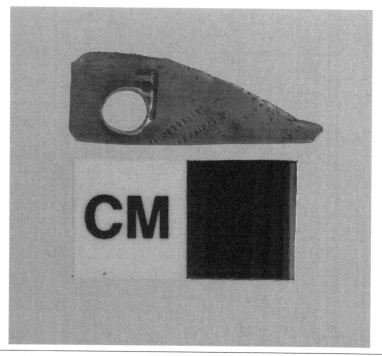

Figure 3. A modified fragment of trade silver perforated for use as an ornament recovered from the Lyne site (20BE10) in close proximity to Fort St. Joseph. Photograph by John Lacko and used courtesy of the Fort St. Joseph Archaeological Project.

In addition, we have identified two clusters of pits filled with carbonized corncobs. These features bear formal similarity to the smudge pits used to tan hides in the Native manner that have been noted at the fort and the earlier Moccasin Bluff site.[37] A sample of the pit contents have been radiocarbon dated to A.D. 1710 ± 50 years, indicating that the pits are roughly contemporaneous with the nearby fort. The co-occurrence of Native style and imported European artifacts on this landform suggests that people with familiarity with both types of goods (e.g., Indians, métis, and/or acculturated French) lived in close proximity to the fort. More extensive excavations of these deposits can provide support for this interpretation and help us to understand the intimate relationships between the French and Natives in the region.

Figure 4. A brass kettle from the vicinity of Fort St. Joseph. Photograph by Roger L. Rosentreter and used courtesy of the Fort St. Joseph Museum, Niles, MI.

In 1998 Western Michigan University archaeologists in partnership with Support the Fort, Inc., the Fort St. Joseph Museum, and the City of Niles initiated the Fort St. Joseph Archaeological Project.[38] The long-term project goals are to use historical and archaeological data to better understand the material and social consequences of the fur trade and colonialism in southwest Michigan.[39] The location of the Fort St. Joseph site was apparently well known to local collectors in the late nineteenth century as they accumulated more than 100,000 European objects that are now curated in local museums (figure 4). However, due to changes in local hydrology associated with a nearby dam, and the establishment of a twentieth-century landfill, which in part conceals the location of interest, the site was difficult to identify on the ground. In 1998, Support the Fort, Inc., a community group dedicated to the identification and preservation of the remains of Fort St. Joseph, invited WMU archaeologists to search for the fort.[40] In an effort to accurately reconstruct the fort in Niles, they sought archaeological information on the fort's location, size, and configuration, along with other architectural details, since neither detailed maps nor thorough descriptions of the fort are known to exist.

Figure 5. A fireplace exposed during excavations at Fort St. Joseph. Photograph by Stephanie Barrante and used courtesy of the Fort St. Joseph Archaeological Project.

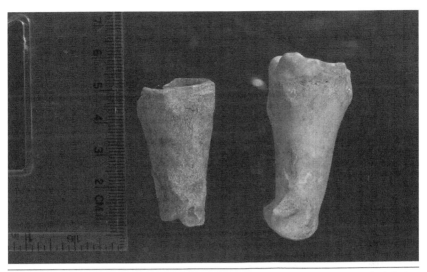

Figure 6. A deer phalanx modified into a cup from a cup–and–pin game is shown on the left. An unmodified comparative specimen is shown on the right. Photograph by Rory Becker and used courtesy of the Fort St. Joseph Archaeological Project.

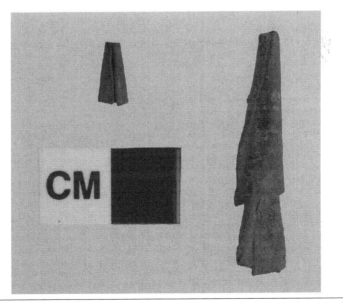

Figure 7. Tinkling cones recovered from excavations at Fort St. Joseph. Photograph by John Lacko and used courtesy of the Fort St. Joseph Archaeological Project.

Since our initial survey revealed definitive evidence of the fort, we have returned repeatedly to the site to conduct more intensive work and evaluate the contexts of our finds. We routinely install a sophisticated well-point drainage system prior to excavation and employ the results of a geophysical survey to examine subsurface anomalies that have potential cultural significance.[41] Since 2002, we have recovered thousands of eighteenth-century artifacts and associated plant and animal remains, and identified numerous features including European-style stone hearths, fireplaces (figure 5), a possible well, post molds, a possible wall trench, several pit features, and middens.

Artifact deposits associated with a broad range of eighteenth-century activities have been uncovered in a majority of our excavation units. What is particularly intriguing is the presence of imported European artifacts and architectural elements, as well as artifacts and activities produced or inspired by Native cultural practices. For example, much of the artifact assemblage consists of European goods employed in the fur trade or used by the fort inhabitants in daily life. Stone fireplaces and hearths testify to European architectural styles. A concentration of more than one hundred gun parts and other metal artifacts has been interpreted as a gunsmith's cache or repair kit. Yet, interspersed among these foreign materials is evidence of the traders' Native spouses, their métis offspring, and activities that represent or mimic Native customs and habits. A number of artifacts suggest Native production and/or use, including several triangular stone arrow points, a bone projectile point, a bone awl, several bone tools of unknown function, a number of local stone and catlinite smoking-pipe fragments, a deer phalanx modified into a cup from the well-known Native cup-and-pin game (figure 6), and two antler gaming pieces or platter dice.[42] Activities that were new to the French include hide tanning, represented by a smudge pit; grease extraction, indicated by fractured animal bones; and the local production of tinkling cones (figure 7), inferred from copper-alloy cutouts.[43] Although we have examined only a small portion of a very large and complex site, we are obtaining tantalizing clues regarding the identities of the fort occupants and the nature of their interactions by juxtaposing the extant documentary and material evidence. A picture of cooperation, interdependence, and métissage begins to emerge and invites us to take a closer look.

In his compelling study *The Middle Ground*, Richard White underscores the importance of the fragile yet enduring alliance that the Algonquians and French maintained for more than a century.[44] He shows that French and Indian success in defending against the Iroquois and their English supporters was dependent on their ability to create bonds of trust and solidarity.

Such relations required that the French protect and supply their allies and, above all, mediate the differences between them.[45] In short, both sides created an elaborate network of political, economic, and social ties to meet the demands of a new cultural milieu.[46] Intermarrying, exchanging gifts, providing services, lowering prices, selling brandy, and accepting deerskins in trade even though they were in limited demand—these were some of the tactics the French used to subsidize the trade and demonstrate their support. The French Crown also provided an interpreter at the site to facilitate communication. In turn, the Indians often conducted themselves according to the expectations of Onontio, the French governor. In addition, the Potawatomis provided the French with warriors in the 1684, 1687, and 1696 expeditions into the Iroquois country.[47]

An examination of the limited documentary sources that discuss Native Americans in the vicinity of the fort, and the emerging archaeological evidence from our investigations can be used to frame an understanding of French and Indian interaction. Moreover, these sources provide an opportunity to evaluate White's claims at a specific historical place on the eighteenth-century frontier.

When Fort St. Joseph was constructed in 1691, it included a small commandant's house, a building that could accommodate up to twenty soldiers, a military storehouse, and some buildings to store trade goods and furs.[48] These buildings were enclosed by a palisade, although it was not especially well constructed, for in 1695 the Iroquois Indians were able to put their guns through gaps in the wall and shoot into the fort.[49] In 1721, the Jesuit priest Pierre de Charlevoix reported that the "commandant's house, which is but a sorry one, is called the fort, from its being surrounded with an indifferent pallisado."[50] This was, apparently, quite a common condition at the smaller forts.[51] From this situation, we can infer that the fort was a more symbolic than defensive structure. Furthermore, community residents lived outside of the palisade walls, as suggested by archaeological materials at the nearby Lyne site. This implies that neighboring Native groups were not perceived as a constant threat. Despite their peaceful coexistence, the fort's commandant in 1750 ordered the construction of a jail measuring 8 by 10 feet, built of square cut stone and provided with "iron work."[52]

Under these conditions, exchanges of services, goods, and personnel were quite common and served to cement the alliances that were so crucial to both groups. For example, the Indians often requested the service of a blacksmith or gunsmith who could repair their metal tools and weapons. Payment records reveal that a gunsmith/blacksmith lived at the fort from 1739 to 1752.[53] Baptismal records show that one resided there as early as

1730,[54] and archaeological evidence of a gunsmith's repair kit postdating 1713 has recently been reported.[55] Written accounts also indicate that resident smiths repaired Native weapons at the king's expense in July 1739 in connection with the Chickasaw war.[56] This pattern was repeated in other conflicts.[57] Dehaistre, one of the documented smiths, had so much interaction with the local Indians that he became familiar enough with their language to act as interpreter for the French in the absence of the official translator.[58] In 1747, the French agreed to build a house in the European style for one of the Indian chiefs.[59] These examples suggest that the French were more than willing to use their expertise in metallurgy and carpentry to accommodate Native desires.

The support of Indian war efforts was not limited to repairing weapons. The French offered feasts to Potawatomi warriors going off to fight,[60] and provided supplies and gifts to the wives left behind.[61] At other times, the French provided gifts of blankets to "cover" a dead Fort St. Joseph Indian at his burial,[62] and in at least one instance made available a coffin for the son of a Potawatomi chief from the fort.[63] All of these expenses were charged to the king's account.

Of course, the glue that bound the Natives and French together in the fur trade was the goods being exchanged. The archaeological record from Fort St. Joseph has yielded hundreds of objects manufactured in France, many of which were intended for use in gift exchange. These imports include glass beads, iron knives, brass kettles, objects of adornment such as finger rings, and a range of other more perishable commodities, including clothing and textiles. Many of these objects have been found in excavations at the fort, where they were stored, as well as at sites where Natives consumed and discarded them.[64]

This is not to imply that the French and Natives always lived apart from each other. It is reported that Indian slaves, some of whom chose to be baptized, lived within the confines of the fort with French families.[65] In addition, marriage and baptismal records indicate that several French fur traders, of the twelve to fifteen living at the fort, were married to Indian women.[66] Intermarriage was a way to fortify French-Indian ties. It is also likely that some French men had so-called "country wives" whom they had married *à la façon du pays*. The Jesuits were generally more accepting of interracial marriage if the wife converted to Catholicism. The baptismal record indicates that Indian women did convert, oftentimes prior to marriage. However, Native children and infants, perhaps the métis offspring of a French father and an Indian mother, more frequently appear in the register.[67] Tribal affiliations mentioned in the baptismal register include Potawatomi, Miami, Abenaki, Sauk, Illinois, and Ottawa.

Some Indian women were chosen to be godmothers for each other's children, implying the sincerity of Native conversion. Godparents were selected to create strong economic and political ties within the community, thus suggesting the role that these women played in society. The selection of godparents served to create fictive kin, which signified as much about exchange relations as the nature of religious faith.[68] Baptism affirmed the value of social relationships and extended the bonds of social solidarity. Baptismal records show Native wives acting as godmothers to the children of socially prominent fort residents, such as the blacksmith and merchants. It would appear that the French women of Fort St. Joseph welcomed Native women into their social spheres, in contrast to relations between English and Native women where boundaries were less permeable. Comparatively speaking, Native relations with the French differ from those with the English. Although the English were known to engage in sexual relations with Native peoples, they did not acknowledge the array of phenotypes and cultural identities that such interactions produced. Instead, they hardened their resolve to place all peoples into literally black and white categories.[69]

It is far too simplistic to see the French as the donor culture and the Indians as merely the recipients. Indeed, the French had much to learn from their Native hosts. According to Bruce Trigger, the Indians taught the French how to make canoes, sleds, snowshoes, winter clothing, and maple sugar; plant maize; harvest wild edible and medicinal plants; and hunt northern animals.[70] Evidence for the French adoption of Native practices, or the presence of Native activities within the confines of the fort, is emerging from the archaeological record. For instance, while guns are well represented at the fort site, we have recovered several well-made triangular Madison arrow points, one associated with a French fireplace. Other artifacts produced in the Native style are several stone smoking-pipe fragments. One is clearly a Micmac variety, perhaps used in the calumet ceremony, whereas two are of red pipestone, possibly catlinite.[71] In proximity to these stone pipes, we also recovered two antler gaming pieces. These disc-shaped platter dice are smooth on one side and have incised symbols on the reverse; they bear formal similarity to those used in the dice game of the Ottawas and Potawatomis as observed by Perrot and Sabrevois.[72] Clifton recorded similar dice in use in the 1960s in a woman's game played by teams from the senior and junior sides of their dual division or moiety, which was only important in organizing the games.[73] The dice consist of six or seven disks and two special pieces representing totems, such as horse, turtle, buffalo, or man.

Another object of recreation is a small deer phalanx carved into the shape of a cup (see figure 6). This object was part of a cup-and-pin game that was popular among Native groups throughout North America.[74]

We have also collected a large assemblage of animal bone remains from sealed deposits at the site. Identification of the bones indicates that while a few pigs, cows, a horse, and other domesticated animals are represented, the majority of the remains derive from wild animal species.[75] This may point to the scarcity of domesticated animals on the frontier during this period, or the fact that some species such as cows and horses were too valuable to slaughter. The high frequencies of deer bones suggest that Native women used familiar food resources, prepared them in traditional Indian ways, and did much of the cooking. Many of the bones have been deliberately splintered, probably pursuant to being placed in brass kettles where they could be boiled to extract grease or tallow, a potentially valuable commodity.

Hides were tanned using Native techniques at the site, based on the identification of a small shallow pit filled with more than five thousand carbonized corncob, cupule, kernel, and stalk fragments. This feature is almost identical to the "corn holes" reported for the Berrien Phase component at Moccasin Bluff and at the Lyne site, and likely represents a context in which these remains were burned to produce a smoke smudge.[76] Cured hides were probably used to make leather shirts, leggings, moccasins, and pouches for trade or for use by the fort inhabitants.[77] Clothing was likely embroidered with imported glass beads in the Woodlands style.[78] Native peoples incorporated glass beads along with beads of shell, stone, bone, and antler to adorn their bodies, clothing, and ritual objects like pipes. Residents of the fort and the neighboring community employed such decorative styles in varying social contexts as a medium to express and negotiate identity.[79] In a multiethnic community like Fort St. Joseph, the visual result would be combinations of European and Native styles of clothing.

Glass, shell, and rosary beads have been recovered from the fort excavations.[80] Rosaries were often given as gifts to Native converts following baptism. Marie Jeanne, a thirteen-year-old slave girl of a prominent Fort St. Joseph merchant, was among the converted. The merchant's wife acted as godmother, and may have instructed the girl in the ways of the Bible.[81] A gift of a rosary would have been common at this event. Though rosaries could have become reinterpreted within a Native worldview, archaeological evidence suggests that at least some devout Catholics of various ethnicities used religious paraphernalia in accordance with sacred beliefs.[82]

Finally, another practice that expresses the close interactions between the French and Natives is the production of tinkling cones (see figure 7).

Used as decorative objects to adorn clothing and bags, tinkling cones are quintessential intercultural artifacts. Both Natives and Europeans typically made them from old, worn-out copper-alloy kettles, apparently in an opportunistic manner.[83] Besides the cones themselves, numerous pieces of cut-out scrap have been found at the fort site, testifying to the importance of this activity. While tinkling cones were made of imported raw materials, their form and use were inspired by Native demands, and they serve to underscore the process of métissage that marked the frontier in eighteenth-century southwest Michigan.

All human groups interact with their neighbors, and encounters can be hostile, particularly between groups with differing worldviews, values, and practices. Yet, under specific historical circumstances, groups can put aside their social, political, and economic differences and establish common ground. In eighteenth-century southwest Michigan, the Potawatomis, Miamis, and French were socially and politically interdependent for a variety of reasons. Perhaps most importantly, they needed each other because they shared a common enemy. To maintain cordial relations, groups participated in a delicately balanced relationship involving gift-giving, service, and mutual respect. Lacking a substantial demographic and military base in the *pays d'en haut*, the French strategy was to establish outposts and create alliances with their Algonquian neighbors to check Iroquoian and English expansion and to secure the interior, if only temporarily.

In this chapter, we have used the documentary and archaeological records to evaluate the extent to which the metanarrative of the middle ground holds for a small corner of New France along the banks of the St. Joseph River in southwest Michigan. The evidence suggests that efforts were made to ensure that Native allies residing around the southern end of Lake Michigan had continued French support in the face of British-sponsored incursions into the region by the Five Nations Iroquois, and to promote the fur trade for mutual benefit.

Material and documentary evidence demonstrates that both groups were accommodating each other. In addition to data on intermarriage and gift-giving, which are frequently cited practices by which the French sought to maintain and strengthen their alliances with Native groups, the fort residents were clearly beneficiaries of Native knowledge and experience in the harvesting and consumption of local resources to sustain themselves. For example, the role of domestic livestock in feeding the community pales in comparison to the sustenance derived from wild animal species. And the practice of extracting bone grease, a valuable commodity on the frontier, is not an activity of French origin, though it was frequently practiced.

Furthermore, the farmers at the fort appear to have adopted the cultivation of maize, and the presence of charred corncobs in smudge pits suggests hide tanning, a Native activity that points to cultural exchange or intermarriage. From resource harvesting to culinary practices and hide-curing, the French residents of Fort St. Joseph benefited daily from interactions with their Native allies.

A picture is emerging of a French population crafting a new culture on the frontier in interaction with their Native allies. Thus, the French were becoming just as acculturated if not more so than the Indians. For example, the production of tinkling cones and stone pipes implies new activities that the French could have only learned on the frontier. The presence of chipped-stone arrow points and antler gaming pieces are also good indicators of cultural mixing, along with the cup-and-pin game and the plethora of wild animal bones. In short, the archaeological evidence points to a cultural hybridization that characterizes the process of ethnogenesis.[84] It challenges us to think in new ways about cultural encounters in the Americas.

Near the end of the French regime in North America, one English subject compared his countrymen's demeanor with that of the French.[85] He noted that "the French have found some secret of conciliating the affections of the savages, which our traders seem stranger to, or at least take no care to put it in practice." He went on to say: "Moreover, the [Albany merchants] lacked the birchbark canoes, the voyageurs to man them, and the prime requisite, the willingness to accept the Indians on their own terms—in short, all the special skills needed for this particular trade."[86] The British who took command of Fort St. Joseph after the French were defeated in 1761 employed very different tactics of diplomacy that ultimately precipitated Pontiac's Rebellion (1763). The British, under General Jeffrey Amherst, ended the practice of treating Indians as allies and assumed that they were subjects, and considered them as such. Presents of tobacco, gunpowder, and other goods, previously used by the French to open and close negotiations and cement alliances, were reduced or eliminated. Incursions onto Indian lands were not negotiated as they had been under the French.[87] The American policy of Indian Removal that culminated in the 1830s was equally intolerant of Native peoples. The legacy of the French in southwest Michigan can teach us lessons about cultural encounters, colonialism, and coexistence that would serve us well in efforts to create multiethnic societies in the twenty-first century.

NOTES

1. Colin Calloway, *The Scratch of a Pen: 1763 and the Transformation of North America* (Oxford: Oxford University Press, 2006).
2. Neal Ferris, *The Archaeology of Native-Lived Colonialism: Challenging History in the Great Lakes* (Tucson: University of Arizona Press, 2008); Gilles Havard, *Empire et métissage: Indiens et Français dans le Pays d'en Haut, 1660–1715* (Paris: Septentrion et les Presses de l'Université Paris-Sorbonne, 2003).
3. Michael S. Nassaney, "Native American Gender Relations and Material Culture in Seventeenth-Century Southeastern New England," *Journal of Social Archaeology* 4, no. 3 (2004): 334–67; Michael S. Nassaney, "Transcending Colonial Borders through the Archaeology of Fort St. Joseph" (paper presented at the 42nd Annual Conference on Underwater and Historical Archaeology, Toronto, Canada, 2009); Stephen W. Silliman, "Culture Contact or Colonialism? Challenges in the Archaeology of Native North America," *American Antiquity* 70, no. 1 (2005): 55–74.
4. The Native American Graves Protection and Repatriation Act (NAGPRA) was passed in 1990. It gives federally recognized Native American groups the right to determine the disposition of ancestral human remains and associated objects. NAGPRA has forced archaeologists and Native peoples to acknowledge that they are both interested in the history and cultures of the Americas prior to European colonialism.
5. Denys Delâge, "French and English Colonial Models in North America," *Le Journal* 18, no. 3 (2002): 4–8.
6. James M. Volo and Dorothy Denneen Volo, *Daily Life on the Old Colonial Frontier* (Westport, CT: Greenwood Press, 2002), xxi.
7. Richard White, *The Middle Ground: Indians, Empires, and Republics in the Great Lakes Region, 1650–1815* (Cambridge: Cambridge University Press, 1991).
8. White, *Middle Ground*, 30.
9. Ian W. Brown, "The Calumet Ceremony in the Southeast and Its Archaeological Manifestations," *American Antiquity* 54, no. 2 (1989): 311–31.
10. Michael S. Nassaney, ed., *An Archaeological Reconnaissance Survey to Locate Remains of Fort St. Joseph (20BE23) in Niles, Michigan*, Archaeological Report No. 22 (Kalamazoo: Department of Anthropology, Western Michigan University, 1999); Dunning Idle, *The Post of the St. Joseph River during the French Regime, 1679–1761* (Niles, MI: Fort St. Joseph Museum, 2003) (originally completed PhD dissertation, Department of History, University of Illinois, Urbana, 1946).

11. R. L. Bettarel and H. G. Smith, comp., *Moccasin Bluff Site and the Woodland Cultures of Southwestern Michigan*, Anthropological Papers No. 49, Museum of Anthropology, University of Michigan, Ann Arbor, 1973; William M. Cremin and Michael S. Nassaney, "Background Research," in *An Archaeological Reconnaissance Survey to Locate Remains of Fort St. Joseph (20BE23) in Niles, Michigan*, ed. M. S. Nassaney, 7–30, Archaeological Report No. 22 (Kalamazoo: Department of Anthropology, Western Michigan University, 1999).

12. Cremin and Nassaney, "Background Research"; Jodie A. O'Gorman, "The Myth of Moccasin Bluff: Rethinking the Potawatomi Pattern," *Ethnohistory* 54, no. 3 (2007): 373–406.

13. Bettarel and Smith, *Moccasin Bluff Site*; William M. Cremin, "Researching the 'Void' between History and Prehistory in Southwest Michigan," *Michigan Archaeologist* 38, nos. 1–2 (1992): 19–37; Cremin and Nassaney, "Background Research"; O'Gorman, *Myth*.

14. William M. Cremin, "The Schwerdt Site: A Fifteenth Century Fishing Station on the Lower Kalamazoo River, Southwest Michigan," *Wisconsin Archaeologist* 61, no. 2 (1980): 280–91; William M. Cremin, "Late Prehistoric Adaptive Strategies on the Northern Periphery of the Carolinian Biotic Province: A Case Study from Southwest Michigan," *Midcontinental Journal of Archaeology* 8, no. 1 (1983): 91–107.

15. William M. Cremin, ed., *Archaeological Investigations in the Lower Galien River Valley of Southwest Michigan*, Technical Report No. 23 (Kalamazoo: Department of Anthropology, Western Michigan University, 1990); William M. Cremin, Gregory R. Walz, and Daniel B. Goatley, *A Report of Significant Data Recovered from Features 6 and 48 on Site 20BE410 during Archaeological Investigations Undertaken by Western Michigan University in the Lower Galien River Valley of Southwest Michigan*, Report of Investigations No. 99 (Kalamazoo: Department of Anthropology, Western Michigan University, 1991).

16. William M. Cremin, "The Berrien Phase of Southwest Michigan: Proto-Potawatomi?" in *Investigating the Archaeological Record of the Great Lakes State: Essays in Honor of Elizabeth Baldwin Garland*, ed. M. B. Holman, J. G. Brashler, and K. E. Parker (Kalamazoo: New Issues Press, 1996), 383–413.

17. James A. Clifton, *The Prairie People: Continuity and Change in Potawatomi Indian Culture, 1665* (Lawrence: Regents Press of Kansas, 1977); James A. Clifton, "Potawatomi," in *Peoples of the Three Fires: The Ottawa, Potawatomi and Ojibway of Michigan*, ed. J. A. Clifton, G. L. Cornell, and J. M. McClurken (Grand Rapids: Michigan Indian Press, 1996), 39–74.

18. Cremin, "Researching"; and Cremin, "Berrien Phase."

19. David S. Brose, "The Direct Historical Approach in Michigan Archaeology," *Ethnohistory* 18 (1971): 51–61.

20. Ronald J. Mason, *Rock Island: Historical Indian Archaeology in the Northern Lake Michigan Basin*, MCJA Special Paper No. 6 (Kent, OH: Kent State University Press, 1986).

21. Mason, *Rock Island*, 218.

22. White, *Middle Ground*, 35.

23. Clifton, "Potawatomi," 726.

24. M. B. Anderson, ed., *Relation of the Discoveries and Voyages of Cavelier de LaSalle from 1679 to 1681: The Official Narrative* (Chicago: Caxton Club, 1901).

25. George Brown et al., *Dictionary of Canadian Biography* (Toronto: University of Toronto Press, 1966), 57–58, 172–84; Cremin, "Berrien Phase," 397; Richard Colebrook Harris, ed., *Historical Atlas of Canada*, vol.1, *From the Beginning to 1800* (Toronto: University of Toronto Press, 1987), plates 38–39; Robert C. Myers and Joseph L. Peyser, "Four Flags over Fort St. Joseph," *Michigan History* 75, no. 5 (1991): 12.

26. Donald J. Berthrong, *An Historical Report on Indian Use and Occupancy of Northern Indiana and Southwestern Michigan* (New York: Garland, 1974); Cremin, "Berrien Phase," 397.

27. Cremin, "Researching," 31, figure 7.

28. W. V. Kinietz, *The Indians of the Western Great Lakes, 1615–1760* (Ann Arbor: University of Michigan Press, 1972), 163, 309; Wayne C. Temple, "Indian Villages of the Illinois Country: Historic Tribes," *Scientific Papers*, vol. 2, pt. 2 (Springfield: Illinois State Museum, 1958), 127.

29. Cremin, "Researching," 33, figure 8.

30. Joseph L. Peyser, trans. and ed., *Letters from New France: The Upper Country, 1686–1783* (Urbana: University of Illinois Press, 1992), 73.

31. Cremin, "Researching"; Cremin, "Background," 399, figure 5.

32. José António Brandão and Michael S. Nassaney, "A Capsule Social and Material History of Fort St. Joseph (1691–1763) and Its Inhabitants," *French Colonial History* 7 (2006): 68.

33. Cremin, "Researching," 35.

34. Michael S. Nassaney, Daniel Osborne, and Stacy Bell, *Salvage Excavations near the Junction of French and St. Joseph Streets, Niles, Michigan*, Report of Investigations No. 108 (Kalamazoo: Department of Anthropology, Western Michigan University, 2000).

35. Arthur Jelinek, "A Late Historic Burial from Berrien County," *Michigan Archaeologist* 4, no. 3 (1958): 48–51.

36. Bettarel and Smith, *Moccasin Bluff Site*, 143.
37. Richard I. Ford, "The Moccasin Bluff Corn Holes," in *Moccasin Bluff Site*, comp. Bettarel and Smith, 188–93; Michael S. Nassaney, José A. Brandão, William M. Cremin, Brock A. Giordano, "Archaeological Evidence of Economic Activities at an 18th Century Frontier Outpost in the Western Great Lakes," *Historical Archaeology* 41, no. 4 (2007): 1–17.
38. Michael S. Nassaney, William M. Cremin, Renee Kurtzweil, and José António Brandão, "The Search for Fort St. Joseph (1691–1781) in Niles, Michigan," *Midcontinental Journal of Archaeology* 28, no. 2 (2003): 1–38.
39. José António Brandão and Michael S. Nassaney, "Suffering for Jesus: Penitential Practices at Fort St. Joseph (Niles, MI) during the French Regime," *Catholic Historical Review* 94, no. 3 (2008): 476–99; Michael S. Nassaney and William M. Cremin, "Realizing the Potential of the Contact Period in Southwest Michigan through the Fort St. Joseph Archaeological Project," *Wisconsin Archaeologist* 83, no. 2 (2002): 123–34; Michael S. Nassaney, "Commemorating French Heritage at Fort St. Joseph, an Eighteenth-Century Mission, Garrison, and Trading Post Complex in Niles, Michigan," in *Dreams of the Americas: Overview of New France Archaeology*, ed. Christian Roy and Hélène Côté (Quebec: Archéologiques, Collection Hors Séries 2, 2008), 96–111; Michael S. Nassaney and José António Brandão, "The Materiality of Individuality at Eighteenth-Century Fort St. Joseph: A Mission-Garrison-Trading Post Complex on the Edge of Empire," in *The Materiality of Individuality*, ed. Carolyn White (New York: Springer Press, 2009), 19–36.
40. Nassaney, *An Archaeological Reconnaissance Survey*.
41. Michael S. Nassaney, William M. Cremin, and Daniel Lynch, "The Archaeological Identification of Colonial Fort St. Joseph, Michigan," *Journal of Field Archaeology* 29, nos. 3–4 (2002–2004): 309–21.
42. Michael S. Nassaney, "Identity Formation at a French Colonial Outpost in the North American Interior," *International Journal of Historical Archaeology* 12, no. 4 (2008), figure 9.
43. Nassaney, "Identity Formation," figure 5.
44. White, *Middle Ground*.
45. Ibid., 31.
46. Ibid.
47. Clifton, "Potawatomi," 728.
48. Marthe Faribault-Beauregard, *La population des forts français d'Amérique* (XVIIIe siècle), 2 vols. (Montreal: Éditions Bergeron, 1982), 175.

49. Pierre Margry, *Découvertes et établissements des Français dans l'ouest et dans le sud de l'Amérique septentrionale, 1614–1754* (Paris: D. Jouast, 1876–86), 5:71.

50. Pierre Joseph Charlevoix, *Journal of a Voyage to North America*, 2 vols. (London: R. and J. Dodsley, 1761), 93.

51. Pierre Margry, *Relations et Mémoires inédits pour servir à l'histoire de la France dans les pays d'outremer* (Paris: Challamel, 1867), 58; Gilles Havard, "Postes français et villages indiens: Un aspect de l'organisation de l'espace colonial français dans le Pays d'En Haut (1660–1715)," *Recherches Amérindiennes au Quebec* 30, no. 2 (2000): 11–22.

52. Peyser, *Letters*, 185.

53. Joseph L. Peyser, trans. and ed., *The Fort St. Joseph Manuscripts: Chronological Inventory and Translations* (Ms. on file, Niles District Library, Niles, Michigan, 1978).

54. Faribault-Beauregard, *La population*, 181.

55. Nassaney, "Identity Formation," 310–11; Nassaney et al., "Economic Activity," 12.

56. Peyser, *Letters*, 166–67.

57. Peyser, *Manuscripts*, records from 1747, FSJ Manuscripts, Doc. 121, 121 [2]; records from 1750 in FSJ Manuscripts, Doc. 141.

58. Peyser, *Manuscripts*, records from 1746, FSJ Manuscripts, Doc. 121 [5].

59. Peyser, *Manuscripts*, records from 1747, FSJ Manuscripts, Doc. 123 [2].

60. Peyser, *Manuscripts*, records from 1750, FSJ Manuscripts, Doc. 151.

61. Peyser, *Manuscripts*, records from 1750, FSJ Manuscripts, Doc. 141.

62. Peyser, *Manuscripts*, records from 1739, FSJ Manuscripts, Doc. 88.

63. Peyser, *Manuscripts*, records from 1747, FSJ Manuscripts, Doc. 123 [2].

64. Imported French and other European objects are common on seventeenth and eighteenth century Native American sites in the western Great Lakes region and the Mississippi River Valley, as documented by Jeffrey P. Brain, *Tunica Treasure*. Papers of the Peabody Museum of Archaeology and Ethnology, Harvard University, vol. 71 (Peabody Museum, Harvard University and Peabody Museum, Salem, MA, 1979); Mason, *Rock Island*, 1986; George I. Quimby, *Indian Culture and European Trade Goods* (Madison: University of Wisconsin Press, 1966).

65. Faribault-Beauregard, *La population*, 186; Idle, *The Post of the St. Joseph River*, 88.

66. Faribault-Beauregard, *La population*; George Paré and M. M. Quaife, "The St. Joseph Baptismal Register," *Mississippi Valley Historical Review* 13 (1926–27): 201–39.

67. Paré and Quaife, "The St. Joseph Baptismal Register," 207–212, 216, 218–19, 230, 232, 237.

68. Susan Sleeper-Smith, *Indian Women and French Men: Rethinking Cultural Encounter in the Western Great Lakes* (Amherst: University of Massachusetts Press, 2001), 43.

69. Gary B. Nash, "The Hidden History of Mestizo America," in *Sex, Love, and Race: Crossing Boundaries in North American History*, ed. Martha Hodes (New York: New York University Press, 1999), 18–20; R. Godbeer, "Eroticizing the Middle Ground: Anglo-Indian Sexual Relations along the Eighteenth-Century Frontier," in *Sex, Love, and Race: Crossing Boundaries in North American History*, ed. Martha Hodes (New York: New York University Press, 1999).

70. Bruce G. Trigger, *The Children of Aataentsic: A History of the Huron People to 1660*, 2 vols. (Montreal: McGill-Queen's University Press, 1976).

71. Nassaney, "Identity Formation," figure 8.

72. Kinietz, *The Indians of the Western Great Lakes*, 268.

73. Clifton, "Potawatomi," figures 5 and 6.

74. Stewart Culin, *Games of the North American Indians*, reprint (New York: Dover, 1975), originally published in *Twenty-Fourth Annual Report of the Bureau of American Ethnology* (Washington, DC: Smithsonian Institution, 1907).

75. Rory Becker, "Eating Ethnicity: Examining 18th Century French Colonial Identity through Selective Consumption of Animal Resources in the North American Interior" (master's thesis, Department of Anthropology, Western Michigan University, 2004); Terrance Martin, "The Archaeozoology of French Colonial Sites in the Illinois Country," in *Dreams of the Americas: Overview of New France Archaeology*, ed. Christian Roy and Hélène Côté (Quebec: Archéologiques, Collection Hors Séries 2, 2008), 184–204.

76. William M. Cremin and Michael S. Nassaney, "Sampling Archaeological Sediments for Small-Scale Remains: Recovery, Identification, and Interpretation of Plant Residues from Fort St. Joseph (20BE23)," *Michigan Archaeologist* 49, nos. 3–4 (2003): 73–85.

77. Peter N. Moogk, *La Nouvelle France: The Making of French Canada—A Cultural History* (East Lansing: Michigan State University Press, 2000).

78. Mortuary remains from Rock Island provide unusually precise contextual information that allows inferences regarding the association of beads with particular garments that clothed men, women, and children. See Mason, *Rock Island*, 128, 139.

79. Bodily adornment was a means by which colonial subjects negotiated their identity in the lower Mississippi Valley. Diana DiPaolo Loren, "The

Intersection of Colonial Policy and Colonial Practice: Creolization on the Eighteenth-Century Louisiana/Texas Frontier, *Historical Archaeology* 34, no. 3 (2000): 85–98.

80. LisaMarie Malischke, "The Excavated Bead Collection at Fort St. Joseph (20BE23) and Its Implications for Understanding Adornment, Ideology, Cultural Exchange, and Identity" (master's thesis, Department of Anthropology, Western Michigan University, 2009).

81. Paré and Quaife, "The St. Joseph Baptismal Register," 218.

82. For more information on the sincerity of religious belief at Fort St. Joseph, see Brandão and Nassaney, "Suffering for Jesus."

83. Brock A. Giordano, "Crafting Culture at Fort St. Joseph: An Archaeological Investigation of Labor Organization on the Colonial Frontier" (master's thesis, Department of Anthropology, Western Michigan University, 2005).

84. Ethnogenesis and its material expressions are discussed by Laurier Turgeon, Denys Delâge, and Réal Ouellet, eds., *Cultural Transfer, America and Europe: 500 Years of Interculturation* (Quebec: Les Presses de l'Université Laval, 1996); Michael S. Nassaney and Eric S. Johnson, "The Contributions of Material Objects to Ethnohistory in Native North America," in *Interpretations of Native North American Life: Material Contributions to Ethnohistory*, ed. M. Nassaney and E. Johnson, 1–30 (Gainesville: Society for Historical Archaeology and University Press of Florida, 2000).

85. William J. Eccles, "The Fur Trade and Eighteenth-Century Imperialism," *William and Mary Quarterly* 40, no. 3 (1983): 352–53.

86. Quoted in Eccles, "The Fur Trade," 352.

87. Gregory Evan Dowd, *War under Heaven: Pontiac, the Indian Nations, and the British Empire* (Baltimore: Johns Hopkins University Press, 2002).

Old Friends in New Territories: Delawares and Quakers in the Old Northwest Territory

DAWN MARSH

THE DELAWARES AND QUAKERS SHARED A UNIQUE HISTORY OF ALLIANCE AND mutual acceptance that began from their earliest diplomatic exchanges in the Delaware River valley at the end of the seventeenth century and remained intertwined throughout the eighteenth century in the Lower Great Lakes region.[1] The Delawares, Algonquian-speaking peoples, lived throughout the drainages and tributaries of the Delaware and lower Hudson Rivers. The Quakers, a Protestant sect, were largely responsible for the English colonization of the Delaware peoples' ancestral lands.[2] Delaware leadership throughout southeastern Pennsylvania successfully negotiated and protected their homelands as Susquehannock, Dutch, Swedish, and English interests all sought to dislodge them from the rich lands of the Delaware River valley throughout the sixteenth and seventeenth centuries. The diplomatic skills employed by their leaders allowed the fairly autonomous Delaware towns to thrive within the expanding web of European colonization. Providing food, alliances and loyalty, and a variety of diplomatic and communication services allowed the Delawares to create a successful political, cultural, and economic niche in their rapidly changing homelands.[3] William Penn was the last in a long list of foreign concerns to seek out the cooperation of Delaware leaders. Penn's well-known interest in establishing a "peaceable kingdom" was not a new idea for the Delawares. Their own diplomacy had already proved reasonably successful in that effort. What was new to the Delawares were Penn's methods and sincere offers of friendship, respect, and fairness. The confluence of their mutual objectives provided the foundation of a shared history that both groups evoked throughout the tumultuous changes and challenges each faced throughout the eighteenth century.

Delaware and Quaker towns peacefully coexisted in the Delaware River valley until the 1730s, when the explosion of the English population and the changes in the economic and political vision of Penn's successors forced most Delaware communities to move incrementally further north and west.[4] Under these combined pressures, the unique Quaker and Delaware alliance frayed and fell apart under the concurrent pressures of colonial expansion and warfare. Both would experience spiritual crises in the mid-eighteenth century brought on by both internal and external pressures. Delaware and Quaker leaders sought solutions to the trials facing their peoples by returning to the traditions of their grandfathers and grandmothers, but in so doing they did not turn to the old alliances their ancestors once shared in southeastern Pennsylvania. The Delawares sought to reinvigorate and renew their roles as peacemakers and negotiators, ultimately turning away from a prophetic message of militant resistance to colonial expansion. In the last quarter of the eighteenth century, most Delaware communities wanted nothing more than the right to live peacefully in their new homelands in the western territories. They did not turn to the Quakers during this period, but most often found friendship and community with another religious family, the Moravians, whose basic tenets advocated pacifism and their mission to the Indian peoples. Facing their own spiritual crisis brought on by the worldly interests of new generations of Quakers, outspoken leaders began to advocate a return to the teachings of their founders and renewal of their dedication to pacifism and living in "the Light."[5] They chose to exhibit their new commitment by working for peace between colonials and Indians on the frontier, and as missionaries to the Indian communities. From the 1750s until the era of the new republic, Quakers stepped forward as de facto diplomats in treaty negotiations in order to encourage fairness for the Indians. However, they did not turn to their old neighbors the Delawares in their new missionary efforts. Instead they offered their agricultural expertise and instruction to the Delawares' new neighbors living throughout the Lower Great Lakes region: the Miamis and Shawnees.

Both Delawares and Quakers responded to the challenges and crises of this period by building on the experience of their earlier alliance. This essay demonstrates that the Delawares and the Quakers both valued and commemorated their historic alliance, but did not renew it. Instead they both constructed new roles and alliances in the western territories. Throughout the French and Indian War and the American Revolution, both faced numerous tests of their spiritual and political identities. But, despite their shared histories, interests, and objectives, neither group turned to the other to renew their old alliances after the American Revolution. Instead, the Delawares turned to another pacifist group, the Moravians.[6] Similarly, the Quakers offered their Indian missionary program to other tribes in the region: Shawnees, Miamis, Oneidas, and Senecas.[7] This essay seeks to understand the complexity of the historic alliance and gain a better understanding of why the Delaware peoples did not seek the support of their old allies as they endeavored to establish and protect their new homelands in the Lower Great Lakes region. A closer look at their shared ideological and spiritual concepts may shed light on why this brief history continues to infuse a mythologized past embraced by both peoples. Despite the availability of Quaker diplomats, missionaries, and well-funded resources throughout the Old Northwest Territory, the Delawares were often found living in close proximity to, and in alliance with, another non-Indian group, the Moravians. The Moravians, like the Quakers, were committed to pacifism and their mission to the Indian peoples. While their dedication to pacifism was not doctrinal, it infused their missionary efforts in Ohio and Indiana. What circumstances and choices led Delaware leaders to tolerate and often ally their towns with the Moravian missions? Delawares did not exploit their historic relationship with the Quakers, despite the Quaker ascendance as treaty diplomats to the new United States. In the late eighteenth and early nineteenth centuries, the Delaware peoples reasserted a historic political strategy that sought out an alliance with another non-Native group, not unlike the Quakers, in order to protect their homelands and their ability to live peacefully in Ohio and Indiana.

The Delawares and Quakers share a history of alliances and cultural acceptance from earliest contact to the present day.[8] Beginning in the 1680s, the Lenapes cautiously welcomed William Penn and his followers into their historic homelands near the site of present-day Philadelphia. The Lenapes who stepped forward to greet Penn's entourage were seasoned and successful negotiators, both within their regional indigenous communities as well as with other European interests who preceded the first encounters with the Quaker refugees. Lenapes successfully negotiated peace, trade, and territorial boundaries with Iroquoian peoples to the north and west. They diplomatically protected the boundaries of Lenapehoking as more distant colonial invasions created new pressures on tribes to reach further south for furs to trade.[9] At the time of Penn's arrival, Lenape peoples lived in small towns and settlements throughout southeastern Pennsylvania and New Jersey. As neighboring and often-belligerent indigenous groups encroached on Lenape homelands, Lenape leaders stepped forward and, with rare exception, protected their boundaries, made new alliances, and prospered. Lenape peoples created a stable economic and political landscape before their first direct encounters with the Dutch, Swedes, and English.[10] Lenapes were known for providing European traders with a broad array of commodities needed for the success of their new ventures.

European observers noted that Lenapes were known for the high quantity of their corn and bean farming. Within decades of their first European encounters, Lenapes dominated the local market by assessing colonial needs and building up tradable stores to meet their newfound economic opportunities. Europeans began to expect a diverse supply of foodstuffs from the Lenape entrepreneurs, which included deer, elk and bear meat, fresh fish of "all kinds," wild turkeys, grouse, fruits and nuts (including apples, peaches, watermelons, chestnuts, walnuts), as well as wild hops used to make beer.[11] As early as 1624, the Dutch West India Company sent agents to Lenapehoking to open trade and negotiate land acquisition with the intention of creating trade centers and colonial settlements.[12] The Lenape people were certainly the key Native group to Europeans venturing into the region. While Lenape leaders may not have conceptualized the European principles of private ownership and land title, they did negotiate for land and resource use in exchange for other goods and alliances. In this their goals were explicit: to continue living in their homelands, to maintain access and control of their resources, and to avoid conflict and warfare. These objectives continued to determine the nature of Lenape diplomacy in their subsequent encounters with all new settlers in the Delaware River valley.[13]

In 1681, prior to his arrival in the colonies, Penn sent a letter to the Indians offering friendship and peace. He acknowledged that the Lenape peoples had reason to distrust the European colonizers from their previous experiences, but he took care to demonstrate his good intentions.

> I am very sensible of the unkindness and injustice that hath been too much exercised towards you by the people of these parts of the world, who sought themselves, and to make great advantages by you . . . but I am not such a man.[14]

Lenape skepticism was short-lived. Very soon after their first meetings, Penn and his agents followed their words with actions that convinced the Lenapes of their intentions. The Quakers introduced themselves as friends to the Indians, journeyed to their communities, and asked permission to live in Lenapehoking and negotiate a trade relationship.[15] For the most part, they were respectful of the Lenape peoples, and Quaker promises were confirmed. Penn was careful to understand the nature of ritual gift exchanges and displayed unprecedented generosity in the quality and quantity of goods he presented to the Lenape sachems. He was equally careful to accept their gifts in return.[16]

Despite their unique approach to colonization, it is unlikely that Penn and his followers fully appreciated Lenape diplomacy or experience, nor did they realize that the members of the Society of Friends and the Lenapes shared more than just an interest in maintaining a peaceful coexistence. By the time of Penn's arrival, the Lenapes were well-versed in European diplomacy. They responded to overtures of trade with exemplary patience, seeking to avoid conflict and hostilities that could have turned Lenapehoking into a landscape of bloody battlefields, not unlike Chesapeake to the south and New England to the north.[17] More than one colonial leader expressed frustration at his inability to dislodge the Lenapes from their key positions as middlemen in the region, and colonists were unable to adequately convince other tribes to wage war against them. Governors Peter Minuet, Johan Printz, and Edmund Andros, representing their respective Dutch, Swedish, and English colonies, all attempted to eliminate, suppress, or remove the Lenapes from their coveted location along the Delaware River and bay. At one point Printz, governor of New Sweden, reasoned that "nothing would be better than to send over here a couple hundred soldiers, and [remain here] until we broke the necks of all of them [Lenapes] in this River."[18] The Quakers and Lenapes shared a common interest in maintaining a stable political and economic landscape where they could enjoy the fruits of the "peaceable kingdom" they both created.[19]

Close interactions between the new and original settlers of the Delaware River valley revealed more commonalities than just the shared goals of promoting peace and prosperity. Both groups expressed a spiritual and ideological set of principles that strengthened their friendship. This spiritual worldview and cross-cultural experience early on in the colonization of England's portion of North American made an impact that was tested and retested throughout the eighteenth century. Delawares living in the Lower Great Lakes region never forgot their former alliances with the Quakers, but ultimately turned away from their missionary efforts. Likewise, after placing Indian missionary efforts in the background for two generations, the Friends revitalized their endeavors, but did not share this new benevolence with their old neighbors and instead offered it to other Indian peoples.

The Lenapes and Quakers both held fast to several shared tenets in their respective philosophies. Three pillars of the Lenape peoples' worldview included kinship, reciprocity, and living a spiritual life. The Lenapes lived in a world shaped by kinship. These relations were not limited to people, but included all animate and inanimate elements of the universe: animals, humans, plants, weather phenomena, and diverse deities.[20] The Lenapes communicated in a world of manitous[21] and spirits that were an active part of their daily lives, exhibiting abilities to change and shape human existence. Lenapes were responsible to all of these elements in varying degrees, and their rituals and ceremonies preserved the balance and restored their world. The living world was populated with forces that were both positive and negative powers. These forces existed simultaneously in their cosmological and temporal realities, and Lenapes' thoughts and actions were inseparable from those forces.

The history of the Lenapes began when the creator, Kishelemukong, formed North America out of the mud on a turtle's back. This omnipotent creator was also responsible for giving life to other divine entities, all members of a sacred family. A spiritual force, Manetuwak, infused all life on Turtle Island.[22] Kishelemukong created a first woman and first man out of the trees that emerged on Turtle Island, from whom all Lenapes descend. According to this tradition, life, from birth to death, is a journey to immortality or reuniting with the creator, and is obtained by living a right life. Heeding the guidance of spiritual helpers, and the faithful practice of ceremonies and rituals to honor the creator and all living things, is fundamental to successfully completing this journey.[23] The ethical underpinnings of this spiritual worldview depend on reciprocity, balance, and peaceful coexistence in the world, and they shaped the Lenapes' spiritual life as well as their social, political, and economic practices.

Similarly, the Society of Friends expressed a unique set of spiritual and temporal tenets that found acceptance in Lenapehoking. While the Quaker cosmology was less populated than the Lenapes' universe, they did have basic tenets that Lenapes recognized through their long history with the Quakers. Friends believed that all humans held a divine spark that linked everyone—Indian, African, and Englishman—in a spiritual brotherhood. This kinship included Quaker obligations to respect and care for the human family, just as the Lenapes were obligated to their various kin. The "Inner Light" created a spiritual link with all people, including the Lenapes.[24] George Fox, founder of the Society of Friends, instructed followers to "answer the light of Christ in every man."[25] The divine spark demanded that all people be treated equally and with respect; therefore the Quakers initiated their earliest dealings with the Lenapes deeply committed to doing their best to be fair in all their negotiations.

An equally important principle in the Quaker faith was the commitment to live a Christ-like life. This commitment required Quakers to exercise kindness, generosity, and humbleness in all their interactions, and it also required they reject violence and warfare. This is known as the "peace testimony" and was the fuel for much of the persecution Quakers experienced in England and North America.[26] Like the Lenapes, the members of the Society of Friends who settled in Lenapehoking lived their belief system daily. Their spiritual and secular worlds were not separate. The two neighbors, Lenapes and Quakers, appeared to be culturally worlds apart, but they both embraced and celebrated a complementary worldview that facilitated a long-lasting alliance based on reciprocity, pacifism, and fairness. Unfortunately, colonial North America was not an ideal proving ground for the Quakers' faith, and the pressures colonization placed on the peoples of Lenapehoking damaged this unique complementary alliance.

During the first quarter of the eighteenth century, Penn's colony grew by leaps and bounds, and the Lenapes were dispossessed of their historic homelands. The population in southeastern Pennsylvania exploded after 1681 and raised their numbers in southeastern Pennsylvania to over 100,000 by 1750; the Lenapes, by then, accounted for only 2 percent of the total southeastern Pennsylvania population.[27] Lenapes were unable to cultivate corn, fish in streams, or take advantage of the resources enjoyed by their ancestors. Husbands and fathers traveled further and further afield to provide food for their communities. Protests by Lenape leaders to Quakers in the provincial assembly fell on sympathetic ears, but provoked few actions. Checochinican, a sachem representing the Brandywine Lenapes, appeared before the Provincial Assembly in Philadelphia during the summer of 1725. He was already well known to the assembly from previous Lenape delegations. He reminded the assembly that the late William Penn had "re-conveyed back a certain tract of land, upon Brandy-wine."[28] Checochinican gave the details of the boundary and declared that the Indians had received documentation of this transaction but the deed was lost in a cabin fire. He recalled that Penn promised the Lenapes the right to occupy the land, without interference by settlers, "whilst one Indian lived, grew old, and blind, and dies, so another to the third generation." Penn's guarantees were not honored, and the Brandywine band and most Lenapes began a westward trek, hoping that distance between their communities and the English colonials would solve their problems. By the 1730s, the Lenapes' diaspora out of southeastern Pennsylvania was nearly complete except for several small enclaves. The majority of Lenapes, known more frequently as the Delawares, settled beyond the Appalachian Mountains and lived scattered throughout western Pennsylvania, Ohio, and Indiana by the second half of the eighteenth century.[29]

The complementary alliance between Lenapes and Quakers lasted much longer in myth, however, than in reality. Penn's time spent with the Lenapes left a lasting impression in Lenape memory. Penn made an effort to learn the Lenape language and personally negotiated several treaties with them. The best known and most mythologized is the Great Treaty at Shackamaxon.[30] Delaware elders remembered the event a century later. They recalled the tradition of Miquon's[31] "first arrival in their country, a friendship formed between them which was to last as long as the sun should shine, and the rivers flow with water"—a sentiment confirmed by Penn's own account.[32] Delaware leaders throughout the second half of the eighteenth century deliberately referenced their old friendship as a symbol of future peaceful alliances.

Other factors led to the dissolution of their venerable friendship. Political contests interrupted Penn's tenure in his beloved colony and kept him away from Pennsylvania except for brief interludes. In his absence, he left the administration and execution of his vision to his closest associates. Ultimately they dismantled William Penn's "peaceable kingdom," his utopian vision of religious tolerance and inclusion, within a decade after his death in 1718.[33] Pennsylvania's rapid growth and prosperity put great pressures on the Lenapes, and Penn's heirs did little to place limits on the Quaker settlers' voracious appetite for land. Penn's benevolent colonialism, despite his unique ideas, had the same impact as all colonialism: the Lenapes lost their lands in southeastern Pennsylvania to new settlers. Penn's heirs abandoned the Quaker religion and continued to control Pennsylvania until the American Revolution.[34]

Quaker prosperity and leadership between Penn's death and the outbreak of the French and Indian War led to ideological shifts in their religious convictions. Many prosperous Quakers in southeastern Pennsylvania turned their attention away from the cultivation of their "inner plantations" in favor of building their "outer plantations."[35] This philosophical shift in promoting outward prosperity and the accumulation of political power and wealth, rather than focusing on the health and well-being of their "Inner Light," caused Quakers to place little priority on their neighborly relationship with the Delawares. Instead they emphasized economic stability and secured alliances with Indian tribes who stood to offer the greatest advantages in trade and expansion. The provincial government of Pennsylvania, dominated by

Quakers, perceived the Delawares as an obstacle to securing land for the colony, while they considered the Iroquois as more strategic friends.[36] Their main concern regarding the Delawares was to dispossess them of their lands and place them under the hegemony of the Iroquois confederacy. Delawares resisted these political maneuvers on most fronts, often reminding Quakers in their appeals to the provincial government of Penn's promise. The Quaker-controlled assembly held Penn's vision in high esteem and invoked it when advantageous, but the practicalities of running a successful colony and reaping the temporal benefits allowed the Quakers to abandon many of their humanitarian goals in favor of newer material objectives and greater political power.

One of the most devastating demonstrations of this new Quaker ideology of prosperity was the Walking Purchase of 1737.[37] Penn's heirs produced a fraudulent treaty as evidence that the Delawares had signed an agreement to sell one of the final, contiguous Delaware holdings along their namesake river. Penn's heirs needed this treaty negotiation to end in their favor to clear unsecured land titles sold to fellow colonists. Delaware leaders repeatedly refused to sell their lands, claiming they were never sold to William Penn. In the end, they were forced to accept the terms when an unsigned treaty was produced. Delaware leaders reluctantly accepted the terms stated in the document. Penn's heirs succeeded in dispossessing the Delawares by trickery, but the fraudulent Walking Purchase Treaty permanently tarnished the Quaker reputation among the Delawares.[38] In the years after Penn's death in 1718, the historic alliance between Lenapes and Quakers came under great strain, but the fraudulent Walking Purchase of 1737 is remembered by the Delawares as the singular event that led to the loss of their ancestral homelands in Pennsylvania.

As the old alliance between Quakers and Delawares frayed and unraveled, another group preaching brotherly love and compassion stepped into the vacuum: the Moravians.[39] In 1741, the German pietists purchased and moved onto some of the lands that Delawares lost in the Walking Purchase Treaty. But the rhetoric of friendship and peaceful coexistence were not enough this time. What ultimately led Delaware individuals and their families to join the Moravians were the actions of the new missionaries. Moravians willingly shared their resources with Indians who came to join them, including food and lodging, and even offering assistance to Delawares in need. By the outbreak of the French and Indian War in 1754, Moravians were playing vital roles as missionaries, interpreters, and government agents.[40] The Moravians did not have a doctrine of nonviolence, but their pacifist tendencies appealed to many Delawares who were forced from their homes in eastern Pennsylvania to avoid conflict with colonial settlers. The symbiotic association of the Delawares and Moravians grew stronger as both groups moved into western Pennsylvania and the Ohio Country. Unfortunately, they also attracted the attention of more militant Delaware leaders who perceived the Moravians as another colonial threat. While the Quakers fastidiously tended their "outer plantations,"[41] relegating the ancient friendship between their colony's founder and the Delawares to a symbolic past, Moravians launched a missionary effort that followed the Delawares along the paths of their diaspora into the new territories of the lower Great Lakes.

The outbreak of the French and Indian War in 1754 pushed both the Delawares and Quakers to question the wisdom of their respective leaders. Each group faced spiritual crises that divided families and communities. For the Delawares, dispossession and the deception of the Quaker-led provincial government pushed them to join other Indian allies like the Shawnees in waging a war throughout Pennsylvania's backcountry borders.[42] A new alliance with the French offered the best solution for the Delawares as they worked to protect their new Lenapehoking, which was formed in western Pennsylvania and Ohio. At the same time, war and dispossession were the fertile soil for a number of prophets, such as Neolin and Papoonan, who emerged with a message that called for a return to Delaware traditions and a retreat from all things European.[43] The messages of renewal offered by the Delaware prophets warned of the dangers of living too close to white settlements. Other Delaware leaders, such as White Eyes and Killbuck, emerged from this period of warfare strengthened by their associations with Moravians, offering leadership that reinvigorated their historic role as peacemakers.[44] The shared objective for Delaware prophets, militants, and leaders advocating coexistence was to secure Delaware homelands in Ohio.

For the Quakers, the beginning of the French and Indian War in 1754 marked their retreat from visible political participation. Their unpopular commitment to pacifism led to schisms within their own ranks as successive wars drew attention to their unpopular stance.[45] Eventually, the Quakers emerged with a reinvigorated ideological core, like the Delawares, and returned to the guidance of their founding theologians. They found political expression by offering their services in Indian treaty negotiations for the British colonizers, and later for the new republic. Quakers also formalized their Indian mission, and by the end of the American Revolution, their missionary efforts were transformed from a personal, individual calling to a highly organized and institutionally funded missionary effort.[46]

The alteration of the Quaker missionary program was one of the many changes experienced during this period.

Neither the Delawares nor the Quakers escaped the changes brought on by continuous warfare between 1754 and 1781. Ironically, neither side would seek the other out in their renewed commitment to peaceful coexistence. Delaware leaders who sought peaceful resolutions turned more often to the Moravian missionaries as allies, and Quakers sought to demonstrate their renewed commitment to the cultivation of their inner plantations by demonstrating their intentions in missions to the Oneidas, Senecas, Shawnees, and Miamis.[47] Quakers, organized around Yearly Meetings headquartered in Baltimore and Philadelphia, agreed to divide their interests in Indian missions. Members of the Baltimore Yearly Meeting focused their efforts in Ohio, and the Philadelphia Yearly Meeting turned its benevolent intention toward the Oneidas and Senecas to the north. For the missionaries sponsored by the Baltimore Yearly Meeting, their efforts with the Shawnees and Miamis were a response to invitations made by those Indian communities. Philadelphia's Quaker missionaries formalized and expanded earlier individual missionary efforts with the Oneidas and Senecas.[48]

The Delawares' spiritual revitalization movement was an effort to return to the traditions of earlier generations.[49] There was no single doctrine offered by the new messengers that would restore the prosperity and power of the Delaware peoples. Instead, the new prophets delivered a series of instructions they received through direct communication from divine sources. The dreams and their interpretations spread throughout the Ohio Country and reinvigorated communities under great pressure to make choices regarding leadership, war, and how they chose to live their lives. Delaware prophet Papoonan rallied his people while demanding both a personal and political commitment from individual Delawares.[50] Papoonan, a self-proclaimed "drunken Indian," emerged from a vision and delivered a message from the "Master of Life"[51] that advised Delawares to abstain from alcohol consumption and remain neutral during the French and Indian War. Papoonan's message of reformation and pacifism did not withstand the imperial firestorm surrounding his community. He advocated peace and urged his followers to return to the "ancient customs and manners of their forefathers." As Papoonan and his followers advocated peaceful coexistence, a new wave of Indian-hating swept through eastern Pennsylvania. In 1763, Presbyterian vigilantes known as the Paxton Boys descended on one of Penn's protected Indian plantations and murdered unarmed Christian Indians.[52] The vigilantes justified the massacre by claiming that the small enclave of Conestoga Indians were harboring spies or supporters of Pontiac's

Rebellion. The attack led Papoonan and his followers to seek the protection of Moravians in Pennsylvania.[53] Eventually, this nativist Delaware prophet converted to Christianity and worked as a Moravian missionary in the Ohio Country until his death in 1775.

Wangomend, the "Assinsink Prophet" living in northern Pennsylvania, delivered a similar message forbidding the "drinking of rum" among his followers.[54] He differed in his political message and openly opposed the British colonials. Wangomend's message of renewal reintroduced older ceremonies as a conduit for rectifying their chaotic world. Moravian missionary Frederick Post reported that Wangomend had revived an "Old quarterly Meeting" in which dreams of the prophet and participants were shared and analyzed.[55] Another fundamental aspect of his message spoke of a separate creation and spiritual path for Indians and whites. Teaching his lessons through a series of pictures, Wangomend included an illustration indicating two separate paths to heaven: one for Indian peoples and the other for white colonials. This message illustrated the source of all their problems in Wangomend's view: turning away from their ancient practices had led them down the wrong path. The right path required them to eliminate all things that diverted them from Indian ways. This mixed message was manifested in many cultural areas, including ceremony, food preparation, and clothing. The most extreme interpretations led to war against white colonials, and witch-hunts among their own people who had accepted Christianity and colonial culture.[56]

Close on the heels of Wangomend's prophetic message came another Delaware prophet, Neolin. By 1761, Neolin's prophecies garnered a following noticed by missionaries and other colonial agents. His message, like Wangomend's, advocated separate paths for Indians and whites. He too saw the path to heaven as different for whites and relayed this message on a map. John Heckewelder, the Moravian interpreter, explained that the map portrayed the many obstacles Indian peoples faced on their journey to heaven, including perilous passages and dangerous obstacles.[57] Neolin preached against the use of alcohol, the worst of "ye vices which ye Indians have learned from ye White people."[58] He advocated turning away from trade with the British, and making political choices that would free them from their dependence on British associations. Like Wangomend, Neolin created new ceremonies and reinvigorated old traditions in an effort to cleanse Indian communities of the detrimental influence of Anglo-American culture.

The messages delivered by Neolin, Wangomend, and other Delaware prophets often inspired armed resistance throughout the Ohio Country during the war-torn period from 1754 up to the beginning of the

American Revolution. The impact of the Delaware-inspired messages of resistance and nativism reached deep into the Lower Great Lakes region and resurfaced again and again until the Removal Era. The nativist Delawares who chose to turn against the children of Miquon faced defeat at the end of the French and Indian War. Their continued militant alliances did not produce the desired result, and instead Delawares lost their lands to British control in the western territories. While nativists faced multiple military losses and witnessed increasing British presence, their message of resistance grew stronger.

The prophets' messages concurred that the path to restore Indian power and independence was to adhere to a prescription of proper behaviors. If Delawares stayed true to this formula (diverse as the components might be), they would be purified and the Indians' world would be restored. Nativist messages continued to gain strength in the midst of multiple military defeats, and the blame was assigned to those Delawares who turned their backs on the nativist prophets. War, dispossession, disease, and starvation divided their communities, while many still believed their survival and salvation could be attained through accommodating Anglo-European culture and religion. Many Delawares tried to remain neutral, aligning with leaders who offered alternative, nonmilitant strategies for their people. The objectives of the accommodation-oriented Delaware leadership were ultimately the same as the nativist objectives: secure their homelands and live freely on their lands.

Delaware leaders seeking peaceful solutions to securing their lands in the Ohio Country found allies in the Moravian missions under the direction of David Zeisberger.[59] As Quakers retreated from public service, Moravians pushed into Ohio Country in the early 1770s and founded a series of mission towns within the heart of the Delaware homelands. For the most part, Moravians were welcomed by the Delawares in Ohio Country because they were perceived as pacifists offering economic and political stability to the war-torn region. Another factor that encouraged alliances between the Delawares and Moravians was their shared, untarnished history based on their previous coexistence in eastern Pennsylvania. Even though the history of their coexistence was relatively shorter than the Delaware-Quaker story, it was unblemished by betrayals and broken treaties. In the collective memory of the Delawares, the Quakers had cheated them out of their lands, while Moravians were remembered for offering friendship and support. The location of active Moravian missionary towns and their fairly consistent pacifist commitment enticed Delaware converts to join the new religion. At the same time, non-Christian Delaware leaders elected to keep their communities close to the missionary towns. They recognized that their political and economic alliance with the Moravians would go far towards securing Delaware lands, and would provide the means for Delaware communities to make the economic and cultural transformation necessary for their peaceful coexistence with their new Anglo-American neighbors. Moravian missions brought vital trade, supplies, and political opportunities to the Delawares who resided in the vicinity.

The vortex of Delaware accommodation was located along the Tuscarawas River in the Ohio Territory. Moravian missionaries in Schonbrunn, New Schonbrunn, Gnadenhutten, Salem, and Lichtenau housed Delaware converts and shared borders with their unconverted relatives in Goschocking and Gekelemukpechink, located in the Ohio Territory.[60] The peaceful coexistence between Moravians and their Delaware neighbors was a pragmatic solution for both sides, expressed in two different ways. Some Delawares chose to convert, living within the mission towns and going through demanding steps to convince the often-skeptical Moravians of their sincerity.[61] Other Delawares were not interested in abandoning the spiritual beliefs of their ancestors, but recognized the benefit of maintaining alliances and borders with the Moravians and their kin in the mission towns.[62] Several Delaware leaders stepped to the forefront, consistently promoting a dialogue of accommodation and solidifying the alliances with the Moravian leaders.

By 1775 Quequedegatha was one leader representing the voice of those neutralist Delawares outside the boundaries of the Moravian missions.[63] As a leader who recognized the importance of alliances, Quequedegatha never converted to Christianity. As a seasoned diplomat, he invoked the memory of William Penn and their old alliance as a symbol of peace, and in 1773 reminded listeners that "we two Brothers the Delawares & the Quakers were brought up together."[64] Out of the ashes of failed militant resistance, Quequedegatha helped construct a new Delaware identity that revitalized their ancient diplomatic role as peacemakers. Referencing the old Quaker alliance was a symbolic gesture meant to place emphasis on peaceful solutions to the shared concerns of everyone involved.

Endless warfare and dispossession transformed the Delawares living throughout the Lower Great Lakes region in the second half of the eighteenth century. Leadership and alliances offered many strategies to achieve the common goal of living freely as Delawares on Delaware lands. Prophets urged armed resistance as well as peaceful alliances, and individual leaders offered a variety of strategies for their people. Some advocated a separation from white colonists, and others embraced coexistence and supported

Moravian missionary efforts. Other Delaware men and women elected to leave their communities and convert to Christianity, seeking safety and salvation within the Moravian mission towns. The choices confronting Delawares were diverse, and all were informed by a spiritual worldview that was changing.

As Delawares met the spiritual and temporal trials confronting them in the new western territories, their former neighbors faced similar challenges.[65] In 1743, the Philadelphia Yearly Meeting authored and distributed a list of twelve questions to be read at the Monthly Meetings.[66] The questions asked the members of the Society of Friends to reflect on their actions and to consider whether or not they were living their faith, one of the basic tenets of their religion. Reform-minded Quakers were disturbed at the growing trend among their prosperous members to ignore or abandon their responsibility to teach and represent "the Truth."[67] Foremost among the trends that troubled elder Quakers was the quest for, and accumulation and display of, material wealth. John Woolman, a Quaker preacher best known for his antislavery stance, reminded his fellow Friends, "Ye cannot serve God and mammon."[68] Early Quaker founders struggled and suffered to advocate against the accumulation of worldly goods in favor of a simple, Christ-like life. For them, accumulation of material possessions corrupted the spirit, and attempts to discipline members on these grounds had grown lax.

This was not an easy message to deliver to an audience reaping the rewards of colonial land acquisition and the blossoming colonial economy. However, the accumulation of wealth was not the only area of concern. During these years, there was a marked increase in the admonishments against members who made a "Practice of taking Strong Drink to Excess," and those members who violated these rules were disciplined less harshly than in earlier years. Quaker records show that between 1742 and 1782, disciplinary action against members for drunkenness increased dramatically.[69] By the last quarter of the eighteenth century, Quaker teachings required their members to abstain from the use of alcohol and prohibited Friends from participating in its manufacture or sale.

Another major reform that came from the Friends' renewed focus on tending their "inner plantations" was the evolution of their official antislavery stance. Early reformers advocated a position against slavery, but many of the most prosperous and politically powerful Quakers profited from owning and/or participating in the slave trade.[70] Woolman and other reformers in the 1750s led the members of the Philadelphia Yearly Meeting to advocate an official policy on the issue and eventually prohibited Quakers from owning or participating in the slave trade. By the 1780s, bringing an end to slavery and the slave trade became the official position of the Society of Friends. Friends who did not respond to the official changes demanded by their leaders faced serious disciplinary action, including disownment.

The adherence to the peace testimony was the most serious challenge to the Quaker constituency at the outset of the French and Indian War. Frontier violence on both sides, and Indian-hating within the colony led the governor of Pennsylvania to declare war against the Delawares in 1756. Quakers resigned from the provincial assembly when it became clear that the Pennsylvania government was determined to wage war on the Indians who had welcomed William Penn and his followers. As a result, the Quakers reaffirmed their pacifist principals but did not completely retreat from their civic responsibilities. Instead they turned to new ways of seeking and promoting peace between whites and Indians. One visible example was the formation of the "Friendly Association for Regaining and Preserving Peace with the Indians by Pacific Measures," also in 1756.[71]

The Quakers devised two strategies to reinvigorate their founders' original intent regarding the Indians. Some Quakers made use of their political networks and stepped forward in a number of negotiations between colonials and Indians. Early in this new effort, they tested their diplomatic influence close to home, but did not venture to offer their diplomatic services in negotiations taking place in the more hostile western territories. Eventually the news of Quaker peacemaking activities reached the Ohio Country, leading Delaware leaders to request their mediation, stating, "We long for that Peace and Friendship we had Formerly."[72] Even as they invoked the symbolism of earlier alliances with Penn, their negations were pragmatic and cautious.

Quakers expressed another aspect of their renewed interest in their Indian brothers and sisters through their missionary programs. Quakers inspired to travel to Indian communities as missionaries were most often responding to an individual calling and not the effort of an institutionalized Quaker mission. Even after the founding of the Friendly Association at mid-century, most missionary efforts were led by individuals who were spiritually inspired to go into Indian communities.[73] Members of the Society of Friends, John Parrish and Zebulon Heston traveled to a Delaware town in the years between the French and Indian War and the American Revolution. Delawares warmly received the missionaries, and Quequedegatha personally presented a wampum belt inviting them to return to the western territories and establish a mission that would instruct the Delawares "in the right way both [in] things of this Life as well as in the world to Come."[74] The Quakers did not answer this invitation to return to the Delaware communities, because the American Revolution upended any plans to promote their renewed interest as peacemakers in Indian country.

Once again, English and American factions tested the Friends' commitment to the Peace Testimony.[75] Most Quakers supported early resistance to the taxation and actions of the Crown, but withdrew from the radical politics and violent actions of the American rebels.[76] Quakers chose to resign from the Pennsylvania Assembly rather than answer the call to arms in the French and Indian War, and the American Revolution demanded the same. From the beginning of the war, Quakers were torn between their commitment to the peace testimony and their loyalties to the colony William Penn founded. There was no middle road for the Quakers, and by war's end most of their fellow citizens perceived the Quakers as untrustworthy. This gave further importance to their interest in reestablishing their mission to the Indians. As missionaries they were able to rebuild their tarnished reputation and secure the trust of the new American government. By promoting peace with Indians through missionary efforts and acting as mediators in treaty negotiations, Quakers found a way to exercise political authority and establish their standing in the new nation.[77]

The Philadelphia Yearly Meeting launched a vigorous campaign to restore their reputation as mediators and missionaries. Philadelphia Friends visited Indian families in their homes and appointed committees to attend treaty councils. There was a marked difference in this new Indian mission that reflected a "corporate concern" rather than depending on the individual callings of the society's membership.[78] Philadelphia was a hub of political activity in the years after the war as the new government struggled to gain control of its western territories. Indian factions in the west disputed the terms of the Treaty of Paris, which ignored Indian territorial claims in the Lower Great Lakes region. In one instance of their mission, Quakers attended a peace conference on the Sandusky River in Ohio in 1793 in response to a direct request from the Miami confederacy. The Indian representatives' request for the presence of a Quaker delegation illustrates how quickly the Friends in Philadelphia had restored their reputation. Despite the failure of these negotiations to bring peace to the Ohio Territory, the Miamis and Quakers developed a friendship that would produce a Quaker Indian mission in Indiana Territory.[79] Friends presented the grievances and requests of various Indian delegates to the President and Congress and authored petitions for the Indian diplomats. As various Indian delegations passed through Philadelphia and Baltimore, Quakers seized the opportunity to develop alliances that would satisfy their mutual objectives. The activities of the Friends produced results, and they became indispensable to the new government.

As the disputes between the American colonists and the Crown intensified, Delaware leaders sought means to secure their lands in Ohio and remain neutral in the escalating hostilities. Netawatwees and Quequedegatha were the main architects of this Delaware diplomatic strategy. In the years leading up to the war, Quequedegatha used Delaware ties to both Moravians and Quakers to further their appeals to the English Crown to recognize their identity and land claims. Delawares asked three Quaker emissaries for assistance in helping "some of their people to England in order to have a conference with the king."[80] They also wanted to remind the English of their historic Quaker friendship by offering a wampum belt "to be shown to the king . . . which they had gotten from old Penn." As they reestablished this old relationship, they also offered their new alliance with the Moravians as proof of their commitment to pacifism and declared that "they were ready to receive" the message offered by the Quakers, because "they hear among the Brethren it is very necessary and healing."[81] Delawares worked hard to convince the Crown of their neutrality and willingness to accept and endorse a peaceful but separate coexistence with colonists.

They failed to reach their immediate goals, and the American Revolution forced Quequedegatha and other Delaware diplomats to find strategies to achieve the same objectives: avoid warfare and secure land title. Delawares attended many of the same treaties that Quakers attended in 1775 and 1776, both working to establish their shared goals as peacemakers. Quequedegatha traveled to Philadelphia and appealed to the new American Congress, requesting they provide the Delawares with a schoolmaster, minister, "a mill, a miller," and a "couple of farmers," hoping to express their sincere interest in the American plan to civilize the Indians.[82] Philadelphia Quakers, Ohio Delawares, and Moravian Delawares attended treaty meetings in Pittsburgh in 1778 at which the Delawares made progress towards their goal of being recognized as a separate and sovereign people. It seemed that the Philadelphia Quakers and Ohio Delawares repeatedly crossed paths and shared common objectives during this period, but no new alliance emerged from their repeated meetings.

The American Revolution tested Delaware neutrality. In the earliest years of the war, Americans urged the Delawares to remain neutral, despite the move of most of their kinsmen in the Lower Great Lakes region to side with British interests. Delawares also stepped forward as peacemakers, counseling other tribes to take a neutral stance. For a while, their efforts met with success, but the American colonists shifted their policy by 1777 and began to pressure Delawares to join the American cause against the British.[83] There was no consensus among the Delaware leaders, and communities made independent decisions. Stuck in a diplomatic no man's land, the Moravian Delawares were perceived as enemies to both the Americans and the British. Heckewelder, Zeisberger, and other Moravian missionaries in the western territories openly declared a pacifist platform, but their commitment to peace did not prevent them from passing along strategic information that aided the Americans' cause. Despite their pro-American leanings, most backcountry settlers only understood Moravians as protectors of Indians. From their perspective, all Indian sympathizers were their enemies. Indian-hating in the backcountry muted any other nuanced efforts to aid the American cause.

The Indian-hating among the backcountry settlers did not allow for any neutrality. American settlers, leaders, and members of the militia expressed the growing sentiment expressed by American colonel Daniel Brodhead that "much confidence ought never to be placed in any of the [Indians'] colour."[84] The Moravian Delawares were distrusted by both sides, and the pro-British Delawares and Wyandots urged their kin to join their side. Americans suspected the Moravian Delawares were passing along information about the locations and status of American militia, while the pro-British Delawares accused their kin of being the cause of internal tribal divisions that were undermining their effectiveness. Buckangahela arrived at Gnadenhutten with eighty of his men and urged the Moravian Delawares to unite with him. The Moravian Delawares at Gnadenhutten and Salem were divided over how they should respond, but by August 1781, a war party that included Delawares, Wyandots, Shawnees, and Ojibwas forced the Christian Indians from Gnadenhutten, Salem, and New Schonbrun to relocate to the Upper Sandusky, where under the watchful eye of the pro-British allies, they posed less of a security threat.

The hurried departures from their towns before harvest left the Moravian refugees without much food, and many eventually returned to their former homes to sift through the remains of their unharvested crops. It was a fatal mistake. In February 1782, Pennsylvania militia left their camps along the Monongahela River in southwestern Pennsylvania with plans to destroy all Indian towns along the Muskingum River. Fueled more by virulent Indian-hating than reliable intelligence, the 160-man militia reached Gnadenhutten on March 7 and imprisoned all of the men, women, and children they found there. The initial plan was to take the prisoners to Fort Pitt, but after an evening's deliberation, the commander, David Williamson, ceded his authority to the chilling, cold-blooded desires of his men. The following day, the mostly Delaware men, women, and children were divided into two cabins, where they prayed and sang hymns, knowing their fate. One by one, the American soldiers—all hailing from William Penn's "peaceable kingdom"—placed ropes around the necks of over ninety innocent Moravian Indians, including thirty-nine children, dragged them to a separate cabin they referred to as the slaughterhouse, and bludgeoned, hacked, and scalped their victims until "the blood flowed like a river." Delawares never forgot their special bond with William Penn, and they never forgot the tragedy at Gnadenhutten. In the months to come, the Delawares would find little solace in taking revenge on several members of the American army they held responsible for the massacre.[85]

With the conclusion of the American Revolution, Delaware efforts to secure land in the Ohio Territory nearly failed. The devastation caused by war in their homeland led to years of famine and epidemics as they struggled to reconstruct their communities in new lands at the end of the eighteenth century. At the end of the century, Delaware towns were found scattered throughout the Lower Great Lakes region. Some attempts were made to consolidate the dispersed communities along the Maumee River in the northwestern quadrant of the Indiana Territory. Other Delaware towns eventually reconsolidated in the southern part of the territory along the White River.[86] While Quakers formalized their mission to civilize the Indians in the years after the war, Delawares struggled to stay alive. Quaker missionaries from the Baltimore Yearly Meeting would not find their way to the Indiana Territory until 1804, and even then their interest was in civilizing Little Turtle's Miamis at Fort Wayne. Preceding that, the Philadelphia Yearly Meeting sent missionaries to New York and the Six Nations, where they founded their first official mission to the Indians with the Oneidas in 1796.[87] Moravians, too, would seize this opportunity to rebuild the trust of the Delaware peoples, but took no action until 1801, when Moravian John Peter Kluge established a mission at Woapmintschi, a Delaware town in Indiana Territory.[88] For the Delawares, neither of their former pacifist allies offered a solution they were willing to embrace.

Delawares were originally drawn to Moravians because their relationship was a mutually productive and positive one, but also because of the consistent presence and participation of Moravian missionaries in Delaware communities. The Delawares were also interested in the message Moravians offered, for the same reason the Quakers had gained their respect in earlier years. The Delawares were moralists, and the principles that provided the framework for their spiritual worldview were not unlike the moral framework guiding Quaker and Moravian missions. Failure to keep ceremonies and adhere to proper behaviors resulted in catastrophe and calamity. The world was set right again by recognizing and rectifying the imbalances. Delawares held deep convictions about justice, fairness, and ethics. They returned again and again to their moral center to determine what choices they made in an era fraught with critical decisions that might determine their very existence in the rapidly shifting world of the eighteenth century. Both Delaware prophets and Moravian missionaries offered remedies to the volatile world the Delaware peoples inhabited in the eighteenth and early nineteenth centuries.[89]

The Delawares eventually withdrew from their close association with the Moravians by the beginning of the nineteenth century. There were several factors that ultimately severed their mutually productive associations, whether as converted Delawares or those who coexisted with their mission communities. Witchcraft and its practitioners were always a part of the Delaware world. During the spiritual crises of the eighteenth century, Delaware prophets often considered the problems facing the tribes as the direct result of inappropriate practices of their medicine men and women. Occasionally these accusations led to witch-hunts that were meant to end inappropriate behaviors that were bringing harm to the people. Accusations of witchcraft also fell on Delawares who associated with Moravian missionaries and favored accommodation. Likewise, prophets were often connected to the special powers associated with positive and malevolent forces. Wangomend, the Assinsink prophet, briefly considered Moravian conversion as a solution to the problems his people faced, but instead became a Delaware witch-hunter. In 1775, he made an appeal before a Delaware council meeting in Ohio and asked followers to join him in seeking out and eliminating witches who caused Delaware corruption and weakness.[90] The appeal of this message had a limited impact at this time, but the logic that produced this supernatural explanation for Delaware problems ultimately inspired their separation from the Moravian communities, and the relationship was never fully restored to its earlier status.

Delaware and Moravian communities moved further west to Indiana following the American Revolution, maintaining their symbiotic relationship. The impact of war and dispossession weakened the value of the Moravians' message to the Indians, and fewer Delawares found reasons to convert. Their association with the Moravian mission towns still served as an economically and politically stabilizing force, but sincere and lasting conversions were not in abundance by the end of the eighteenth century. Accusations of witchcraft continued to resurface in Delaware communities as they moved further into Indiana Territory and settled along the White River. Moravians were unable to stem a series of epidemics that swept through the Delaware towns during this period, and rumors of witchcraft surfaced to explain the most recent catastrophes. In 1802 Delawares accused and executed two women charged with using their supernatural powers to cause epidemics. In 1805, more epidemics led Delawares to blame witches, but many also found an explanation by blaming Christian Delawares *and* the Moravian missions as the source of the ills that plagued their communities.[91] Moravian missionaries worried that few Delawares listened to their message and those who did were harassed by other Delawares. The Moravians concluded that those sentiments "cannot work anything but great harm to us."

As Delawares grew increasingly dissatisfied and suspicious of their relationship with the Moravians, another prophetic message reached Delaware towns along the White River. The Shawnee prophet Tenskwatawa offered a path to restore power and independence to all Indians who were willing to adhere to his authority.[92] His message echoed the sentiments of earlier prophets. The Shawnees and all Indian peoples were corrupted by the teachings and material world of the white settlers. In order to restore the Indian world, Tenskwatawa admonished his followers to rid themselves of corrupting influences. They were also required to adhere to his guidelines and perform the new rituals he created. Tenskwatawa's agenda to cleanse Indian peoples of corruption inspired more witch-hunts targeting the Delawares, already under pressure to understand the source of their continued misfortunes. Tenskwatawa's accusations found supporters, but they were inconsistent. As could be expected, he accused Moravians of harboring witches and also leveled accusations against Christian Delawares. At the same time, he made accusations against traditional Delaware elders who rejected the Shawnee Prophet's authority and refused to adhere to his new rituals and practices.

After a brief but damaging period of accusations and executions, the prophet's interest in witch-hunting was cut short as more pressing political concerns demanded his attention along the Wabash River. Still, the Delawares along the White River were profoundly changed by the most recent assaults on their communities. Those traditional leaders who rejected the Shawnee Prophet's edicts also concluded that their close association with Moravians diverted them from performing the great public ceremonies of their ancestors. These leaders concluded that a source of their problems rested in their failure to maintain their sacred ceremonies. After the departure of Tenskwatawa and his followers, Delawares along the White River asked the Moravians to leave their mission, and subsequently reinstated the big house and green corn ceremony.[93] The last Moravian mission established in the Delaware town of Woapimintschi, located along the White River, lasted only five short years. John Peter Kluge was unable to restore the trust of Delawares that the Moravians had formerly enjoyed. Moravians were no longer invited to sit at council meetings, and attempts to teach Delawares the Anglo-American agricultural arts also met with resistance. Delawares continued to farm on small plots, to hunt and fish as they always had, and to find a variety of means to support their families in Indiana, but not by adapting to the Jeffersonian civilization program offered by the Moravians. By 1806 the mission was permanently abandoned.

Quakers all but ignored their ancient friends the Delawares, extending their Indian missions into New York, Ohio, and Indiana. Quakers established a series of demonstration farms, spreading their terms of civilization by "Kindness and Necessity."[94] Their program advocated a fence-and-farm strategy that required a complete rehabilitation of gendered work roles. Quakers asked Indian women to abandon their fields and practice the home-centered domestic arts of weaving and homemaking. Similarly, Quaker missionaries required that Indian men come out of the forests and into the fields to cultivate crops that would sustain their communities.[95] Indian communities conditionally accepted the Quakers' help for many reasons. Starvation and land loss were the major threats to Indian communities in the aftermath of the Americans' ascendance. The Quakers offered their skills as mediators, advocating on most counts a preservation of Indian lands, much as their founder William Penn had done. Secondly, Quakers did not proselytize. They did not require a religious conversion from the Indians who accepted their missionary efforts. Instead, what the Quakers required was that their followers change their mode of living to reflect their own. Unlike Moravians, Quakers moved in and out of these missions at a relatively quick pace—three years at Oneida, six years with the Senecas, less than one year with the Miamis. Once the demonstration farms were established, and outward appearances convinced members that the lessons were understood, they left their tools and equipment with the Indians and found a new community to share their wisdom with. Quakers met with varying degrees of "success" in their mission, but in the end their former reputation as mediators and pacifists were restored. Quakers continued to provide their services to the government until the late nineteenth century.[96]

The story of the friendship shared between the Delawares of southeastern Pennsylvania and William Penn and his followers is still recalled by citizens of the modern Delaware nation, as well as members of the Society of Friends in Philadelphia. As peacemakers, mediators, and diplomats, both groups struggled to find their place in a world that held little tolerance for peace and mediation. Delaware leaders repeatedly recalled their trust in William Penn as they attempted to prove their neutrality and independence in the most trying years of the eighteenth century. Similarly, the Quakers' commitment to the peace testimony undermined the trust of their fellow colonists and caused the Quakers to find new strategies to live the spiritual life they professed. Despite the common ideals that infused these communities, they did not find mutual comfort from each other during the spiritual and political crises of mid-century.

Quakers emerged from the American Revolution acting as mediators at treaty councils and missionaries to Indian communities. They turned to other tribes like the Oneidas, Senecas, and Shawnees, who were more receptive, to demonstrate their program for Indian civilization. The Quakers needed to prove themselves to their new government, and they were careful to select tribes who offered the most chance for success. The Delawares were rare recipients of their efforts, partially because they did not seek Quaker help, but also because Delawares created a new alliance with the Moravians in the years before the Revolution. This alliance continued to bolster Delaware neutrality, but ultimately the war forced both the Delawares and the Moravians to choose sides, and the intensity of Indian-hating on the western frontier and the 1782 massacre of Delawares in Gnadenhutten proved the final undoing of their alliance. Delawares continued their diaspora to the western territories in Ohio and Indiana, placing greater distances, ideologically and geographically, between their communities and those colonists who once offered a shared vision of coexistence. Until the removals of the early nineteenth century, the Delawares largely rejected the offers of civilization that Quakers and others continued to make.

The "ancient friendship" cited by both Delawares and Quakers from the eighteenth to the twenty-first century is a rich and complex story that cannot be understood in one telling. This essay focused in particular on the period of history when both Quakers and Delawares faced common challenges and internal crises. The Quakers withdrew from a very public political and economic life in the first half of the eighteenth century. Their own success and prosperity threatened to undermine their spiritual ideals of modesty and charity. The French and Indian War, followed quickly by the American Revolution, put Quakers further under public scrutiny because of their commitment to pacifism. As the new American nation took shape in the wars' aftermath, Quakers found new footing as diplomats and missionaries in Indian country. Their relative success in both arenas owes much to their long friendship and alliances with the Delawares. During this same period, the Delawares also sought to find their political and spiritual place in the rapidly changing landscape of the new western territories of the American republic. Delawares largely withdrew from the battlefields of the old Northwest Territory and concentrated their efforts on finding and protecting homelands where they could live as Delawares. Many Delaware leaders understood the value of aligning their communities with missionary settlements. The economic and political ties created stability in a landscape where the Delawares had little leverage in treaty negotiations. They were guests in a country not their own, and alliances that provided stability were essential to their success. Delawares also faced a spiritual crisis during this period, and some selectively embraced the Moravian lessons; but more often than not, their relationship to their most recent Christian ally was a fickle one, not lasting beyond the mid-nineteenth century.

NOTES

1. Delawares and Lenapes are interchangeable names for the same people and are used to reflect the common usage as it changed throughout the eighteenth century. Quakers and Friends are interchangeable names for the members of the Society of Friends used throughout the essay.
2. For general histories of the Lenapes and Quakers in Pennsylvania, see C. A. Weslager, *The Delaware Indians* (New Brunswick, NJ: Rutgers University Press, 1991); and Gary B. Nash, *Quakers and Politics: Pennsylvania, 1681–1726* (Princeton, NJ: Princeton University Press, 1968).
3. Dawn G. Marsh, "Hiding in Plain Sight: Hannah Freeman, a Lenape Woman in Penn's Peaceable Kingdom" (PhD dissertation, University of California, 2003), 104–13.
4. For demographic details, see James Lemon, *The Best Poor Man's Country: A Geographical Study of Early Southeastern Pennsylvania* (Baltimore: Johns Hopkins University Press, 1972); Thomas Sugrue, "The Peopling and Depeopling of Early Pennsylvania: Indians and Colonists, 1680–1720," *Pennsylvania Magazine of History and Biography* 116 (1992): 3–31.
5. Note: The "Inner Light" is the belief that all humans carry the divine spark within. See Edwin B. Bronner, *William Penn's "Holy Experiment": The Founding of Pennsylvania, 1681–1701* (Philadelphia: Temple University Press, 1963), 12–13; Canby T. Jones, ed., *"The Power of the Lord is Over All": The Pastoral Letters of George Fox* (Richmond, IN: Friends United Press, 1989), 25.

6. Herman Wellenreuther and Carola Wessel, eds., *The Moravian Mission Diaries of David Zeisberger, 1772–1781* (University Park: Pennsylvania State University Press, 2005), 1–89.

7. Rayner W. Kelsey, *Friends and the Indians, 1655–1917* (Philadelphia: Associated Executive Committee of Friends on Indian Affairs, 1917), 89–109, 132–40.

8. Amy C. Schutt, *Peoples of the River Valleys: The Odyssey of the Delaware Indians* (Philadelphia: University of Pennsylvania Press, 2007), passim; Personal interview with Nancy Webster, Swarthmore College, July 9, 2008.

9. Some Delawares and scholars recognize Lenapehoking as the Delaware name for their historic homeland.

10. Dawn G. Marsh, "Hiding in Plain Sight," 2–5, 50–105.

11. Robert Juet, "The Third Voyage of Master Henry Hudson, 1610," in *Narratives of New Netherland, 1609–1664*, ed. J. Franklin Jameson (New York: Charles Scribner's Sons, 1909), 11–28; Johannes de Laet, "New World," in *Narratives of New Netherland*, 29–58.

12. Matthew Dennis, *Cultivating a Landscape of Peace* (Ithaca, NY: Cornell University Press, 1993), 127; Ives Goddard, "Delaware," in *Handbook of North American Indians*, vol. 15, *Northeast*, ed. Bruce G. Trigger (Washington, DC: Smithsonian Institution, 1978), 220.

13. For Swedish commercial and cultural relations with the Lenapes, see Gunlog Maria Fur, "Cultural Confrontation on Two Fronts: Swedes Meet Lenapes and Saamis in the Seventeenth Century" (PhD dissertation, University of Oklahoma, 1993), 99. For Dutch and English relations with the Lenapes before Penn, see C. A. Weslager, *The English on the Delaware: 1610–1682* (New Brunswick, NJ: Rutgers University Press, 1967).

14. "William Penn's First Letter to the Indians," in *Early American Indian Documents: Treaties and Laws, 1606–1789*, vol. 1, *Pennsylvania and Delaware Treaties: 1629–1737*, ed. Alden T. Vaughan (Washington, DC: University Publications of America, 1979), 55.

15. Robert W. Harper, *John Fenwick and Salem County in the Province of West Jersey: 1609–1700* (Pennsville, NJ: Associated Printers, 1978), 54–57.

16. "Deed from the Delaware Indians," in *The Papers of William Penn*, ed. Mary Maples Dunn and Richard S. Dunn (Philadelphia: University of Pennsylvania Press, 1981), 261–66.

17. Wilcomb E. Washburn, "Seventeenth-Century Indian Wars," in *Handbook of North American Indians*, vol. 15, *Northeast*, ed. Bruce G. Trigger (Washington, DC: Smithsonian Institution, 1978), 88–92.

18. Amandus Johnson et al., *The Instruction for Johan Printz, Governor of New Sweden: The First Constitution or Supreme Law of the States of Pennsylvania and*

Delaware (Philadelphia: Swedish Colonial Society, 1930), 117–18; Marsh, "Hiding in Plain Sight," 55–85.

19. The "peaceable kingdom" trope celebrates William Penn's mythologized relationships with the Delawares in the Quaker colony. The best-known reference is in a series of paintings by the nineteenth-century Quaker artist William Hicks.

20. For Lenape religious beliefs and practices, see John Bierhorst, *Mythology of the Lenape: Guide and Texts* (Tucson: University of Arizona Press, 1995), 5–12; Daniel G. Brinton, *The Lenape and Their Legends* (Philadelphia, 1885); John Heckewelder, *History, Manners, and Customs of the Indian Nations* (Philadelphia: Historical Society of Pennsylvania, 1876), 249–57.

21. Manitous are spiritual forces that take many forms. For further information, see Gladys Tantaquidgeon, *Folk Medicine of the Delaware and Related Algonkian Indians* (Harrisburg: Pennsylvania Historical and Museum Commission, 2001), 6–12.

22. Turtle Island is a common Algonquian name for planet Earth.

23. Bierhorst, *Mythology*, 5–12.

24. Edwin B. Bronner, *William Penn's "Holy Experiment,"* 12–15.

25. Jones, *Power of the Lord*, 25.

26. Religious Society of Friends, *Faith and Practice* (Philadelphia: Philadelphia Yearly Meeting, 1984), 34–36, 89–92. For more on the peace testimony, see Elisha Bates, *The Doctrines of Friends* (Providence: Knowles & Vose, 1840); Edwin B. Bronner, "The Quakers and Non-Violence in Pennsylvania," *Pennsylvania History* 35, no. 1 (1968): 1–22.

27. Lemon, *The Best Poor Man's Country*, 48.

28. C. A. Weslager, *Red Men on the Brandywine* (Wilmington, DE: Hambleton, 1953), 24–32.

29. C. A. Weslager, *The Delaware Indians' Westward Migration* (Wallingford, PA: Middle Atlantic Press, 1978), 3–77.

30. Francis Jennings, "Brother Miquon: Good Lord!," in *The World of William Penn*, ed. Richard S. Dunn and Mary Maples Dunn (Philadelphia: University of Pennsylvania Press, 1986), 195–214.

31. The Delawares called Penn "Miquon," meaning feather or pen. The Iroquois called him "Onus," meaning the same thing in their language. He arrived in their country in 1682. See Francis Jennings, *The Ambiguous Iroquois Empire* (New York: Norton, 1983), 230–31.

32. Heckewelder, *History, Manners*, 66.

33. Francis Jennings, "Miquon's Passing: Indian-European Relations in Colonial Pennsylvania, 1674–1755" (PhD dissertation, University of Pennsylvania, 1965), 100.

34. Jack D. Marietta, *The Reformation of American Quakerism, 1748–1783* (Philadelphia: University of Pennsylvania Press, 1984), 150–69.

35. Jones, *Power of the Lord*, 407; Frederick B. Tolles, *Meeting House and Counting House: The Quaker Merchants of Colonial Philadelphia, 1682–1763* (Chapel Hill: University of North Carolina Press, 1948), 3–29.

36. C. A. Weslager, *Westward Migration*, 171–94.

37. For the Walking Purchase, see Francis Jennings, "The Scandalous Indian Policy of William Penn's Sons: Deeds and Documents of the Walking Purchase," *Pennsylvania History* 30, no. 1 (1970): 19–39.

38. Francis Jennings, *The Ambiguous Iroquois Empire: The Covenant Chain Confederation of Indian Tribes with the English Colonies from Its Beginnings to the Lancaster Treaty of 1744* (New York: W.W. Norton, 1983), 329–33, 336–39.

39. Herman Wellenreuther and Carola Wessel, eds., *The Moravian Mission Diaries of David Zeisberger, 1772–1781* (University Park: Pennsylvania State University Press, 2005), 1–87.

40. Note: David Zeisberger, John Heckewelder, and Christian Frederick Post are the three most well-known Moravians who spent their lives working with the Indians in the eighteenth century. See Weslager, *The Delaware Indians*, 42–44, 223, 237–38.

41. "Outer plantations" is the term George Fox used to describe Quaker interests in world affairs and goods, relative to the "inner plantations," which referred to their Inner Light and spiritual well-being.

42. Anthony F. C. Wallace, *King of the Delawares: Teedyuscung* (Philadelphia: University of Pennsylvania Press, 1949), 56–266; Weslager, *The Delaware Indians*, 221–60.

43. Gregory Evans Dowd, *A Spirited Resistance: The North American Indian Struggle for Unity, 1745–1815* (Baltimore: Johns Hopkins University Press, 1992), 23–46.

44. Ibid., 68–69.

45. On the history of the Quaker Hicksite schism, see Bruce Dorsey, "Friends Becoming Enemies: Philadelphia Benevolence and the Neglected Era of American Quaker History," *Journal of the Early Republic* 18, no. 3 (1998): 395–428; Sydney V. James, "The Impact of the American Revolution on the Quakers' Ideas about Their Sect," *William and Mary Quarterly* 19, no. 3 (1962): 360–82.

46. Kelsey, *Friends*, 70–84.

47. Ibid., 89–109, 132–61.

48. Ibid.

49. Charles E. Hunter, "The Delaware Nativist Revival of the Mid-Eighteenth Century," *Ethnohistory: The Bulletin of the Ohio Valley Historic Indian Conference* 18 (1971): 39, 42.

50. Dowd, *Spirited Resistance*, 31–32.

51. In a vision, Papoonan received his message from a supernatural presence he named the "Master of Life." See Dowd, *Spirited Resistance*, 31–32.

52. William Penn provided reserved lands for Indian communities that he called plantations. These were lands that were protected for Indian use until the Indians abandoned them. See Weslager, *The Delaware Indians*, 35–42. For the Paxton Boys and the Paxton Massacre, see Brooke Hindle, "The March of the Paxton Boys," *William and Mary Quarterly* 3, no. 4 (1946): 462–86. For Pontiac's Rebellion, see Gregory Dowd, *War under Heaven: Pontiac, the Indian Nations, and the British Empire* (Baltimore: Johns Hopkins University Press, 2002).

53. Dowd, *War under Heaven*, 32, 35, 42, 45; Weslager, *The Delaware Indians*, 247–48.

54. Hunter, *The Delaware Nativist Revival*, 42–43.

55. Christian Frederick Post, quoted in Dowd, *The Spirited Resistance*, 32.

56. Alfred A. Cave, "The Failure of the Shawnee Prophet's Witch-Hunt," *Ethnohistory* 42, no. 3 (1995): 445–75; Dowd, *The Spirited Resistance*, 69, 194, 38–40.

57. Roger L. Nichols, *The American Indian*, 6th ed. (Norman: University of Oklahoma Press, 2008), 109.

58. Dowd, *The Spirited Resistance*, 33.

59. Earl P. Olmstead, *David Zeisberger: A Life among the Indians* (Kent, OH: Kent State University Press, 1997).

60. The anglicized names for these towns are Coshocton and Newcomer's Town, respectively. See Helen Hornbeck Tanner and Miklos Pinther, *Atlas of Great Lakes History* (Norman: University of Oklahoma Press, 1987), 75, 80, 85, 88; Wellenreuther, *Zeisberger Diaries*, 130–32.

61. Wellenreuther, *Zeisberger Diaries*, 57.

62. Ibid., 239–45.

63. Also known by the anglicized George White Eyes. See Richard White, *The Middle Ground* (Cambridge: Cambridge University Press, 1991), 359.

64. Dowd, *The Spirited Resistance*, 69.

65. Bruce Dorsey, "Friends Becoming Enemies: Philadelphia Benevolence and the Neglected Era of American Quaker History," *Journal of the Early Republic* 18, no. 3 (Autumn 1998): 395–428.

66. John M. Moore, ed., *Friends in the Delaware Valley: Philadelphia Yearly Meeting, 1681–1981* (Haverford, PA: Friends Historical Association, 1981), 27.

67. Ibid.

68. Ibid.

69. Marietta, *The Reformation of American Quakerism*, 105–10.

70. Ibid., 160–87.

71. Ibid., 169–72.

72. Weslager, *The Delaware Indians*, 236.

73. Kelsey, *Friends and the Indians*, 94.

74. John Lacey, "Memoirs of Brigadier-General John Lacey of Pennsylvania," *Pennsylvania Magazine of History and Biography* 25, no. 1 (1901): 4–9; John Parrish, "Extracts from the Journal of John Parrish, 1773," *Pennsylvania Magazine of History and Biography* 26, no. 4 (1892): 443–48.

75. The "Peace Testimony" is the name of the Quaker doctrine of pacifism.

76. Arthur J. Meekel, *The Relation of the Quakers to the American Revolution* (Washington, DC: University Press of America, 1979), 123.

77. Dorsey, *Friends Becoming Enemies*, 401.

78. Kelsey, *Friends and the Indians*, 89.

79. Ibid., 132–40.

80. Schutt, *Peoples of the River Valleys*, 159.

81. Ibid.

82. Ibid.

83. Ibid., 172.

84. Correspondence, Colonel Daniel Brodhead to General Washington, October 17, 1780, in *The Olden Time*, vol. 2, ed. Neville B. Craig (Pittsburgh, PA: Wright and Charleton, 1874), 374–75.

85. Schutt, *Peoples of the River Valleys*, 172–73.

86. Ibid., 176–77.

87. Kelsey, *Friends and the Indians*, 95.

88. Lawrence Henry Gipson, *The Moravian Indian Mission on White River* (Indianapolis: Historical Bureau, 1938), 13–17; Weslager, *The Delaware Indians*, 336–37.

89. Cave, "The Failure of the Shawnee Prophet's Witch-Hunt," 448–49.

90. Heckewelder, *History, Manners*, 293–95; Dowd, *The Spirited Resistance*, 37–38; Hunter, *Delaware Nativist Revival*, 39–49.

91. Gipson, *Moravian Indian Mission*, 230–31.

92. R. David Edmunds, *The Shawnee Prophet* (Lincoln: University of Nebraska Press, 1983); Dowd, *The Spirited Resistance*, 135–46.

93. Cave, "The Failure of the Shawnee Prophet's Witch-Hunt," 459; Gipson, *Moravian Indian Mission*, 420–21, 624.

94. Karim M. Tiro, "'We Wish to Do You Good': The Quaker Mission to the Oneida Nation, 1790–1840," *Journal of the Early Republic* 26 (Fall 2006): 363.

95. Robert F. Berkhofer Jr., *Salvation and the Savage: An Analysis of Protestant Missions and American Indian Response, 1787–1862* (Lexington: University of Kentucky Press, 1965), 23–35.

96. Tiro, "We Wish to Do You Good," 360–65.

Delawares in Eastern Ohio after the Treaty of Greenville: The Goshen Mission in Context

AMY C. SCHUTT

CLEARING "HIGH TIMBER AND THICK UNDERWOOD," A GROUP OF Native Americans began the hard work of building a town "on a level, high ground" west of the Tuscarawas River in autumn 1798. This town lay within the Old Northwest Territory, but soon, in 1803, would be part of the new state of Ohio, in an area west of Steubenville and south of present-day Canton. A fair amount of information is available about this town, called Goshen, because it was a Moravian Christian mission and, as such, was the subject of detailed missionary record keeping, in both English and German languages. Between 1798 and 1821, Goshen was home to a dynamic population of Indians. Linguistically almost all of them would be categorized by scholars as Algonquians. More specifically, the majority were Delawares or Lenapes (also known as Lenni Lenapes), peoples whose homelands in the seventeenth century had been in the lower Hudson and Delaware valleys.[1]

Although revealing different viewpoints of the Goshen mission, two examples suggest why Goshen remained a small settlement. Stories circulated that Goshen was a dangerous place. About 1804 a Wyandot leader reportedly received a prophecy from a spirit "in the likeness of a woman," who came "to make known various things to the Indians, & among the rest to warn them, if they valued their lives, not to remain in . . . [the] neighborhood" of Goshen. Meanwhile, Euro-American Moravian missionaries expended much effort in trying to regulate Indians' lives at Goshen, and to cleanse the community of what they considered "sinful" influences.

The following words of the missionary David Zeisberger seemed to draw a clear distinction between the converted and unconverted, with a view toward Goshen being only for the former. He told one Indian man, Ska, a frequent visitor at Goshen, "that it was time for him to resolve whether he would stay here or not." "If you desire to stay here," Zeisberger said, "you must quit your sinful life, and begin to think seriously about yourself, for what purposes you was created, and what you live for. . . . If you want to live among us, you must resolve with your whole heart to be converted." Given Wyandot reports of warnings about Goshen's dangers, and Zeisberger's stark language, Goshen seemed unlikely to attract a large number of Indians. At its peak it had seventy-one residents officially registered by the missionaries, but during many years the town's "official" numbers dropped into the twenties.[2]

Furthermore, Goshen's location seemed to marginalize and isolate it from indigenous peoples whom missionaries could have approached in order to expand the mission. With the defeat of the northern Indian Confederacy in 1794 and the Treaty of Greenville the next year, Native American dispossession in the Ohio Valley—already far along—continued apace. As the threat of war with Indians diminished, Euro-American newcomers to Ohio arrived, especially from Pennsylvania, Virginia, and New England. Particularly in southern and eastern Ohio, the displacement of Indian peoples, especially Delawares and Shawnees, was marked. Underscoring this trend, one historian refers to Euro-Americans "having ousted the Native Americans" from the lower Muskingum Valley by the early 1800s. Yet the story of the Goshen mission complicates this familiar narrative of dispossession in eastern Ohio. Although by missionary reckoning their numbers were small, the Goshen Delawares participated in, and contributed to, the life of the Lower Great Lakes–Ohio Valley region in many ways—in large part through their wide range of social and economic connections that helped offset their small numbers.[3]

The significance of Goshen becomes clearer when we look beyond questions of Moravian success or failure in gaining converts who would then be expected to live in the mission town. Delawares' worldviews provided a wider perspective. "Algonquians conceptualized native space," according to scholar Lisa Brooks, "as a network of villages connected by rivers and relations." Hunting grounds were also part of this landscape. The Goshen mission records reveal how Indians assumed this expansive view, which was much greater than the boundaries of one mission town. Goshen Indians traveled widely, allowing them to maintain a variety of contacts on both sides of the Greenville Treaty line. Their connections extended north to the

Canadian side of Lake Erie, west to the White River in Indiana Territory, east to the panhandle of present West Virginia, and in some cases south to Marietta, Ohio. Many Indians visited and stayed at Goshen, besides those whom the Euro-American Moravians considered official, converted residents. Typically, Goshen Indians' own journeys kept them in touch with kin, but they also had various contacts with Euro-Americans throughout the region. Recent studies have turned new attention to the roles of Native Americans in the Midwest. Despite this welcome emphasis, Indians of eastern and central Ohio in the post-1795 period have received less attention than other groups. Yet their story provides a significant opportunity for close examination of Native Americans' participation in a "network of villages," hunting areas, and trading centers in the Lower Great Lakes–Ohio Valley region after the Treaty of Greenville.[4]

Delawares, like other Indian peoples in the Lower Great Lakes region, were mobile, but also intent on gathering their people in specific communities. During some of the years of Goshen's existence, Ohio-area Shawnees resided at Wapakoneta on the Auglaize River, and in the Greenville area. Wapakoneta was the town of the Shawnee leader Black Hoof and became the site of a Quaker mission. For a time, the Greenville area was home to the Shawnee prophet Tenskwatawa, who urged Indian peoples to turn away from Euro-American customs and to "live as did the Indians in olden days." At the end of 1805, Shawnees were "gathering together" near Greenville and, "upon the advice" of Tenskwatawa, proposed "to build a large town," to which they had "also invited the Delawares." Greenville was on the upper end of the Miami Valley, a fertile region linked with Cincinnati and, as historian Andrew R. L. Cayton writes, "by far the most dynamic" part of Ohio at the start of the nineteenth century. As the Euro-American population expanded in the Miami Valley, the Greenville Shawnees moved west to the Wabash River. Another important area for Lower Great Lakes Indian communities was along the Sandusky River south of Lake Erie. In the early nineteenth century, Wyandots, Delawares, Senecas, and Cayugas all lived in this region, although they faced increasing pressures to give up these lands and relocate to the west.[5]

East of Upper Sandusky were lands that were ceded to the United States at the Treaty of Fort Industry in 1805. These lands bordered Lake Erie and included a portion of north-central Ohio where presently the towns of Norwalk, Medina, and Mansfield are located. Names of Delawares, Shawnees, Wyandots, Potawatomis, Ottawas, and Ojibwas appear on the treaty. Euro-American settlement of this isolated area proceeded slowly at first, and Indian peoples continued to live there in the early nineteenth century.

These included Delawares who resided at Pettquotting on the Huron River near Lake Erie. Southeast of Pettquotting and still within the Fort Industry cession, Delawares lived in two other communities, Jerometown and Greentown, which Congress set aside as reservation lands in 1807.[6]

Like Goshen, Jerometown and Greentown were in the Muskingum River valley, an area that in the early nineteenth century still included Indian hunting grounds. Indian peoples' growing indebtedness to Great Lakes traders undoubtedly increased pressures to use these hunting areas. In 1802, a "traveller from New York state who came down the Muskingum by water," reported that on the banks of the river there were so many carcases [*sic*] of deer that had lately been killed by the hunters, that the air was tainted thereby." Predominant in these particular hunting parties were Anishinabeg (Ottawas and Ojibwas), who, like Wyandots and Delawares, sought game in this region. Some of this hunting occurred on or near the United States side of the Greenville Treaty line. For example, Wyandots hunted in 1801 on the Stillwater and One Leg creeks flowing into the Tuscarawas River, and in 1804 near the Mahoning River southeast of Cleveland.[7]

Moravian Indian mission records are voluminous and offer many details about religion, the economy, and other aspects of everyday life. They describe Delawares' conversion experiences, participation in trading networks, and struggles to maintain contacts with far-off friends and kin. Valuable as they are for their richness of detail, it is important to read these records critically by considering biases and omissions. Focusing on successes or failures in converting Native Americans, Euro-American missionaries tended to judge individuals on this basis, so that they appear in a positive or negative light according to this standard. Individuals who were often at Goshen, but whom the Moravian missionaries never considered converted, appear in the records as outsiders. A close examination, though, reveals that such persons made a mark on the Goshen community in important ways and deserve a place in the mission's story. Another point to recognize is that on the many occasions when Goshen Indians were absent, missionary record keepers would have had little, if any, knowledge about what these Indians were doing. Yet this time away from Goshen was crucial for visiting relatives, hunting, bartering, and finding paid employment. As with other early European records documenting Native American lives, gender bias needs to be considered. Relative to records for some earlier Moravian missions, Goshen records place less emphasis on women's roles and contributions. Close readings and a broader understanding of Delaware cultural practices can help mitigate this problem, but frequently we have to admit that the Goshen records leave out much that scholars would like to know about the history of women and girls. Each of these considerations is important in constructing a meaningful interpretation of Goshen's history.[8]

German-speaking Moravians, Pietists whose organization was formally known as the Unity of the Brethren, had begun mission work among the Delawares and nearby Mohicans in the 1740s in New York and Pennsylvania. Following a period of growth, particularly in the upper Lehigh Valley of Pennsylvania, Moravian missions experienced divisions and depletions during the violent period between the mid-1750s and the mid-1760s. By 1765, with the Seven Years' War–Pontiac's War era coming to an end, most Delawares had been dispossessed of homelands in the east. Relocating to the Susquehanna and Ohio valleys, Delawares encountered concerted mission-building efforts by Euro-American Moravians, especially the missionary David Zeisberger. This rebuilding phase, which resulted in substantial Moravian mission towns among the Delawares in the Muskingum River valley of the Ohio Country, ended during the Revolutionary War. The greatest blow came in 1782, when militia out of western Pennsylvania slaughtered an estimated ninety-six Moravian mission Indians. After this massacre, the Moravian mission to the Delawares was in chaos. For a few years, a remnant of the mission Indians lived on the Clinton River in Ojibwa country north of Detroit. Subsequent Moravian mission sites were along the southern shore of Lake Erie and then on the Thames River in Upper Canada, where the town of Fairfield was founded.[9]

Throughout the postwar period, Euro-American Moravians and some Delawares sought to return to the Muskingum Valley, where, according to one missionary's estimate, well over 350 Indians had resided among three Moravian sites in the year before the massacre. In 1786, Moravian bishop John Ettwein petitioned Congress to assist in reestablishing a mission in the Muskingum Valley. Subsequently, Congress reserved three tracts at the site of the former mission towns for the Moravians to use "for civilizing the Indians & promoting Christianity." Here, Indians were expected to raise livestock, grow crops, and adopt Euro-American gender roles, with men taking on agricultural work traditionally handled by women. They were to serve as an example to other Indians that they, according to congressional records, "may see the great difference of a civilised Christian life and the life of savages." This action was in keeping with U.S. policy to urge the use of Euro-American-style agricultural practices, and to discourage hunting among Indian peoples. The idea was that through these changes, Indians "would be weaned from the land-extensive search for game," as one historian writes; more lands would be available for Euro-American settlement, leading to the expansion and economic growth of the United States. Early national policymakers enlisted missionaries to promote these ends.[10]

Despite the promise of land, Moravian Indians did not return to live in the Muskingum Valley until about a decade later, when they set up Goshen. Until then, the dangers seemed too great to attempt resettlement. Indian peoples were angered by their treatment in the period after the Revolutionary War. "The greatest complaint they made against the American people," stated Moravian John Heckewelder, "was that 'at treaties, they charged them, with the injuries they had done to the Americans; while *they*, (the Americans) neither said a word, nor would hear any thing about injuries they had done to Indians! That, finally, they took their land . . . from them, alledging [*sic*] to them, crimes which properly had been caused by, or committed by themselves.'" Violence and destruction of property occurred in confrontations between Euro-American Kentuckians and Indian peoples during raids across the Ohio River in the 1780s and 1790s. In 1790 and 1791, the Washington administration tried and failed to eliminate confederated Indian opposition to advancing Euro-American settlement. The northern Indian confederacy, consisting of Miamis, Shawnees, Ottawas, Delawares, and others, won victories over forces led by Josiah Harmar and Arthur St. Clair. It was not until after the Battle of Fallen Timbers and then the Greenville Treaty settlement of 1795 that conditions seemed secure enough for the Moravians to attempt another mission on the Tuscarawas River in the Muskingum Valley.[11]

As the message in the Wyandot prophecy indicated, though, Goshen still seemed a volatile place to many Indians. Probably most terrifying were the memories of the massacre that had occurred in this area. Delawares who lived at Goshen continually heard from other Indians that "if they adopted the manners of the white people, and believed the gospel, they should die," like the Moravian mission Indians in 1782. Heightening anxieties was the evidence that the murderers from the massacre could be nearby. A group of Euro-Americans traveling from western Virginia to the Tuscarawas River in 1800 included a person who "threatened to kill" the Indian man Ska, to whom he "boasted . . . that he was one of the murderers" from "18 years ago." Missionaries repeatedly tried to counter Native arguments that Christianization endangered Indians' lives, and that the Christian gospel was "only for the white people," and "not for the Indians." Native prophets for many years had made this point that whites and Indians were completely different and should follow different beliefs.[12]

A mixture of factors must have influenced Delawares who decided to join the mission community. After years of land dispossession, some may have seen Congress's designation of reserved space in Ohio as the very least that was owed to them after their horrible treatment in 1782. Specifically named in a congressional letter as especially deserving of these lands were the following: Gelelemend (or William Henry), a leading Delaware supporter of the United States during the war; his family members; and the family of the deceased Delaware leader, Quequedegatha (or White Eyes). Gelelemend had sacrificed a great deal when he had sided with the United States, including losing the support of many Delawares who resented their treatment by U.S. forces. For a long time he had been constructing his political and religious life around alliances with the Moravians and the United States. Gelelemend probably hoped that the land grant confirmed he had made the right choice. Despite the many naysayers, Goshen Delawares, in the midst of poverty and struggle, also hoped that Goshen offered access to spiritual power, which could bring them healing and comfort. One such individual was White Eyes's widow, now remarried, who was baptized at Goshen. This woman, called Mary, explained that she had suffered from an illness making it difficult to walk. Hoping for relief, "she had now and then sacrificed a deer or bear and given a dance" as part of a traditional ceremony. "But," she said, "this had not at all helped her" condition. With gratitude, she explained that, since living at Goshen, her life had changed, and "she . . . had become completely healthy." Delawares would have found a variety of meanings in Moravian rituals and teachings, which they interpreted through their own frames of reference. Some may have appreciated missionaries' struggling efforts to learn the Delaware language and incorporate it into religious services. Like those Delawares who heeded Native prophecies, Delawares at Goshen were seeking spiritual aid at a time when they faced many threats, including starvation, disease, and possible renewed warfare.[13]

Previously, in eastern homelands, Delawares had utilized a variety of means to gain a livelihood. They grew corn, beans, squash, and other crops, with women primarily responsible for this work. Men had special responsibility for hunting, but women and children also traveled with hunting parties. Fishing and the collection of wild foods were additional means of support. This mixed economy involved trading furs for European-made wares. In addition, Delawares sold baskets and brooms to neighboring Euro-Americans. A diversified approach was important at Goshen, where Delawares faced lean times. Drought, flooding, and insects all took a toll on agriculture. Outbreaks of "intermitting fevers," probably malaria, right at harvest time sometimes made it impossible for Delawares to gather in all of their crops. To survive, they participated in varied ways in the region's economy. When crop yields were low, hunting became even more vital. In summer, Goshen Indians could obtain "various sorts" of fish from the Tuscarawas. In the fall, "women gathered hickory nuts, to make soup of" and located berries in the summer. With access to "excellent sugar trees" on their tract, Goshen Indians devoted much attention to producing maple syrup, which they "accounted extremely wholesome."[14]

In keeping with governmental policy, Goshen missionaries wanted Indians to reorganize their lives around agriculture and animal husbandry so that men would assume primary farming duties and de-emphasize hunting. Yet hunting continued to be a necessary and expected part of survival at Goshen. Deer and bear were the principal game for Goshen Indians, although elk, beaver, raccoons, and otters were also hunted or trapped. The primary deer hunt occurred in the fall when the animals were "fat . . . and the leaves" were "falling off the trees," allowing hunters to keep an eye on their quarry. In November and December, a missionary explained, "deer are taken in greatest numbers, and their skins are most valuable for every kind of use, and fetch the highest prices." The hot summer months were the secondary period for deer hunting. Because of "the frequent resort of the deer to the rivers and creeks about this time, in order to cool themselves," hunters knew where to locate game. Goshen hunters especially sought out fattened bears during winter months when the animals were hibernating.[15]

Some hunting occurred fairly close to home, thus probably limiting contact with outsiders. In January 1800, a group of twelve hunters had a "camp 10 miles from" Goshen, from which site they "killed 6 bears, besides a few deer." "After a fall of snow," four years later, six Goshen residents "went a hunting near" the mission "and each brought home a deer." Frequently, however, hunting widened the range of contacts beyond the mission community. Comments of English-born missionary Benjamin Mortimer reveal these regular absences from Goshen and the possibilities for outside connections that hunting provided. "*The spending of the far greater part of their time in the woods, at a distance from us*," he worried, "*is a vast impediment to us in the prosecution of our missionary labors.*" Sometimes away from missionary preaching for weeks at a time, hunters would have had opportunities to meet non-Moravian whites and Indians. One group of Goshen Indians planned to hunt "far up the Muskingum and to [its] smaller branches," while another company came back to Goshen after a three-week hunting trip. Goshen men hunted in the vicinity of a road leading to Georgetown, Pennsylvania, along which they would have encountered a variety of travelers. The Georgetown road hunting ground was about twenty-five miles from Goshen and lay on a route between the Tuscarawas and the Ohio River used by traders and migrants.[16]

Hunting parties from Goshen were often all male, but in some cases consisted of entire families. In this way, women, men, and children would have had increased chances for contacts beyond the mission. Just as he frowned on long absences, Mortimer did not favor family hunting trips, although he did not try to ban them. He liked to think that mission women "generally prefer staying at home" in contrast to the "wild Indian" whose "wife & children generally accompany him" in hunting. Similar to other missionaries of the time, he showed his bias in favor of gendered occupations of domestic duties for women and farm work for men. Nevertheless, Goshen Delawares did not completely adopt this model. In November 1802, Mortimer stated that "nearly all our people . . . went with their families to the hunting-camps." About a month later he wrote, "This is their principal hunting season, the spirit of which seems this year to have entered into the sisters as well as brethren, as many of them as can possibly leave home, having for some weeks past, taken up their abode at the hunting-camps, with their children." Goshen Indians explained that this method would "save the men the trouble of bringing home the meat they kill, which sometimes takes place very sparingly," and family members could "assist them in frying out the bears-fat."[17]

Hunting trips also brought non-Goshen Indians into the region of the mission, where they shared hunting grounds with Goshen residents. In 1798, one such individual came and offered "bear's meat and venison" to Gelelemend, which then was distributed at Goshen. From another area of Delaware settlement—Pettquotting on the Huron River south of Lake Erie—Delawares frequently traveled to the Muskingum Valley to hunt. "Pettquotting and other Indians" were said to "come into these parts at the [hunting] season, on account of the great plenty of game . . . within the hilly country" in 1806. Although some of these visitors were part of a small Moravian mission at Pettquotting, others probably were not. Both Moravian and non-Moravian Indians around Pettquotting suffered because "every thing . . . [was] scarce in that part of the country."[18]

Hunting was essential during frequent shortages of corn and other provisions. Soon after Goshen was established, the community's "small stock of corn & meat was nearly exhausted." Parties of Goshen hunters provided meat at such times, but they also provided skins that could be traded for food and other goods. "We cannot restrain our people" from hunting, a missionary wrote, "because they need clothes and provisions." These were typically obtained through trade.[19]

Mission records are filled with examples of contacts between Native hunters and Euro-American traders. The earliest trading route for the mission led to Charlestown (present Wellsburg, West Virginia), which was about sixty-five miles away on the Ohio River north of Wheeling. Moravian records often referred to this area as Buffalo because it was near the mouth of Buffalo Creek. Euro-American traders from Charlestown frequently came to Goshen with flour and corn to exchange for pelts. In 1798, for example, a Mr. Griffin from Charlestown left with "three horse loads of pelts" after an eight-day visit to Goshen. Often, Goshen Indians traveled to Charlestown themselves, either on foot or possibly by horse, if one was available. Besides flour and corn, items available at Charlestown included potatoes, bacon, hatchets, and gunpowder. For a time, Charlestown was the site of Goshen's nearest postal station and blacksmith. Goshen Indians on occasion canoed down the Muskingum to Marietta, at the mouth of the river, in order to trade. In May 1799, seven Goshen men went there to obtain "corn, provisions, and different things for planting." Sometimes a Euro-American trader from Marietta came to Goshen.[20]

The Goshen Indians occupied only one of the tracts set aside by Congress. Soon the Moravian church opened up the other two tracts for settlement by Euro-American Moravians from the east. Beginning in fall 1799, Goshen Indians had the option of buying or trading at a nearby Moravian-run store across the Tuscarawas River and downstream at Gnadenhütten, where Euro-American Moravians were starting to settle. Goshen Indians did not depend on the Gnadenhütten store, preferring instead to select from a range of trading options within the region. Although much closer than Charlestown, the Gnadenhütten store was not always easily accessible. The rising Tuscarawas River at certain times impeded travel back and forth between Goshen and Gnadenhütten. Also, the advantage of proximity was offset by the disadvantage of higher prices. Mortimer complained that "traders from the northward, who stroll about the country, and live in the Indian manner, can generally afford [to offer] their goods at a much lower price" than at Gnadenhütten. These same traders "give a higher price for most kinds of skins." For seed corn, Goshen Indians went to Native settlements at Pettquotting or the nearby Walhonding River, where they could obtain preferred varieties not sold by Euro-Americans. On one occasion the gunpowder sold at Gnadenhütten displeased Goshen Indians, so they went the longer distance to Charlestown for a better product. In 1802, Goshen residents decided to go to Pettquotting for clothing, which was "much cheaper than in Gnadenhütten." As they checked for quality and price, Goshen

Indians utilized an extensive range of trading contacts throughout the Great Lakes and Ohio Valley region.[21]

This statement should not imply that Goshen Indians could trade whenever and wherever they wanted or that they always received the best prices for their goods. Game shortages, exacerbated by competition from Euro-American hunters, hurt trade. During the War of 1812, it was dangerous for Goshen Indians to hunt throughout the area, with so much hostility growing toward Indians in general. In some cases, an insufficient number of horses could make it more difficult to carry pelts to market and goods in return. Reports of killings of Native Americans by Euro-Americans must have also made Goshen residents wary about moving freely through certain areas.[22]

Trade deals ill favored Indians when alcohol was involved, as had been true in the Delawares' eighteenth-century eastern communities. "Our [Euro-American] neighbors make a game out of the poor Indians," John Proske, the last missionary at Goshen, complained of the liquor trade; "then they always get their goods for half price." Mortimer concluded that it was "the practice of most Indian traders, to endeavor to obtain vent for their goods, by first making the Indians drunk." A couple of notorious whites at nearby New Philadelphia, who later were found to be part of a counterfeiting scheme, took advantage of the season when Goshen residents were making maple syrup. These men sold whiskey to the Indians "and took of them in payment their sugar and clothing at a very low valuation." Apparently while Indians were drinking, these same whiskey traders robbed the Goshen tract of timber. Corn whiskey and distilleries were very common in the Ohio Valley during this time. The Gnadenhütten store, where whites as well as Indians traded, featured "scenes of drunkenness" and "loud noise," much to the disgust of some Goshen Indians. Mortimer noted in 1806 that "a few miles S[outh] from" Goshen, "a white man given to intoxication, murdered his neighbor with the hoe with which he had been working with him in a corn-field."[23]

Although the Goshen Indians did not trade at Gnadenhütten as often as the storekeeper there would have liked, Goshen Indians were vital to the origins of this Moravian settlement—a place that Mortimer called home to "some of our poorest brethren from the mountainous parts of Pennsylvania, whose former lands did not repay the labor they bestowed on them." These new arrivals were part of a movement of German-speaking people into the Muskingum area. Downriver near the market town of Zanesville, a Quaker missionary in 1804 noted that "many Germans are making settlements here." Goshen Indians constructed buildings for incoming rural

Euro-American families. In so doing, Indians supplemented their own families' material support. Men from Goshen "set up rafters on a new house" there. In August 1799, Goshen Indians participated "in raising the large building" that would become the store and residence of David Peter, the storekeeper. The following year, Goshen residents were "employed in sawing boards for" a Gnadenhütten structure. It was typical for entire Indian families to stay at Gnadenhütten while this construction took place. The Goshen Indian most recognized for his building skills was a man named Ignatius, who had once lived at Fairfield in Upper Canada. He was "a good carpenter," who worked on contract to build a residence at Gnadenhütten. Along with family members, Ignatius obtained extra income by making "clapboards for sale" at the neighboring Moravian town.[24]

Goshen residents participated in the area's economy in other ways. Ignatius used his construction abilities to make and sell a canoe to a Gnadenhütten resident. In addition, Goshen Indians made deerskin moccasins to sell at Charlestown. Before the War of 1812, though, there was a shortage of options for marketing items made at Goshen. "We wish much that our Indians could find means of selling canoes, and other articles which they can manufacture, as they did formerly on the river Huron [at Pettquotting] and in Fairfield," Mortimer wrote. After the war, however, Goshen Indians were more active in selling handmade baskets at Pittsburgh and other areas along the Ohio River. Some Goshen Indians found various types of temporary employment, such as assisting a surveyor or guiding Euro-American travelers through the area. When cattle or horses strayed from Euro-Americans, owners sometimes called upon Goshen Indians to help locate them. Records are generally silent about what Indians might have received in return for much of this work, although it was reported that a Delaware man, John Thomas, "was handsomely rewarded" for finding a lost horse of a Gnadenhütten inhabitant. Like Euro-Americans in Ohio at this time, Goshen Indians dug up ginseng roots and sold them to merchants trading with China, where the plant was used medicinally. In many ways, both large and small, Goshen Indians were an active part of the local and regional economy, taking an adaptive approach to the challenges of living in the Ohio Valley.[25]

Goshen Indians' closest contacts usually would have been with other Delawares, with whom they were linked by kinship and culture. Certain Indians were especially known for moving from place to place, sharing news and keeping the Goshen population informed about Native friends and family—especially those in Canada, on the Pettquotting, at Sandusky, and on the White River in Indiana. One such individual was Ska, possibly one source of information about the Wyandot warning against Goshen. A missionary mentioned this warning after noting that Ska had just returned "from the Northward"—probably where Wyandots lived. When Ska arrived from Pettquotting in November 1804, Goshen residents learned that "the season has been very sickly there." From Sandusky, Ska "brought distressing news" in 1810 "of the failure of crops of corn," which would have adversely affected friends and relatives of Goshen residents. When, in spring 1812, many local Euro-Americans suspected Ohio Indians of having pro-British sympathies, Ska brought important news that Native peoples at Sandusky and Greentown (about twelve miles from Mansfield, Ohio) were "peaceably disposed towards the United States." Among other places, Ska journeyed to the White River, Charlestown, and Pittsburgh. Goshen Indians would have relied on this well-traveled man to help them participate in a network of communities.[26]

Indians throughout the area kept in contact through oral messages transmitted by travelers. At Goshen there were frequently new arrivals, especially from Pettquotting, Fairfield, the White River, and Sandusky. These travelers were sources of informal news reports such as those brought by Ska. On one occasion, an Ojibwa visitor reported "news . . . [of] disputes between the United States and the Wiondats [Wyandots]," which aroused great fear of war breaking out. Other times, there were formal messages from chiefs, accompanied by strings of wampum that underscored the importance and authority of their words. In 1800, Tulpe Najudam, "messenger from the chief and grand council of the Delawares on the Woapikamikunk [or White River]," relayed a call for the Goshen Indians to relocate to the west. "We have a large district . . . that belongs to us," the message said. "Therefore I take you Gelilemind [Gelelemend], . . . and your friends softly by the hand, and lift you up, and place you here near to me on the Woapikamikunk." To make this point, the messenger, "according to custom," imparted "a long and beautiful string of wampum." The next year, thirteen Indians from Goshen were part of a new Moravian mission that started on the White River in Indiana, although Gelelemend was not among them.[27]

As Tulpe Najudam showed, Delawares did not just communicate with oral language, but they also used objects, such as wampum, to express themselves. Increasingly, Goshen Indians added alphabetic writing to their options for communicating with each other. For example, one January day in 1800, two Indians, named Joachim and Michael, "arrived from Fairfield, as express, and brought . . . letters . . . from many" Indian men there. Moravian-affiliated Indians had access to some formal schooling in which alphabetic reading and writing were taught. It is uncertain, however, to what degree Goshen missionaries encouraged females to write, compared to males. Earlier in the eighteenth century, Moravian missions offered separate classes for girls and boys, with female and male instructors respectively. At Goshen, though, records suggest that there was just one class and one male teacher, with writing instruction stressed more for males than for females. On one occasion, "many [adult] Indian brothers" composed "letters to their acquaintances," and Goshen boys also sent letters to Fairfield. Women and girls may have written letters on this occasion as well. "The young people . . . exercise themselves diligently in this art," Mortimer stated, but he did not specifically mention the gender of these writers. In 1809, Goshen schoolchildren held a demonstration for their parents, and Mortimer's account of this event suggests greater attention to boys' education. Although Mortimer used the gender-neutral word "children" to refer to the pupils, there are hints that males dominated the school event. The only student that Mortimer specifically named in describing this event was a boy called Clemens. Parents observed children being examined "in English reading & spelling," and listened to both group and individual recitations. They heard the children sing memorized "hymns & verses" in Delaware. Then six of the children showed "specimens of English writing done . . . on paper or on slates." Given other evidence of gender bias, it seems probable that all or nearly all of these writers were boys. Moravian records from 1809 indicate that of the fourteen children at Goshen, six were male—coincidentally or not, the exact number of those providing writing specimens at the school demonstration.[28]

The Goshen mission existed at a time of spiritual intensity in the region. On the one hand, Goshen Indians knew of the teachings of the Shawnee prophet Tenskwatawa, and Tecumseh's associated confederacy opposing U.S. expansion. On the other hand, they witnessed how Methodists and other white evangelicals involved in the Second Great Awakening held camp meetings in the Goshen area. "Methodists . . . roared into Ohio," historian John Wigger writes, aided by young itinerant preachers expounding upon sin and salvation as they traveled their lengthy circuits. In 1811, "a camp meeting of the methodists . . . about six miles" from Goshen "drew together considerable numbers of people from distant parts." At this four-day meeting, which resulted in about thirty baptisms, "ten preachers were present, who . . . alternately sung, preached, prayed & exhorted, from early in the morning till late at night." The strong earthquake of late 1811, with aftershocks in 1812, contributed to spiritual agitation. "An Indian chief" hunting in the Goshen area said, "The late earthquakes took place because the great Spirit was not pleased that the white people had taken possession of so much of the Indian country"—comments that were similar to views of the Shawnee prophet Tenskwatawa. Meanwhile, "prognostications" of an individual called a "prophet among the whites in Virginia" contributed to local beliefs "that the end of the world was near at hand."[29]

Goshen Indians added to the religious diversity of the region. They did not rely on Euro-American missionaries to hold all of their ceremonies, but rather sometimes arranged their own. Probably combining elements of traditional Delaware healing rituals with Christian messages, "for several weeks in succession" Goshen Indians "met in a private house, and sung verses together till late at night." These meetings occurred "commonly . . . where there was a sick child" present. In an era when white evangelical preachers were known for holding open-air revival services, Gelelemend offered his own public interpretation of Moravian teachings to a Native audience one day along "the banks of the river." Here he met a group of visiting Indians, and as they sat in "a circle," he was heard to preach "evangelical discourses" to them. Euro-American Moravians observed rather than participated in this event.[30]

Despite their creative and varied efforts to sustain themselves in eastern Ohio, Delawares found that the continuation of Goshen was in grave doubt during the War of 1812. Euro-Americans from nearby New Philadelphia accused Goshen Indians of harboring Indian spies for the British. When Kaschates, an Indian with ties to the Sandusky area, arrived in July 1812 wearing a red coat, New Philadelphians became alarmed. The red coat, as it turned out, had actually been sewn six years before at Goshen and had nothing to do with the British, but that assurance did little to calm emotions. For their part, Goshen Indians had to face militia marching through their town, which no doubt aroused fearful memories of 1782 when militia invaded their towns and massacred their people. After the loss of Detroit by U.S. forces under Brigadier-General William Hull in August 1812, returning militia passing through Goshen were especially hostile. "Some of the men from Genl. Hull's army . . . declared the Indians at this place to be in great danger of their lives from their incensed comrades," Mortimer wrote. "Some parties . . . spoke loudly before they came here . . . that they would kill every Indian here, and take their horses to ride home on."[31]

When peace returned, Delawares continued to live at the Goshen mission, but life there was increasingly difficult. John Henry, son of Gelelemend, described conditions in 1820 in a letter to John Heckewelder: "We wish to tell you what is causing us dissatisfaction here. It proceeds from the land upon which we live, because already so many whites have settled on the Goshen tract. Yes! On the same land, which, to start with, was given to us and for our use." Because of these encroachments, game became scarcer. In 1818, "two Indians who had been bear hunting came home with nothing." Later that same year, even though it should have been the prime deer-hunting season, some Goshen hunters "unfortunately shot only a few deer." In 1820, Delawares at Upper Sandusky attempted to convince Goshen Indians to move to them. A Delaware leader, Welansiquwechink, or Captain Pipe, told the Goshen Indians: "Remember the Time that our Old Men had told one another that they should like to live close together. I am now here for this purpose to bring in your remembrance their words." Philipp, a man from Upper Sandusky who was "related to most of the inhabitants at Goshen," arrived in the summer of 1821 and pressed Goshen Indians to relocate. Clearly resenting the missionaries' influence, he convinced a number of his family members to leave Goshen for Upper Sandusky in late July. These were tense times at Goshen. Euro-Americans were actively trading in brandy, which resulted in heavy drinking and some violence between Goshen residents and their white neighbors. An epidemic of fevers spread through the area, sickening both Goshen Indians and Euro-American missionaries. Following this turmoil, the members of the Moravian Society for Propagating the Gospel decided to end the mission at Goshen, which by now they viewed as an expensive and unsuccessful endeavor. In 1823 the land was sold to the United States.[32]

By this point, the main place remaining for Delawares in Ohio lay at Upper Sandusky, but this was merely nine square miles set aside out of an 1817 treaty cession. This Treaty of the Maumee Rapids (or Fort Meigs Treaty) stripped Indians of most of their remaining lands in northwestern Ohio. The small Delaware reservation, which included Captain Pipe's town, adjoined a twelve-square-mile tract left to the Wyandots at the treaty. At this time, two small reservations were designated for Ottawas on the Blanchard and Little Auglaize Rivers, and Shawnees ended up with reservations as well, including one that they shared with Senecas at Lewistown. In the context of the Fort Meigs Treaty, Philipp's call for his relatives to leave Goshen and relocate to Upper Sandusky likely reflected a combination of frustration at dispossession and an effort to hold on to remaining Delaware lands in northwestern Ohio. Meanwhile, taking advantage of new opportunities for land acquisition, the non-Indian population of Ohio continued to grow. In 1800 Ohio's overall population was 45,365 and by 1820 had reached 581,434. Slow to grow at first, northeastern Ohio's population received a boost from the Erie Canal's completion in 1825, which connected Lake Erie to the Hudson River traffic. With ongoing pressure to leave Ohio, some Sandusky Delawares joined other Delawares from Indiana to resettle on the White River in Missouri. Removal pressures mounted under the policies of the Jacksonian era. Facing violence and discrimination, Shawnees ceded Ohio reservation lands in 1831. Wyandots held on to their Upper Sandusky reservation with much difficulty until a treaty cession in 1842 and their removal to Kansas the following year. By then, Delawares were also living in Kansas, including some who had been neighbors of the Wyandots at Upper Sandusky.[33]

When Delawares reestablished themselves in the Muskingum Valley in 1798, they did not limit themselves to the town of Goshen, but rather participated in the changing economic, social, and religious life of a sizable region. In short, they situated themselves within an expanding and connected world of the Lower Great Lakes and Ohio Valley. There is no doubt that Goshen was a small mission, but Goshen should not be viewed merely in terms of Euro-American missionaries' official population totals. Frequently individuals, especially Native Americans, passed through and sometimes made extended stays at Goshen, making it a link in the transmission of news throughout the area. From the Euro-American missionaries' perspective, many of these individuals from distant and not-so-distant places were outsiders who "encamped" around Goshen and were "heathen" unwilling to convert.[34] Yet, to Delawares, many of these individuals were friends and family members who helped them survive the many hardships facing Ohio Indians in the nineteenth century. These individuals enlarged the world of the Goshen mission, even as the Goshen Delawares themselves promoted connections throughout the Lower Great Lakes–Ohio Valley region.

NOTES

1. Goshen diary, October 7 (second quotation), 9 (first quotation), and 10, 1798, English, Mortimer, based on Zeisberger's notes, item 1, folder 2, box 171, reel 19 (hereafter written as 1:2:171:19), *Records of the Moravian Mission among the Indians of North America* (hereafter *RMM*, all Goshen diary references below are from *RMM*), photographed from original materials at the Archives of the Moravian Church, Bethlehem, PA, microfilm, 40 reels (New Haven, CT: Research Publications, 1970). Eighteenth-century Moravian Indian mission records were typically written in old German script. For Goshen, some records are in German and many are in English. I have indicated the language of specific documents in my endnotes. Translations from German into English are mine, unless otherwise noted. Helen Hornbeck Tanner, ed., *Atlas of Great Lakes Indian History* (Norman: University

of Oklahoma Press, 1987), [98–99]; Ives Goddard, "Delaware," in *Handbook of North American Indians* [hereafter *HNAI*], ed. William C. Sturtevant, vol. 15, *Northeast*, ed. Bruce G. Trigger (Washington, DC: Smithsonian Institution, 1978), 213–39. Earl P. Olmstead, *Blackcoats among the Delaware: David Zeisberger on the Ohio Frontier* (Kent, OH: Kent State University Press, 1991) includes discussion of the Goshen mission, but especially in terms of the missionaries and their viewpoints. On experiences in the homelands, see Amy C. Schutt, *Peoples of the River Valleys: The Odyssey of the Delaware Indians* (Philadelphia: University of Pennsylvania Press, 2007), chapters 1 and 2.

2. Goshen diary, April 13, 1804, English, Mortimer, 1:1:173:20; ibid., October 2, 1799, English, signed by Zeisberger and Mortimer, 1:5:171:19 (Zeisberger quotations). On totals, see Goshen diary entries for December 31 for the following years: 1800, 1801, 1802, 1803, English, Mortimer, 1:8, 9, 11, and 13:171:19; 1804, 1805, 1806, and 1807, English, Mortimer, 1:1, 2, 3, and 4:173:20; 1808, German, excerpt, 1:5:173:20; 1809, 1810, and 1811, English, Mortimer, 1:6, 7, and 8:173:20; 1812 and 1813, German, Luckenbach, 1:10:173:20; 1814, German, Luckenbach, 1:11:173:20; 1815, 1816, 1817, 1818, and 1819, German, Luckenbach, 1:1, 2, 3, 4, and 6:175:20; 1820, German, duplicate, 2:7:175:20.

3. Schutt, *Peoples of the River Valleys*, chapter 6 and epilogue; William H. Bergmann, "A 'Commercial View of This Unfortunate War': Economic Roots of an American National State in the Ohio Valley, 1775–1795," *Early American Studies* (Spring 2008): 137–64; Kim M. Gruenwald, *River of Enterprise: The Commercial Origins of Regional Identity in the Ohio Valley, 1790–1850* (Bloomington: Indiana University Press, 2002), 25 (quotation); Tanner, ed., *Atlas*, [80], [98–99], 101; R. Douglas Hurt, *The Ohio Frontier: Crucible of the Old Northwest, 1720–1830* (Bloomington: Indiana University Press, 1996), 189; Patrick Griffin, "Reconsidering the Ideological Origins of Indian Removal: The Case of the Big Bottom 'Massacre,'" in *The Center of a Great Empire: The Ohio Country in the Early American Republic*, ed. Andrew R. L. Cayton and Stuart D. Hobbs (Athens: Ohio University Press, 2005), 11–35, especially 29–30; and Andrew R. L. Cayton, *Ohio: The History of a People* (Columbus: Ohio State University Press, 2002), 13–15, 40–43 (p. 15 on the background of newcomers).

4. Lisa Brooks, "Two Paths to Peace: Competing Visions of Native Space in the Old Northwest," in *The Boundaries Between Us: Natives and Newcomers along the Frontiers of the Old Northwest Territory, 1750–1850*, ed. Daniel P. Barr (Kent, OH: Kent State University Press, 2006), 99. I explore the history of Delawares' constructions of relationships and connections, especially in the seventeenth and eighteenth centuries, in Schutt, *Peoples of the River Valleys*.

Euro-American Moravians had their own version of an expanded perspective, one that placed themselves and their missions within a larger global evangelical project. See views of Moravians within the Atlantic World in Michele Gillespie and Robert Beachy, eds., *Pious Pursuits: German Moravians in the Atlantic World* (New York: Berghahn Books, 2007). For recent scholarly studies on midwestern Indians, see the essays in Barr, ed., *Boundaries Between Us*; and R. David Edmunds, ed., *Enduring Nations: Native Americans in the Midwest* (Urbana: University of Illinois Press, 2008). The one chapter devoted to Ohio Indians (Griffin, "Reconsidering the Ideological Origins") in the collection edited by Cayton and Hobbs (*Center of a Great Empire*) focuses on the pre-1795 period.

5. James H. O'Donnell III, *Ohio's First Peoples* (Athens: Ohio University Press, 2004), 103; Tanner, ed., *Atlas*, 103, [99]; Lawrence Henry Gipson, ed., *The Moravian Indian Mission on White River* (Indianapolis: Indiana Historical Bureau, 1938), 392 (quotations about Shawnees); Cayton, *Ohio*, 21; Charles Callender, "Shawnee," in *HNAI*, 15:631; William Sturtevant, "Oklahoma Seneca-Cayuga," in *HNAI*, 15:537; Elisabeth Tooker, "Wyandot," in *HNAI*, 15:402.

6. Goshen diary, English, Mortimer, February 17, 1809, 1:6:173:20; Tanner, ed., *Atlas*, 116, 101; "Indian Land Cessions in the United States, 1784 to 1894," in J. W. Powell, *Eighteenth Annual Report of the Bureau of American Ethnology to the Secretary of the Smithsonian Institution, 1896–1897*, part 2, printed as *H.R. Doc. No. 736*, 56th Cong., 1st sess., 666–67, http://lcweb2 loc.gov/ammem/amlaw/lwss-ilc.html; Charles C. Royce, comp., Ohio map, in ibid.; "Treaty with the Wyandot, etc., 1805" [Fort Industry Treaty], in *Indian Affairs: Laws and Treaties*, vol. 2, *Treaties*, comp. and ed. Charles J. Kappler (Washington, DC: Government Printing Office, 1904), 77–78, http://digi tal.library.okstate.edu/KAPPLER/VOL2/treaties/wya0077.htm; Hurt, *Ohio Frontier*, 316, 165.

7. Phyllis Gernhardt, "'Justice and Public Policy': Indian Trade, Treaties, and Removal from Northern Indiana, 1826–1846," in *Boundaries Between Us*, ed. Barr, 179–81; Goshen diary, July 7, 1802, English, Mortimer, 1:10:171:19 (quotation); ibid., April 17, 1801, English, Mortimer, 1:8:171:19; J. B. Mansfield, *The History of Tuscarawas County, Ohio . . .* (Chicago: Warner, Beers & Co., 1884), 215, http://books.google.com/books?id=5DguAAAAYAAJ; Gerard T. Hopkins, *A Mission to the Indians, from the Indian Committee of Baltimore Yearly Meeting, to Fort Wayne, in 1804* (Philadelphia: T. Ellwood Zell, 1862), 15, http://books.google.com/books?id=SB4oAAAAYAAJ; Royce, comp., Ohio map (full).

8. Beverly P. Smaby, "'No one should lust for power . . . women least of all': Dismantling Female Leadership among Eighteenth-Century Moravians," in *Pious Pursuits*, ed. Gillespie and Beachy, 159–75; Jane T. Merritt, "The Gender Frontier Revisited: Native American Women in the Age of Revolution," in *Ethnographies and Exchanges: Native Americans, Moravians, and Catholics in Early North America*, ed. A. G. Roeber (University Park: Pennsylvania State University Press, 2008), 165–74; Amy C. Schutt, "Female Relationships and Intercultural Bonds in Moravian Indian Missions," in *Friends and Enemies in Penn's Woods: Indians, Colonies, and the Racial Construction of Pennsylvania*, ed. William A. Pencak and Daniel K. Richter (University Park: Pennsylvania State University, 2004), 87–103; Jane T. Merritt, "Cultural Encounters along a Gender Frontier: Mahican, Delaware, and German Women in Eighteenth-Century Pennsylvania," *Pennsylvania History* 67 (2000): 502–31.

9. Rachel Wheeler, *To Live upon Hope: Mohicans and Missionaries in the Eighteenth-Century Northeast* (Ithaca, NY: Cornell University Press, 2008); Jane T. Merritt, *At the Crossroads: Indians and Empires on a Mid-Atlantic Frontier, 1700–1763* (Chapel Hill: University of North Carolina Press for the Omohundro Institute of Early American History and Culture, 2003); Schutt, *Peoples of the River Valleys*, chapters 4–6 and epilogue; Hermann Wellenreuther and Carola Wessel, eds., *The Moravian Mission Diaries of David Zeisberger, 1772–1781*, trans. Julie Tomberlin Weber (University Park: Pennsylvania State University Press, 2005); Eugene F. Bliss, trans. and ed., *Diary of David Zeisberger, a Moravian Missionary among the Indians of Ohio*, 2 vols. (Cincinnati: Robert Clarke & Co., 1885); Linda Sabbathy-Judd, ed., *Moravians in Upper Canada: The Diary of the Indian Mission of Fairfield on the Thames, 1792–1813* (Toronto: The Champlain Society, 1999), xix–xxi, xxv–xxvi; Tanner, ed., *Atlas*, [80]; and Goshen diary, April 13, 1800, English, Mortimer, 1:6:171:19.

10. Goshen diary, September 3, 1799, English, signed by Zeisberger and Mortimer, 1:4:171:19; Schutt, *Peoples of the River Valleys*, 171–73; Charles Thomson to John Ettwein, August 15, 1787, in *Letters of Delegates to Congress, 1774–1789*, ed. Paul H. Smith et al., 25 vols. (Washington, DC: Library of Congress, 1976–2000), 24:404–5 (first quotation), http:// lcweb2.loc.gov/ammem/amlaw/lwdg.html. In the second quotation in this paragraph, Thomson seems to be quoting Ettwein. Thomson to Ettwein, August 26, 1786, in *Letters of Delegates to Congress*, 23:532n, 532–33; *Journals of the Continental Congress, 1774–1789*, ed. Worthington C. Ford et al., 34 vols. (Washington, DC, 1904–37), 34:485–87, http://lcweb2.loc.gov/ ammem/amlaw/lwjc.html; Karim Tiro, "'We Wish to Do You Good': The Quaker Mission to the Oneida Nation, 1790–1840," *Journal of the Early*

Republic 26 (Fall 2006): 355 (third quotation); Ginette Aley, "Bringing about the Dawn: Agriculture, Internal Improvements, Indian Policy, and Euro-American Hegemony," in *Boundaries Between Us*, ed. Barr, 200–203; Bernard W. Sheehan, *Seeds of Extinction: Jeffersonian Philanthropy and the American Indian* (Chapel Hill: University of North Carolina Press and Institute of Early American History and Culture, 1973), 120–29.

11. John Heckewelder, *A Narrative of the Mission of the United Brethren . . .* (Philadelphia: McCarty & Davis, 1820), 379 (quotation), 381–88, 405; Bergmann, "A 'Commercial View of This Unfortunate War,'" 146–49, 154–56, 159–63; Hurt, *Ohio Frontier*, 100–111; Donald F. Carmony, ed., "Spencer Records' Memoir of the Ohio Valley Frontier, 1766–1795," *Indiana Magazine of History* 55 (December 1959): 323–77.

12. Goshen diary, July 6, 1799 (first quotation) and July 11, 1799, English, signed by Zeisberger and Mortimer, 1:4:171:19; Lawrence Henry Gipson, ed., *The Moravian Indian Mission on White River* (Indianapolis: Indiana Historical Bureau, 1938), 131, 141, 155; Goshen diary, April 8, 1800, English, Mortimer, 1:6:171:19 (second quotation). Probably under pressure from other Euro-Americans fearful of his inciting violence, this man later apologized and said he had not participated in the killings. Ibid., April 27, 1800; Langundo Utenünk diary, German, Zeisberger, January 2, 1771, 1:2:137:8, *RMM* (last quotation); Goshen diary, November 19, 1798, German, Mortimer, based on Zeisberger's notes, 3:2:171:19; ibid., June 6, 1802, and May 29, 1803, English, Mortimer, 1:10 and 13:171:19; ibid., January 6, 1804, English, Mortimer, 1:1:173:20; Gregory Evans Dowd, *A Spirited Resistance: The North American Indian Struggle for Unity, 1745–1815* (Baltimore: Johns Hopkins University Press, 1992), 30.

13. Schutt, *Peoples of the River Valleys*, 161–70; Goshen diary, German, Mortimer based on Zeisberger's notes, December 17, 1798, 3:2:171:19 (quotation); ibid., October 10, 1798, English, Mortimer, based on Zeisberger's notes, 1:2:171:19. On Indians' experiences of Moravian Christianity, see Wheeler, *To Live upon Hope*, 95–116; Merritt, *At the Crossroads*, 89–128; and Amy C. Schutt, "'What will become of our young people?' Goals for Indian Children in Moravian Missions," *History of Education Quarterly* 38 (Fall 1998): 268–86.

14. Schutt, *Peoples of the River Valleys*, 7–21, 95, and epilogue; Goshen diary, April 30, and June 12 and 13, 1807, English, Mortimer, 1:4:173:20; ibid., August 24, 1802, English, Mortimer, 1:10:171:19; ibid., July 29, September 15 ("intermitting fevers") and 28, 1801, English, Mortimer, 1:9 and 10:171:19; Olmstead, *Blackcoats*, 142; Goshen diary, July 7, 1801, English, Mortimer, 1:9:171:19 ("various sorts"); ibid., October 24, 1799, English,

signed by Zeisberger and Mortimer, 1:5:171:19 ("hickory nuts"); ibid., October 26, 1802, English, Mortimer, 1:11:171:19; ibid., March 16, 1800, English, Mortimer, 1:6:171:19 (on maple syrup).

15. Goshen diary, October 31, 1799, English, signed by Zeisberger and Mortimer, 1:5:171:19; Schutt, "Female Relationships," 92–93; Goshen diary, April 27, 1799, German, Mortimer, from Zeisberger's notes, 1:3:171:19; ibid., September 19, 1799, English, signed by Zeisberger and Mortimer, 1:4:171:19; ibid., December 16, 1799, and March 23, 1800, English, Mortimer, 1:6:171:19; ibid., October 20, 1798, English, Mortimer, based on Zeisberger's notes, 1:2:171:19 (first quotation); ibid., November 12, 1799, English, signed by Zeisberger and Mortimer, 1:5:171:19 (second quotation); ibid., June 20, 1802 (third quotation), and July 29, 1800, English, Mortimer, 1:10 and 7:171:19; ibid., January 8, 1799, German, Mortimer, based on Zeisberger's notes, 1:2:171:19; ibid., January 18 and 20, 1800, English, Mortimer, 1:6:171:19; Archer Butler Hulbert and William Nathaniel Schwarze, eds., "David Zeisberger's History of the Northern American Indians," in *Ohio Archaeological and Historical Publications* (Columbus, OH: Fred J. Herr, 1910), 19:13, 58.

16. Goshen diary, January 20, 1800, English, Mortimer, 1:6:171:19 ("camp 10 miles"); ibid., January 4, 1804 ("After a fall"), English, Mortimer, 1:1:173:20; ibid., September 22, 1812, English, Mortimer, 1:9:173:20; ibid., March 9, 1801 ("The spending," underlined in original), March 23, 1800 ("far up the Muskingum"), March 23 and July 7, 1801, English, Mortimer, 1:8, 6, and 9:171:19; ibid., October 24, 1799, English, signed by Zeisberger and Mortimer, 1:5:171:19; ibid., October 26, 1802, English, Mortimer, 1:11:171:19; ibid., September 19, 1799, English, signed by Zeisberger and Mortimer, 1:4:171:19.

17. Goshen diary, December 10, 1799, English, Mortimer, 1:6:171:19 ("generally prefer"); ibid., November 13 ("nearly all") and December 5 ("This is their," abbreviations expanded in quotation), 1802, English, Mortimer, 1:11:171:19; ibid., English, signed by Zeisberger and Mortimer, August 24, 1799, 1:4:171:19; ibid., August 3, 1803, and November 14, 1804, English, Mortimer, 1:13:171:20 and 1:1:173:20. For examples of male hunting parties, see Goshen diary, October 11, 1798, English, Mortimer, based on Zeisberger's notes, 1:2:171:19; ibid., November 29, 1798, and April 22, 1799, German, Mortimer, based on Zeisberger's notes, 3:2:171:19 and 1:3:171:19; ibid., August 6 and 16, 1799, and October 7, 1799, English, signed by Zeisberger and Mortimer, 1:4 and 5:171:19; ibid., January 10 and April 17, 1804, and October 26, 1802, English, Mortimer, 1:1:173:20 and 1:11:171:19.

18. Goshen diary, December 2, 1798, German, Mortimer, based on Zeisberger's notes, 3:2:171:19 (first quotation); ibid., December 1, 1806 ("Pettquotting and other Indians"), and March 5, 1806 ("every thing"), English, Mortimer, 1:3 and 2:173:20.

19. Goshen, October 21, 1798, English, Mortimer, based on Zeisberger's notes, 1:2:171:19 ("small stock"); ibid., November 29, 1798, German, by Mortimer, based on Zeisberger's notes, 3:2:171:19 (second quotation).

20. Goshen diary, May 22, 1800, English, Mortimer, 1:7:171:19; ibid., October 17, 1798, English, Mortimer, based on Zeisberger's notes, 1:2:171:19; ibid., December 10, 1798, January 1, 1799, and April 5, 1799, German, Mortimer, based on Zeisberger's notes, 3:2:171:19 and 1:3:171:19; ibid., November 29, 1798, German, Mortimer, based on Zeisberger's notes, 3:2:171:19 (first quotation); ibid., March 29, 1799, and April 4 and May 24, 1799, German, Mortimer, from Zeisberger's notes, 1:3:171:19; ibid., English, Mortimer, April 3 and January 8, 1800, October 20, 1800, 1:6 and 7:171:19; Goshen conference minutes, 1803, German, 1:4:174, session 3, p. 37, *RMM*; Goshen diary, February 16, 1799, German, Mortimer, based on Zeisberger's notes, 3:2:171:19; ibid., May 7, 1800, English, Mortimer, 1:7:171:19; ibid., May 13, 1799 (second quotation), and June 3 and 7, 1799, German, Mortimer, based on Zeisberger's notes, 1:3:171:19; ibid., July 28, July 30, and August 5, 1799, 1:4:171:19; Joseph Doddridge, Narcissa Doddridge, John S. Ritenour, and William T. Lindsey, *Notes on the Settlement and Indian Wars of the Western Parts of Virginia and Pennsylvania . . .* (Pittsburgh, PA, 1912; reprint, Parsons, WV: McClain Printing Co., 1976), 252, http://books.google.com/books?id=FXl5AAAAMAAJ.

21. Olmstead, *Blackcoats*, 111; Mansfield, *History of Tuscarawas County*, 310; Goshen diary, November 11 and 26, 1799, English, signed by Zeisberger and Mortimer, 1:5:171:19; ibid., June 30, 1800, English, Mortimer, 1:7:171:19; Mortimer to Rev. James Birkby, November 28, 1799, 4:3:172:19, *RMM*; Goshen diary, January 24 and March 27, 1800, November 23, 1802, June 3, 1800 ("traders from the northward"), December 22, 1803 (on price comparison), June 11, 1802 ("much cheaper"), English, Mortimer, 1:6, 11, 7, 13, and 10:171:19; ibid., April 22 and April 15, 1799, German, Mortimer, based on Zeisberger's notes, 1:3:171:19.

22. Goshen diary, December 16, 1799, English, Mortimer, 1:6:171:19; Stephen Aron, "Pigs and Hunters: 'Rights in the Woods' on the Trans-Appalachian Frontier," in *Contact Points: American Frontiers from the Mohawk Valley to the Mississippi, 1750–1830*, ed. Andrew R. L. Cayton and Fredrika J. Teute (Chapel Hill: University of North Carolina Press and the Omohundro Institute of Early American History and Culture, 1998), 175–204; Goshen diary,

English, Mortimer, August 5 and 31, 1812, 1:9:173:20; ibid., February 3, 1813, German, Luckenbach, 1:10:173:20.

23. Schutt, *Peoples of the River Valleys*, 72; Goshen diary, January 8, 1802, and May 16, 1804, English, Mortimer, 1:9:171:19 and 1:1:173:20; ibid., May 3, 1806, and April 11, 1800, English, Mortimer, 1:2:173:20 and 1:6:171:19; ibid., August 21, 1821, German, Proske and Bardill, abbreviated copy, 2:8:175:20 (first quotation); ibid., December 15, 1799, German, Mortimer, from Zeisberger's notes, 1:3:171:19 (second quotation); ibid., March 12 ("took of them") and 5, 1806, April 13 and 20, July 24, 1806, June 12, 1806, December 29, 1805 ("scenes"), and June 12, 1806 ("a few miles"), English, Mortimer, 1:2:173:20; Robert Leslie Jones, *History of Agriculture in Ohio to 1880* (Kent, OH: Kent State University Press, 1983), 52–53.

24. Mortimer to Birkby, November 28, 1799 (first quotation); Hopkins, *Mission to the Indians*, 25 (second quotation); Goshen diary, April 8, 1799, German, Mortimer, from Zeisberger's notes, 1:3:171:19 (third quotation); ibid., August 25 ("raising the large") and 28, 1799, and August 31, 1800 ("sawing boards"), English, Mortimer, 1:4 and 7:171:19; Goshen diary, September 9 ("good carpenter") and 30, 1799, English, signed by Zeisberger and Mortimer, 1:4:171:19; ibid., April 16 and May 4, 1800, July 2, 1801 (last quotation), and January 18 and July 24, 1802, English, Mortimer, 1:6, 7, 10, and 9:171:19.

25. Goshen diary, March 9 (first quotation) and July 7, 1801, English, Mortimer, 1:8 and 9:171:19; ibid., November 15, June 20, July 25, August 8, 1820, January 22, 1821, February 13, 1821, German, duplicate, 2:7:175:20; ibid., August 23, 1799, English, signed by Zeisberger and Mortimer, 1:4:171:19; ibid., July 2, 1800, English, Mortimer, 1:7:171:19; ibid., July 8, 1799, English, signed by Zeisberger and Mortimer, 1:4:171:19 (second quotation); ibid., September 13 and 19, 1803, English, Mortimer, 1:13:171:19; ibid., August 14 and September 8, 1821, German, Proske and Bardill, 1:8:175:20; Gruenwald, *River of Enterprise*, 30–31.

26. Goshen diary, April 13, 1804, English, Mortimer, 1:1:173:20 (first quotation); ibid., August 4, 1812, English, Mortimer, 1:9:173:20; ibid., November 24, 1804 (second quotation), November 2, 1810 (third quotation), and May 24, 1812 (fourth quotation), English, Mortimer, 1:1, 7, and 9:173:20; Schutt, *Peoples of the River Valleys*, 181 (on Greentown); Goshen diary, September 17, 1807, English, Mortimer, 1:4:173:20; ibid., December 22, 1808, German, excerpt, 1:5:173:20; ibid., August 29, 1805, and July 29, 1806, English, Mortimer, 1:2:173:20; ibid., October 2 and 24, 1799, English, signed by Zeisberger and Mortimer, 1:5:171:19.

27. Goshen diary, June 1, August 21, and September 11, 1802, and January 6 and March 31, 1800, English, Mortimer, 1:10 and 6:171:19. In May 1800, for example, Mortimer wrote that there were "several camps" of Indians around Goshen, including some arriving from Sandusky. Ibid., May 19 and May 22, 1800 ("news"), English, Mortimer, 1:7:171:19; ibid., April 14, 1800, English, Mortimer, 1:6:171:19 ("messenger"); Gipson, ed., *Moravian Indian Mission on White River*, 67.

28. Goshen diary, January 31, 1800 (first quotation), May 27, 1800, English, Mortimer, 1:6 and 7:171:19; ibid., January 9, 1799, German, Mortimer, based on Zeisberger's notes, 3:2:171:19 (second quotation); ibid., October 15 and 8 ("The young people"), 1799, English, signed by Zeisberger and Mortimer, 1:5:171:19. Defining *writing, reading*, and *literacy* is problematic, as Kristina Bross and Hilary Wyss point out. They note that "there is much debate over what actually constitutes writing. Are carvings or painted images part of literary systems? Are pictures? Clothing? Tatoos? Weaving?" When I include the terms *writing, writing instruction*, and *reading* in this section, I am referring to alphabetic forms, but I do not mean to suggest that "literary systems" must be defined this narrowly. Kristina Bross and Hilary E. Wyss, ed., *Early Native Literacies in New England: A Documentary and Critical Anthology* (Amherst: University of Massachusetts Press, 2008), 3–5 (quotation on p. 4). On earlier examples of Moravian schooling: Schutt, "'What will become of our young people?,'" 282–85. Goshen diary, August 31 (class demonstration) and December 31, 1809, English, Mortimer, 1:6:173:20. On gender differences in writing instruction for the colonial period, see E. Jennifer Monaghan, *Learning to Read and Write in Colonial America* (Worcester: University of Massachusetts Press, 2005), 25, 367–68, 373–74.

29. Gipson, ed., *White River Mission*, 392–93; Goshen diary, September 20, 1811, English, Mortimer, 1:8:173:20; John Wigger, "Ohio Gospel: Methodism in Early Ohio," in *Center of a Great Empire*, ed. Cayton and Hobbs, 62–80 (quotation on p. 74); Goshen diary, July 12, 1811, and August 30, 1811 ("camp meeting"), English, Mortimer, 1:8:173:20; ibid., February 15, 1808, German, excerpt, 1:5:173:20; ibid., December 16, 1811, and January 23, 1812 ("late earthquakes"), English, Mortimer, 1:8:173:20; ibid., February 7, 1812, 1:8:173:20 ("prophet among the whites"); R. David Edmunds, *The Shawnee Prophet* (Lincoln: University of Nebraska Press, 1983), 28–41.

30. Goshen diary, July 21 ("several weeks") and August 7 ("banks of the river"), 1799, English, signed by Zeisberger and Mortimer, 1:4:171:19; Schutt, *Peoples of the River Valleys*, 27–29.

31. Goshen diary, August 14 and July 22, 1812, English, Mortimer, 1:9:173:20; Goshen diary, August 28 (first quotation) and August 29 (second quotation), 1812, English, Mortimer, 1:9:173:20; Carl Benn, *The Iroquois in the War of 1812* (Toronto: University of Toronto Press, 1998), 44–50.

32. John Henry to Heckewelder, September 23, 1820, German, 12:12:175:20, *RMM*; Goshen diary, April 12, 1818 (second quotation), November 11 (third quotation) and 16, 1818, German, Luckenbach, 1:4:175:20; ibid., February 12, 1814, and November 22 and 27, 1814, German, Luckenbach, 1:11:173:20; Pipe's Speech, [June 1820], English, 9:12:175:20, *RMM*; Goshen diary, German, duplicate, June 1, 1820, 2:7:175:20; ibid., July 27, 1821, German, Proske, 1:7:175:20 (last quotation); ibid., July 27, 1821, German, Proske and Bardill, 1:8:175:20; ibid., June 30, 1821, July 14 and 16, 1821, and August 31–October 25, 1821, German, Proske, 1:7:175:20; J. Taylor Hamilton and Kenneth G. Hamilton, *History of the Moravian Church: The Renewed Unitas Fratrum, 1722–1957* (Bethlehem, PA: Interprovincial Board of Christian Education, Moravian Church in America, 1967), 290; "Indian Land Cessions in the United States," 704–5.

33. Hurt, *Ohio Frontier*, 362–65; Cayton, *Ohio*, 15, 30; Schutt, *Peoples of the River Valleys*, 182; Stephen Warren, "The Ohio Shawnees' Struggle against Removal, 1814–30," in *Enduring Nations*, ed. Edmunds, 87–89; Tooker, "Wyandot," 402–3; O'Donnell, *Ohio's First Peoples*, 124–25.

34. Goshen diary, March 16, 1800, and September 22, 1810, English, Mortimer, 1:6:171:19 and 1:7:173:20; ibid., September 13, 1799, English, signed by Zeisberger and Mortimer, 1:4:171:19; ibid., August 18, 1801, August 19, 1806, and January 11, 1810, English, Mortimer, 1:9:171:19, 1:2:173:20, and 1:7:173:20.

Miami Resistance and Resilience during the Removal Era

MELISSA RINEHART

The Indian Removal Era marks a painful period for Native Americans with ancestral homelands east of the Mississippi River. Over sixty Native communities, or approximately 50,000 Native Americans from different linguistic families of the Eastern Woodlands cultural region, were intentionally relocated or removed during the 1830s and 1840s, and many of these communities were removed more than once. Twenty-five Native communities alone signed removal treaties between 1825 and 1843. This forced migration to the "Great American Desert" affected community cohesion and made a permanent imprint on tribal histories.[1] Although historical parlance often memorializes these removals, such as with the Cherokee Trail of Tears and the Potawatomi Trail of Death, even these titles do not encapsulate the life-changing events leading to removal, how it affected the community, who made decisions for the community, who benefited from removal, and how this shaped Native identities throughout the process.

The Miami Indian Removal of 1846, although never described as a Trail of Tears or a Trail of Death, physically split the community in half, accelerated cultural change within the community, and permanently affected the political status of Miami peoples. Simply put, Miami removal had grave consequences for community maintenance, but the Miamis were not passive agents throughout this process. Instead, through strategic leadership and the sociopolitical involvement of various community members, they delayed removal sixteen years past the passage of the 1830 Removal Act while ethnically reorganizing their community. The Miamis, American settlers, traders, and bureaucrats alike were major players during the Removal

137

Era, and each operated from self-interest premised upon maintaining an ancestral land base, securing farmlands, exchanging commodity goods, and Western expansion respectively.[2] While this essay details the roles each of these groups played during the Removal Era, it also illustrates how Miami peoples persevered in spite of very difficult circumstances.

Active ethnic reorganization abounded in the Miami community during the Removal Era, and it is a particularly effective way to assess Miami community maintenance and the ways they asserted their identities.[3] Although sociocultural changes resultant from intertribal contact predated their first encounters with Europeans ca. 1650, colonization sped up this process immensely among the Miamis. As such, under significant social, economic, and political pressures, Miami community boundaries were stretched continuously and variably from clan to clan. Nevertheless, this persistence enabled Miami leadership and other community members to avoid removal for their families, and as a result, only half the community was forcibly removed from Indiana—making them one of the last tribes to be removed from the Lower Great Lakes region.

Miami ancestral lands include present-day Indiana, Ohio, Illinois, southern Michigan, and Wisconsin. At the time of European contact, the greater Miami community included six bands—the Atchatchakangouens, Kilatikas, Mengakonkias, Pepikokias (Tepicons), Piankashaws, and Weas—all of whom spoke similar Miami dialects from the Algonquian language family, recognized one another's leadership and ritual practices, and intermarried. Miami peoples were intrinsically linked to riverine areas throughout the Lower Great Lakes, and as such, their origin story begins with their emergence from a pool of water known as "Saakiiweesiipi" or "the Coming Out Place" located at the portage between the Kankakee and St. Joseph Rivers in South Bend, Indiana. Soil fertility in these riverine environments was ideal for a mixed economy that included horticulture, hunting, gathering, fishing, maple-tapping, and rice cultivation. Tribal member and linguist Daryl Baldwin describes the importance of these rivers to Miami communities as "central to our ancestors' place of being . . . [as] these river systems formed the heartland of our ancestral territory."[4]

Wooded areas surrounding rivers were equally important, and in 1790 British traveler Henry Hay reported, "For it must be observed that they have nothing here to live upon—everything they possess & have is in the woods." Miami knowledge of trails and river systems throughout this region far exceeded that of non-Indians, and as tribal member Dani Tippmann once remarked, "We were runners." Their mixed economy relied on cumulative ecological knowledge; therefore, land was not owned, but shared and respected. Baldwin offers: "From the land, our traditional beliefs and knowledge systems developed and evolved, giving meaning to our ancestors' lives. . . . Their relationships were based on mutual respect not superiority."[5]

Relationships with the environment provided history, place, and meaning to Miami communities. Not surprisingly, Miami spiritual and ritual organization focused on various aspects of their physical environment as they honored the sun and other deities, such as the Master of Life and Great Hare. Several manitous representing animals and other natural phenomena were revered as well.

The Miamis recognized the vulnerability of their relationships with the land as American settlement increased throughout the region from 1813 to 1830, following the end of the British-American War of 1812. They also witnessed how this led to the removal of surrounding Native communities. The first Indian removal in Indiana occurred in 1821 with the Delawares, and in 1838 another large removal took place for eight hundred Potawatomis. The Potawatomi journey west was stricken with much sadness, food insecurity, exposure, illness, and death. "Eyewitnesses in the main felt sympathetic toward those who formed the 'sad sight.' The Indians were disarmed . . . and available government wagons apparently frightened the natives, and most of them preferred to walk." Rumors about the possibilities of continued Indian removals in the region ran rampant, and although rumors were scrutinized, they now offer a window into community ideologies.[6] Native communities were fearful of removal, and their fears at times led to action. The Grand River Ottawas and Little Traverse Bay Ottawas fled Michigan for Canada in fear of removal, and Miami clans such as the Wauwasees, Papkeechis, and the Eel River (Thorntown) band left Indiana for Michigan and Canada to avoid removal.

Native communities and American settlers were anxious about potential conflict and violence. One American surveyor abruptly ended his work in Indiana because of such hostilities. Native communities and American settlers were both guilty of horse-stealing and vandalism to personal property, and violent conflicts erupted periodically, including the Diamond Island Tragedy of 1803, the Fall Creek Tragedy, the Deer Lick Creek Massacre of 1824, and the Blackhawk War of 1832, as well as others. As a result of the Blackhawk War alone, "the whites of sparsely populated northern Indiana erected forts, while the wary Indian took to the woods to avoid reprisals." Similar tragedies befell Indians and Americans in neighboring Michigan and Ohio; thereby, rumors abounded about continued violence. While these events deepened settlers' fears in the Old Northwest, settlement continued, albeit cautiously. "With more Indians than whites in the areas, and the closest supporting military force in Kentucky, there was an undertone of danger." As such, several settlers eventually lobbied the state and federal governments for defensive security and economic relief.[7]

By 1829, fearful and frustrated Americans petitioned the Indiana state legislature for securing more land in Indiana. The legislature passed a resolution urging Congress to remove all Indians immediately—thus freeing up lands for agricultural pursuits and internal improvements like canal and road construction. "The continuance of these savages within our limits, who claim so large a space of the best soil . . . tends to materially impede a system of internal improvements . . . and jeopardizes the peace and tranquility of our frontier, which is our right and duty to secure." Legislative opinion concurred that the best remedy for the situation was the "speedy concentration of Indians in some permanent situation." Several appeals followed, and in 1835 state legislators requested the federal government to deal with the "Indian problem"; three years later, another petition requested Miami land cessions for continued internal improvements and American settlement. Persistent bureaucratic nudging supported the ideology that a "territory sufficient to support a thousand Indians by hunting and fishing, would furnish homes for hundreds of thousands of industrious white men."[8] Not only did state legislation marginalize Miami peoples, it also homogenized their identities, grouping different Miami bands as "Miami," thereby creating further tensions within the greater Miami community.

Six treaties were signed before Indiana achieved statehood in 1816, and six additional treaties thereafter. Their first land cessions were made with the Treaty of Greenville in 1795, and with each subsequent treaty, their land base diminished further. In spite of this slow but steady dispossession, the Miamis continued, although with difficulty, to plant their crops, gather, hunt, fish, and attend their maple stands on reserved lands. This reservation system disrupted traditional subsistence practices and forced them to reorganize economically. It fully immersed them in a market economy, beyond their engagements with the fur trade, where land had become a commodity. By 1813, land sales in Indiana soared by 57 percent, and after statehood was established, the settler population stood at 65,000. By 1820, the population had increased to 147,000, and a decade later climbed to over 343,000.[9]

The ways the Miamis were acknowledged in treaties were inconsistent. At times, such as with the Treaty of Fort Wayne in 1803, the government engaged with the "Miami" and Miami bands, such as the Eel River band, Weas, and Piankashaws individually, and in other treaties with only the Miamis. This was done intentionally to create political divisions within the greater community by weakening the authority of smaller bands and clan chiefs, and centralizing power with a principal chief, thereby easing negotiations with the federal government. This did not mean the Miamis did not recognize their individual band/village identities, but that the federal government "superimposed external political structure on the Miami and, in so doing, forged political divisions."[10] As the Miami population declined, community boundaries reorganized to ensure more just political representation, which lay in the hands of one principal chief. This reorganization of the Miami political structure, although disruptive, prepared them for removal, as two political bodies assembled, one among the Eastern Miamis and the other among the Western Miamis, after removal.

The Treaty of 1826 changed the physical landscape for the Miamis further as it secured 926,000 acres of land for settlement and construction for the Wabash-Erie Canal. This treaty also changed the social landscape in Indiana by attracting new settlers and canal workers of Irish, German, Dutch, and American descent. In addition to traders who dealt liquor, alcohol flowed alongside canal construction, wreaking further havoc in surrounding Miami communities until it was eventually slowed by pressures from the temperance movement. By 1829, President Andrew Jackson proposed relocating eastern tribes to lands west of the Mississippi River in his first annual address to Congress, and one year later Congress passed the Indian Removal Act. This act specified that treaties should not only provide additional lands and resources, but isolate Indians on reserved lands. Upon passage of this act, the Miamis were well aware of ensuing pressures for their removal. Chief Jean Baptiste de Richardville and other leaders "resisted agreeing to any specific mention of removal in treaties with the federal government" during the 1830s.[11]

The possibility of removal haunted Miami leadership, but Richardville refused it steadfastly. He boldly proclaimed, "Father, I have told you . . . that your red children would not go to the Mississippi country—they wish to stay on their ancient lands. . . . The Miamies will never consent to leave the homes of their fathers . . . we will not sell, and still you ask us for land." As chief, Richardville understood the impact removal would have on the Miami community. Miami culture, traditions, and language were intimately connected with the land, and any separation from this would be devastating to community identity maintenance. Removal would equate to even greater sociocultural reorganization than had been experienced up until this point, and the uncertainties about the subsequent fallout were more than concerning. Richardville recognized the monetary value of Miami land, but it was the deeper connections to the land he acknowledged most. "We know the value of our soil as well as the white man can tell us. Here the Great Spirit has fixed our homes. Here are our cornfields and cabins. From this soil and these forests we derive our subsistence, and here we will live and die I repeat, we will not sell an inch of our lands." Nevertheless, Richardville and others were eventually persuaded by General William Marshall, the United States chief negotiator, to sign another treaty in 1834 at the Forks of the Wabash. Unlike previous treaties, seven tracts of land were ceded for $208,000, and six small land grants were converted to patents in fee simple for several tribal members and leaders like Richardville.[12]

The Treaty of 1834 did not pacify President Jackson's desire to move the Miamis westward, and he refused to forward it for ratification to the United States Senate. His objections involved three problematic statements, including a federal agreement to pay tribal debt through treaty appropriations, helping the Miamis in (re)securing lands given to the State of Indiana for internal improvements, and additional land grants made to individual tribal members.[13] To the dismay of Miami leadership, President Jackson's disapproval led to a new round of treaty negotiations in 1836.

Marshall was sent back to renegotiate a treaty with the Miamis, but he was unsuccessful, as was his successor, Henry Ellsworth. In March 1836, a third negotiator, Jonathan Keller, resumed negotiations. Keller took a highly unusual, if not unethical, approach in these negotiations, as he avoided discussions with a formal council and worked only with a select group of Miami leaders, including Richardville, Francis Godfroy, and Magineca. Keller made revisions in this treaty to address President Jackson's first two concerns, but he was unable to address Jackson's third concern, because individual land grants had already been made. Rather than proceeding under normal protocol involving negotiation between Miami representatives and government officials, Keller convinced the three Miami leaders to sign a one-paragraph agreement-in-principle to his proposed treaty revisions. He then sent this agreement-in-principal to his supervisors in the War Department, parent agency of the Indian Affairs Office, who made further suggestions and then sent it back to Keller for further revision. Keller submitted the third treaty draft to the new president Martin Van Buren. This draft was never reviewed, evaluated, agreed to, or signed by a full tribal council, let alone any Miami representative. Van Buren passed it on to the Senate along with a brief explanation of Keller's protocols, and it was assigned to the Senate Committee on Indian Affairs, where it received support. It was then taken up on the Senate floor under the lead of Indiana Senator Oliver H. Smith. The original treaty was unanimously rejected, and instead the Senate ratified Keller's third version of the treaty based upon the endorsement of the Committee on Indian Affairs. The Miamis had never tacitly or actively supported the amended treaty, and both Joel R. Poinsett, secretary of the War Department, and President Van Buren noted in the public record that it should be "again submitted to the chiefs and warriors of the Miami tribe for their sanction." This occurred, but not until November 1837, when a general tribal council of thirty-one leaders evaluated the changes and signed a statement under significant pressure, thereby agreeing to it.[14]

In December 1838, President Van Buren forwarded the negotiated treaty to the Senate for confirmation, along with a letter from Poinsett apologizing for not requiring removal, but urged ratification of the 1838 Treaty as a necessary step toward removal. The Senate voted, but was unable to get the necessary two-thirds of the votes; however, through successful lobbying, the Senate voted a second time and it was ratified on February 8, 1839. The 1838 Treaty ceded three reserves of land equating to 170,000 acres south of the Wabash River in exchange for $335,680. Richardville also received $6,800 and Francis Godfroy $2,612 for their claims against the Miami tribe. Thirty-four individual land grants were made, with many going to the Richardville and Godfroy families as allotted in previous treaties. By this time, the only lands collectively held by the Miamis were their winter hunting grounds on the Big Miami Reserve and one small reserve for the Eel River band. While the 1838 Treaty called for guaranteed lands west of the Mississippi River "suited to their wants and conditions," it did not require their removal, and settlers were quickly dissatisfied because they felt this left a loophole for legally evading removal.[15]

After the 1838 Treaty was ratified, a commission within the Office of Indian Affairs was established to conduct a year-long investigation on tribal debt. Debt was an ever-present burden on the Miamis, and nearly half the money awarded to the Miamis for ceded lands in the 1838 Treaty, or $150,000, was set aside for tribal debt. The exploitative nature of the trade strapped the Miamis financially as inflated pricing of commodity goods and alcohol led to insurmountable debt. According to Indian agent John Tipton in 1827, seven of every ten families in the Fort Wayne area depended on the Indian trade, and "Anyone who could transport to Fort Wayne enough kegs of whiskey, blankets, shawls, and other Indian goods could set up a store. The Indian customers were plentiful and for the most part gullible . . . the whites who traded . . . were a transient and rather worthless lot."[16] Investigators for the Claims Commission found "that the close proximity of the Indians with whites such as the Ewings, coupled with federal policies that allowed such economic abuses against the native peoples, dramatically altered the Indian way of life." In 1832 alone, the Ewing brothers, unscrupulous traders with the Miamis and other Native communities, made over $30,000 from the Miamis in Fort Wayne alone. Miami reliance on trade goods led to a total debt of over half a million dollars, which was alarming given that the Miami population was only around seven hundred persons. Nevertheless, merchants continued to trade and extend credit as long as the government continued to reimburse the Miamis through treaty annuities. Claims commissioner Nathaniel West reported in 1837 that "the Miamies are fast falling away from their true character, imbibing more. . . . Indolence, extravagance, and a love of display pervade the whole nation. . . . They hunt but little, do not work, and the whole nation may be said to live from sources drawn from the store of the trader." Later that year, he observed that nothing significant had changed. "They were fast sinking into those wretched habits originating from intoxication, and too great intercourse with the white people. . . . will . . . entirely destroy them, unless removed west of the Mississippi. . . . They are fast diminishing in numbers . . . more than sixty have died . . . by violence."[17] Claims investigations ended in 1842, and by September, the federal government adjusted the commissioners' reports and readjusted the claims owed to traders.

By this time, settler demands for Miami removal gained even more momentum. They "wistfully hoped" that if credit to the Indians was stopped, it would create one of two situations—either the Miamis would starve, or they would be forced to leave Indiana immediately. The situation was tense, and in August 1841, John Bell of the Office of Indian Affairs noted there was "a state of things which subjects a portion of the citizens of Indiana to great present annoyance and distress, and which, unless the appropriating power of Congress be promptly interposed, may, without exaggerating consequences, eventuate in actual hostilities."[18] While the Treaty of 1838 formally opened discussions on Miami removal, it did not detail how this would occur.

Chief Richardville was approaching his eightieth birthday and in failing health, so Samuel Milroy, Indian agent for the Miamis, and Allen Hamilton, Richardville's attorney and frequent business partner, acted on Richardville's seeming vulnerability. Milroy and Hamilton requested permission from their supervisors in Washington to draft a treaty with the Miamis, and despite numerous appeals, they were denied on the grounds that the Senate had not authorized such negotiations with the tribe.[19] Nevertheless, Milroy and Hamilton unofficially brokered a deal with Richardville specifying removal, and took the opportunity afforded by the annual annuity meeting to have a general tribal council ratify their proposed treaty. This signed treaty was soon sent to the Senate. Once again, traditional protocol was dispensed with as methods similar to those used by Keller three years earlier were employed by Milroy and Hamilton. Their practices usurped Miami political organization that had come to recognize Richardville as their principal chief, but still required council consultation during treaty negotiations.

With apologies for the unusual protocol, or lack thereof, President Van Buren urged the Senate to ratify this treaty because the "terms appear to be so advantageous and the acquisition of these lands are deemed so desirable." In late January 1841, the Senate Committee on Indian Affairs reviewed the treaty and proposed additional amendments. One provision was added promising that their 500,000-acre reservation out West would be bounded by other lands reserved for the Weas, Kaskaskias, Potawatomis, and Senecas. A second amendment included application of an additional $50,000 of the total settlement amount of $550,000 to go toward debt payments, leaving less for annual annuity payments.[20] In February, the full Senate took up the matter and voted to ratify the amended 1840 Treaty, and only three months before he died, Richardville and thirty-one other Miami chiefs ratified the Treaty of 1840. With ratification by both parties, Miami removal was officially sanctioned and the terms of removal established.

In the 1840 Treaty, the Miamis agreed upon removal to their reserve in the Kansas Territory within five years, and emigration expenses plus subsistence measures were to be provided by the federal government during removal and for twelve months thereafter. The Miamis ceded to the United States their remaining tribal lands, including 511,000 acres of their winter hunting grounds on the Big Miami Reserve for $550,000. Of these funds, nearly half or $250,000 were to be used to pay off tribal debts, and what remained would be paid in annuity payments over twenty years—and additional funds were taken out of the annual annuity thereafter as well.[21]

Chief Richardville, in the course of eight years, reconsidered and ultimately changed his opinion about removal. Presumably, he was motivated by several contributing factors. Allen Hamilton exerted significant influence over Richardville, especially near the end of his life. Richardville even named Hamilton coexecutor of his will, as did Richardville's daughters. Irrespective of the true nature of their relationship, Hamilton benefited financially from his relationships with the Richardvilles. He persistently assured Richardville that removal was the best answer to dealing with exorbitant debt and growing alcoholism within the tribe. Earlier, Hamilton reported his concerns for their socioeconomic standing to the Senate, stating that removal would move the Miamis "beyond the influence of those [white] men around them, or a total extinction of the race would be the consequence of their remaining." This projected notion of imminent tribal extinction ran deep, as T. Hartley Crawford, commissioner of Indian Affairs, wrote that "principal chief [Richardville] was desirous, before the close of his life, now drawing near, to effect a negotiation, as in his opinion the emigration or extinction of the tribe were the alternatives before them."[22] Fatalistic sentiment, in spite of any underlying sincerity, justified removal further.

Jean Baptiste de Richardville was a complex man. He was formally educated, both trilingual (Miami, French, and English) and literate (French and English), and a successful trader like his parents, Antoine Joseph Drouet de Ricardville and Tacumwah. His successes in commerce instilled jealousies within and outside the tribe. Fellow Miamis used their annuity payments to buy supplies at his stores, which were conveniently located at payment sites. Although this enabled Richardville to keep more Miami money within the community, this practice led to burgeoning resentment of his comfortable life with large homes, elegant clothing, and plentiful food. Richardville centralized power and wealth within the community, but he was also noted for his charity to those in need. The benefits Richardville secured from every treaty he marked resulted in his amassing even more land and wealth, which deepened intertribal resentment. Most likely, Richardville recognized, during treaty negotiations for the 1834, 1838, and 1840 treaties, that removal loomed closely. The treaty provisions he secured for himself, as well as his earnings through the trade, inevitably enabled him to prepare for removal incrementally. While some Miami clans were skeptical of his intentions, traders and settlers were even more concerned. The latter saw Richardville's role as a principal chief and merchant as a conflict of interest. Even Richardville's connections with the Catholic Church bothered some. John Forsythe, an American clerk at Richardville's Fort Wayne store, found Richardville hypocritical. "The old Fox professes the same religion [Roman Catholic]. . . . [He] is somewhat bigoted in the principals [*sic*] of the sect and no person can convince [me] to the contrary." Additionally, Protestant missionaries were concerned about Richardville's wealth and connections with the Catholic Church, and feared he would leave his property to the Church.[23]

Richardville anguished over the changes taking place in his community, and this is indicated through speeches he gave, as well as by changes he made in his life. Although literate, he signed multiple treaties with only his mark and worked only through interpreters; even his personal correspondence was penned by others. Additionally, Richardville reportedly wore only traditional clothing and staunchly refused to speak English in his latter years. His personal decisions to identify more with his Miami heritage intimates how he managed the deleterious effects of rampant ethnic reorganization. Hugh McCulloch, attorney, bank operator, and future secretary of the Treasury, reflected that the "greatest mistake of his [Richardville's] life was made . . . when he yielded his own judgment to that of a Catholic priest . . . and sent two boys away from home to be educated." After their return to Fort Wayne, Richardville found they had "lost their taste for Indian life, and they had no disposition to engage in the pursuits of white men," and "soon passed from listlessness to dissipation." Richardville concluded, "Education very good for white boys; bad, very bad for Indians."[24]

The liquor trade concerned Richardville as well because many Miamis were addicted and the harmful effects of alcohol rippled throughout the community. Alcoholism disrupted family organization and strained social relations. Even his son-in-law and successor, Francis LaFontaine, was a notable drinker. Bureaucrats, land speculators, and settlers "repeatedly used over-consumption of alcohol as a primary rationale for removing the Miami," suggesting they would be better off out west, away from their present circumstances. Concerns about alcohol consumption predated statehood, however, as various local laws regulating alcohol trade with Indians were passed during Indiana's territorial days. Traders found numerous loopholes, though, and if caught, were only punished with a fine. Enforcing these laws after statehood was achieved was difficult, and once canal work began, alcohol poured into the region in even greater abundance. The temperance movement under the direction of Presbyterian Pastor James Chute lobbied for state legislation that would "halt the flow of liquor" in 1832. He also got canal contractors to agree, under the threat of losing their contracts, to cease providing whiskey for their workers as partial payment for their labor.[25]

Local federal agents and businessmen were appalled at the Miami propensity for drinking. Thomas Dowling, Miami removal contractor, was outspoken about the debilitating effects alcohol had among the Miamis and wrote to the commissioner of Indian Affairs, Thomas Crawford, in June 1844: "There are 269 Miamies here [Peru, Indiana], big, little and small, being a increase of deaths over births last year of 16, which shows that if the same ratio continues they will be extinct as a tribe in less than 20 years. Liquor, dissipation and idelness are the principal causes of their decay." Four months later, Dowling found little had changed, in that "the condition of these Indians is deplorable and that every sincere friend of the tribe will rejoice at the prospect of their speedy removal beyond the reach of the demoralizing influences which surround them. The use of intoxicating drinks is the prolific source of all this misfortune." Indian subagent John Hays was equally concerned and pleaded for government intervention to prohibit the sale of alcohol to the Indians. "Of all the troubles an agent had to contend with, this was the first and last and most insoluble. The Indians would part with anything they had to secure whiskey." Allen Hamilton reported to the commissioner of Indian Affairs that "the cheapness of whiskey, the easy access to obtaining it keeps their poor degraded beings under its influence almost constantly." His admonishment of unscrupulous traders was the norm of the time, and he once commented that "Among their present traders are men so low as to associate with them in every way."[26]

Annuity payment centers proved most concerning as merchants were situated nearby ready to sell their goods and alcohol. At one center fifty miles from Fort Wayne, four hundred Miamis were reportedly drunk the day after their annuities were paid. In 1831, Richardville moved tribal headquarters from Fort Wayne and built a new trading post at the Forks of the Wabash to centralize Miami commerce and to get away from traders. Previously, though, Indian subagent John Tipton moved the Indian agency from Ft. Wayne to Logansport, despite trader outcry in 1828. He also moved the agency because "it was too close to numerous grogshops and to the traders who sold his wards whiskey, encouraged them to run up debts which must later be deducted from annuities, and cheated them in a hundred different ways"; however, alcohol soon arrived at Logansport. Tipton had personal interests in securing agency removal near the junction of the Wabash and Eel Rivers, as he and his partners were orchestrating control of the Indian reserves in that region. It is no coincidence that shortly thereafter, the town of Logansport was platted on one of those reserves.[27]

The temperance movement experienced variable success in Fort Wayne, Logansport, and Peru. In Peru, one missionary described temperance activities as "lively," but still deemed it an intemperate community, noting, "Peru must be a very wicked place till these Indians. . . . are removed." One Ft. Wayne physician estimated that for every two gallons of whiskey consumed in 1830, only a pint was consumed two years later.[28] While this demonstrated a marked improvement in overall alcohol consumption, it remained a pervasive problem throughout Northern Indiana.

Although Chief Richardville secured exemption from removal for his family and the Godfroy and Metocina families in the 1840 Treaty (approximately 130 individuals), he had accomplished this previously for his family in the Treaty of 1838. This was granted to him because he was considered "very old and infirm, and not well able to endure the fatigue of a long journey, it is agreed that the United States will pay to him and his family the proportion of the annuity of said tribe . . . at Fort Wayne." Although Richardville died prior to removal, his family remained exempt, and everyone, including the Godfroy and Metocina families, legally retained their annuities in Indiana. Many of the legally exempt Miamis were of mixed ancestry, Christians, and successful businessmen; therefore, they avoided the accrual of significant debt and social stigmatization, unlike other Miamis. Furthermore, "The state legislature petitioned Congress not to disturb these men in Indiana under the rationale that they could continue to pay taxes on their farming lands."[29] It was much easier for state government to endorse individual Miamis who were viewed as assimilated, in the sense that their behavior conformed to American norms by farming, earning an income, and paying taxes. In other words, they were not deemed as much a threat as other less-assimilated Miamis.[30]

Another official exemption for a Miami family was accomplished through congressional appeal. Maconaquah (Frances Slocum), a former white captive, petitioned the federal government for her family's exemption once her identity was confirmed. With the support of her Miami and birth relatives, she claimed to be too old to move to Kansas. She also reported the hardship removal would have caused her since she had just found her birth family. Congress agreed and granted an exemption for Maconaquah and twenty-one family members in 1845.[31] Ultimately, her entire village was granted exemption, bringing the total count of officially exempted Miamis to approximately 154.

Some settlers supported other Miamis who sought exclusion from removal. One petition was filed jointly in January 1846 by 101 American settlers and 10 Miamis. Another petition was filed by 291 settlers in July that same year. These petitions failed, as there were far more settlers who longed for Miami removal than those who did not. John Bell of the Office of Indian Affairs noted tensions between settlers and the Miamis during the winter of 1846, and suggested conducting removal earlier. He noted there was "a state of things which subjects a portion of the citizens of Indiana to great present annoyance and distress, and which, unless the appropriating power of Congress be promptly interposed, may . . . eventuate in actual hostilities."[32] Missionaries were also conflicted about Miami removal. Quaker missionaries blamed corrupt traders for their failed attempts at conversion, and other Protestant religious leaders saw removal as a reminder of their failure to assimilate the Miamis. Six months before the Miamis left Indiana, one Protestant even wrote of the frustrations he and others felt about the Miamis' "impending exile" in a poem.[33] However, some Presbyterian missionaries rejoiced at the prospects of Miami removal because they believed once the Miamis were gone, traders would follow, and any remaining settlers would be more amenable to the possibilities of conversion.

On May 6, 1844, Thomas Dowling of Terre Haute accepted a contract of $53,000 to remove the Miamis west. His responsibilities included issuing rations at assembly, assuming emigration expenses totaling $55,000, providing rations for one year after removal, and paying assistants along the journey. There were questions surrounding Dowling's true interests in removing the Miamis, as he bragged to his brother that the profit from the contract would "rear the superstructure of an independence for myself, family, and relatives."[34] He also used his contract as equity in securing a $6,000 loan, for which he then sold the contract to Robert Peebles of Pittsburgh. By March 1846, the removal contract was sold again, to a group of four men including brothers William and George Ewing, owning a third of the contract, with the remaining two-thirds divided between Samuel Edsall and Alexis Coquillard. The latter became the actual removal conductor.

Traders were lobbying to keep the Miamis in Indiana. This tried Coquillard's patience, so he suggested to the secretary of war, William Wilkins, that the Miamis would never consent to emigrate unless their annuities were cut off. He also suggested their next annuity be made in the West, destroying traders' hopes for future dealings and collections. Traders, in response to the aforementioned efforts, claimed that Coquillard allied himself with traders intentionally so that he would become aware of the full exploitative nature of their enterprise.[35] These claims required further investigation, delaying removal once again. Removal was stalled due to resolving land titles and patents for reserves, and land issues including ownership, transfer, and disposal of property proved to be the primary obstacles preventing removal. The Miamis then stepped forward asking for more time to sell off personal property and belongings. By early 1846, the federal government and settlers alike were becoming increasingly more anxious for their removal. In fact, the federal government agreed to pay Miami debts off in yearly installments out of their annuities to hasten the process, and by February, questions emerged from Washington about why removal had not occurred.

In 1845, Richardville's successor, Francis LaFontaine, requested that a delegation go to Kansas to inspect their new lands as guaranteed by the 1838 Treaty. As a stalling tactic, it proved successful. Where officials at the Indian Affairs Office had previously surveyed and found the reserved lands acceptable, other evidence suggests that the Kansas Territory was harsh and unsuitable; "it was a miserable despicable country." The heat was notably unbearable and the soil was "poor and unfriendly, it [would] be impossible to raise corn on more than one tenth of the land, and only land on which we could raise corn would be the bottoms."[36] The Great American Desert in the West held little appeal for the Miamis.

With one successful delay already achieved, LaFontaine decided to try it again. In late June, 1846, LaFontaine—with a contingent of six village chiefs, including Pimyotamah; the agency doctor; and an interpreter—made an unofficial trip to Washington, DC, under the pretense of "making some arrangements in relation to the removal of their people west of the Mississippi." The delegation sought another extension for removal, and exemption from removal for four leaders (Meaquah, Rivarre, Coesse, and White Loon) and their families from President James Polk. The delegation, however, returned to Indiana in August unsuccessful in their efforts.[37] By August, military support was called in from Cincinnati to enforce removal, and by September 21, troops arrived in Peru. Coquillard insisted to Lafontaine that nonexempt Miamis had to report to his camp within forty-eight hours or the troops would begin their search for fugitives. LaFontaine realized future delays were futile.

Miami removal began at the canal docks in Peru on October 6, 1846. Removal occurred over various waterways by canal boats and steamboats and took nearly a month to complete. Three canal boats awaited the Miamis in Peru, as well as accompanying Indian Affairs agents, removal contractors, Father Julien Benoit, traders, and a detachment of United States soldiers under the command of Captain Jouett. LaFontaine requested Father Benoit to accompany the removal party, and although he did not want to, a federal officer told him, "Unless you go with them, they will not go and I will be obliged to hunt them down like wild beasts and kill them."[38]

Not surprisingly, many Miamis fled the region prior to removal. The Wauwasee and Papkeechi families left Indiana for Southern Michigan to live with the Pokagon Potawatomis. The Eel River Miamis also fled, but the following year were permitted, through a state court decision, to remain in Indiana since they were "Eel River" Indians and not "Miami" Indians.[39] Other Miamis simply refused to assemble. "All the things that you can imagine that you could do to, stay if you wanted to stay were . . . taking place. . . . The Miami didn't want to go . . . only with force and threats of force was the move made. They didn't have any choice." One Peru resident recalled, "Many of the Indians had to be brought forcibly to the place of rendezvous. . . . Many had to be hunted down like wild animals, some were actually found in the tops of trees, others secreted themselves in swamps and many fled from the locality, coming back only after the emigration had taken place, only to be forwarded as prisoners to their new home." Several Miamis who boarded the canal boats were sick, so anxiety over removal surely compounded their illnesses. Western Miami Rose Carver once described it as: "They didn't want to leave their land . . . they just picked up a little handful of dirt and put it in a tobacco sack and take that with 'em [*sic*]." Historical records concur with oral history in that the late Western Miami chief Forest Olds once claimed "that the Miamis would break and run. They had been to visit the graves of their loved ones, and they were carrying a clod of dirt or small stone that they had picked off the graves. . . . [and] they loaded them like cattle on canal boats."[40] With Indiana soil in one hand and their belongings in the other, nearly half the tribe left their ancestral homelands that fateful autumn day. The following day, on October 7, the canal boat reached Fort Wayne, a journey of 65 miles. Here awaited more Miamis with two additional canal boats. John Dawson, eyewitness to the Miami departure from Fort Wayne, described the scene as a very somber event. "I remember the sober, saddened faces, the profusion of tears, as I saw them hug to their bosoms a little handful of earth which they had gathered from the graves of their dead kindred . . . many a bystander was moved to tears at the evidences of grief he saw before him."[41]

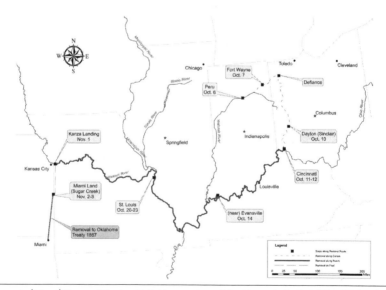

Myaamia (Miami) Removal Route, 1846. Map courtesy of the Myaamia Project, Miami University, Oxford, Ohio.

The boats followed the newly constructed Wabash-Erie Canal to its junction with the Miami-Erie Canal in Junction, Ohio. The canal boat caravan headed south for the next three days, passing through Piqua, Ohio, until they reached Dayton, Ohio, on October 10, a distance of over 140 miles. On the following evening, the caravan reached Cincinnati, Ohio, about 66 miles south of Dayton. While in Cincinnati, according to Sinclair, two Miami men sleeping on the baggage deck were accidentally injured as their boat passed under a low-lying bridge. On October 12, the removal party boarded the steamboat the *Colorado* and headed west on the Ohio River. It took two days to reach Evansville, Indiana—a distance of over 225 miles. The *Colorado* continued along the Ohio River and then up the Mississippi River until landing at Bloody Island at the port of St. Louis, Missouri, on October 20. Reportedly, during the latter part of their steamboat journey, an infant and elder died.[42]

The Miamis stayed on Bloody Island for three days until they boarded a second steamboat, the *Clermont No. 2*. From Bloody Island, they headed toward Kanza Landing, or present-day Kansas City, Missouri. During this part of the journey, four Miamis died and two-thirds of the removal party had become extremely ill. The Miamis reached the West Port of Kanza Landing on November 1. After their arrival, LaFontaine lamented that "This country does not please me. It would have been much better if my people had moved by land moving by water does not suit the habits of my people." Interestingly, this same sentiment was reflected a year later by Coquillard during the Potawatomi removal in 1838, when he commented, "Boats do not agree with Indians and we will likely lose a good many in that way." From Kanza Landing, the removal party walked approximately 50 miles over the course of two days to reach their Sugar Creek Reserve in eastern Kansas.[43]

By November 5, the Miamis reached their new reservation lands and checked in with subagent Alfred Vaughan, at the Osage River Sub-Agency. They were met there by Joseph Comparet, who had brought ninety of their horses from Indiana to Kansas. One Indian trader who accompanied the removal party commented on their despair once they arrived at Sugar Creek. "I am . . . unused to the melting mood, but when the young braves at my parting with them burst into tears and begged like children to be taken back to their old home, I could not help crying also." The actual number of Miamis removed is difficult to discern as statistics vary from source to source. It is clear, though, that more Miamis remained in Indiana, officially and otherwise (over 350) than were removed (approximately 325). A local newspaper reported that 325 "Indians" arrived on November 5. Unbeknownst to removal conductors and accompanying Indian agents, thirteen other Indians of unknown tribal affiliation accompanied the caravan; therefore, it is likely that the total number of removed Miamis is even lower than what Sinclair recorded.[44]

Although the Treaty of 1840 promised the Miamis a 500,000-acre reserve, the actual size of their reserved lands turned out to be less than 325,000 acres. Hugh McCulloch commented on how the Miamis must have felt when they reached Kansas. "To them it was a desert over which the fierce winds were constantly sweeping, without trees, and without game. The change from a country like Northern Indiana . . . was indeed disheartening."[45] Not even a full month after arriving at their reserve, a group of Miami tribal leaders wrote to President Polk about their new home. "We have emigrated to our new home, and we have pitched our tents on the land set apart for us west of the Mississippi. . . . Dear to us was that home of our children, still dearer to us were the ashes of our forefathers, and how could we expect to find anywhere the aught that would compensate for such a loss."[46] Despair prevailed among the Western Miamis and worsened once LaFontaine left for Indiana.

As a member of the Richardville clan, LaFontaine and his family were exempt from removal. So, after living with the Miamis for several months in Kansas, he headed back to Indiana along with four other leaders—Meaquah, Rivarre, Coesse, and White Loon—in April 1847. On the return trip, a very ill LaFontaine passed away in Lafayette, Indiana, and although there was significant debate on the cause of his death, Meaquah, Rivarre, Coesse, and White Loon were busily submitting their petition for exemption from permanent removal. They had previously negotiated a unique agreement with a federal Indian agent where in exchange for their assistance in removing the Miamis west, they could return to Indiana temporarily for their fall harvest and then relinquish their lands and return to Kansas at their own expense. While these four leaders eventually harvested their crops, they only did so after submitting their petition for exemption from removal. This process took over a year and a half, but with the support of the Indiana state legislature, the federal government conceded that Meaquah, Rivarre, Coesse, and White Loon and their families could not be forcibly removed to Kansas; however, the federal government refused to pay them their annuities if they remained.[47] The Indiana state legislature again advocated for the Miamis and reminded Congress that these families were paying taxes on lands they retained through treaties. The state endorsed this because it broke up any power base these leaders may have shared with leadership remaining in Kansas; plus they were deemed as assimilated enough to remain and become productive Indiana citizens.

Commissioner of Indian Affairs William Medill was concerned that permitting more exemptions would cause dissent among those removed. There were also concerns that this would lead others to try the same. "The remaining of those permitted to do so, operates injuriously upon those who have been removed. They naturally prefer their old homes, and think it unjust, that, while they were compelled to remove, others were permitted to remain." To permit more exemptions would only foster continued "discontent, and lead to expectations, that . . . others will be permitted to return and remain . . . thus to defeat the beneficial policy adopted by the government for their improvement and welfare."[48] While Medill may have been correct in his presumption, dissent was present among the Western Miamis long before Meaquah, Rivarre, Coesse, and White Loon secured their de facto exemptions.

Another Miami removal, albeit smaller, took place in 1847. The purpose of this was to remove those who had evaded the 1846 removal, such as the Wauwasee band. Trader Edekial French was contracted to track members from the Wauwasee band who fled to Michigan. By the spring of 1847, Coquillard opened a camp in Kosciusko County where thirty Miamis convened from Columbia City, Huntington, South Bend, Manchester, and Peru. Altogether Coquillard gathered seventy-eight individual Miamis for removal, even charging the tribe for his search of missing or escaped Indians from the previous removal.[49] Several Potawatomis who married into Miami bands were also included with the removal party. Seventeen Natives were declared "Wea" and not "Miami," so they were exempt from removal, which left the total emigration party at sixty-one, the number reported to the western reservation in September 1847. Removal took place over land and began eleven miles north of Peru, with the caravan passing through Winamac and Ottawa, Illinois, eventually arriving at Sugar Creek, Kansas.

The events leading to removal, emigration, and the fallout experienced thereafter played a significant role in how Miami identity was defined and experienced. Settlers desired Miami land for agriculture, while the State of Indiana wanted bureaucratic control of everything within its boundaries for internal improvements and commerce. The federal government continuously endorsed a policy calling for removal of eastern Native peoples to solve the "Indian problem," while the Miamis found themselves engaged in policymaking, often involving unethical practices clouded by seeming concerns over the effects tribal debt and alcoholism had on their community. While these concerns may have been legitimate, they also justified Miami removal away from such problematic circumstances.

The federal government's decision to treat with select leaders usurped the power of many and thereby created dissent. Furthermore, the ways Miami bands were arbitrarily ignored during treaty negotiations consolidated various Miami groups with different traditions and dialects. This showed a distinct movement toward homogenizing Miami identities, but in doing so instilled greater division. Although treaties guaranteed reserved lands, they often carried various stipulations—such as the Treaty of 1826 that gave the government right of way for a canal if necessary.[50] This commodification of land ran counter to Miami land-management practices, and when the federal government made additional amendments to guaranteed lands, it dismissed Miami connections to the land further.

Traders introduced new goods, replacing traditional practices and, perhaps most importantly, integrating a full market economy into Miami communities. Traders and canal workers also provided a steady supply of alcohol, which changed family and group dynamics considerably. Although far more traders wanted the Miamis to remain in Indiana than those who did not, they complicated Miami lives immeasurably—the very clientele traders relied upon. As missionaries integrated into Miami communities, several traditional rituals faded and became obsolete. Missionaries devalued Miami beliefs, and while many Miamis syncretized Catholicism and Protestantism with Miami traditions, this nevertheless led to a shift away from consummate traditional practices. Marriages to American settlers during the Removal Era also led to additional reorganization of Miami women's roles, especially their roles as economic providers. Other influences leading to rampant ethnic reorganization included formal education. Indian treaties attempted to assimilate the Miamis through education, such as the 1826 Treaty that ensured Miami entrance to the Choctaw Academy in Kentucky, where Richardville and others eventually sent their children. The 1840 Treaty also guaranteed an educational fund for those removed to Kansas.

Dispossession, persistent public pressure, debt, and alcoholism left the Miamis extremely vulnerable. The cultural changes that occurred throughout the Miami community were extensive, and Richardville was well aware of the impact these changes were having on the community. Richardville himself was the product of mixed Miami-French parentage, and he enjoyed many luxuries as a child. Undoubtedly, this aided in his role as principal chief, as his expert knowledge of living in two worlds would have proven advantageous. In spite of the land cessions Richardville made in various treaties, his steadfast decision to keep the Miamis—if even a select few, including his own family—in Indiana after 1846 proved successful. But, other Miamis in non-leadership roles resisted in their own ways, too.

LaFontaine, in the tradition established by his late father-in-law, delayed removal by ensuring the fulfillment of secured treaty stipulations. Maconaquah used her whiteness to exempt herself and her family from removal, while Meaquah, Rivarre, Coesse and White Loon negotiated an agreement to assist with Miami removal, ensure a return to Indiana, and eventually remain, even without federal benefits, in Indiana.[51] The Miamis also resisted by asserting their identities, such as Richardville's adherence to Miami traditions during his latter years, and Maconaquah's refusal to visit her American family in Pennsylvania.

Removal was physically and emotionally divisive throughout the Miami community. The Western Miamis were disgruntled about removing to Kansas as others were permitted to remain in Indiana. The late chief Floyd Leonard of the Western Miamis once commented, "I would be less than honest if I did not say that many Western Miami still resent the fact that some, by some special permission got to stay here [in Indiana]." However, the Western Miamis also grieved over their separation from kin and ancestral homelands. Community maintenance became especially concerning as increased cultural and linguistic isolation occurred. Western Miami Rosa Boington Beck once remarked, "The Tribe it seemed like they just drifted apart. . . . And it was divided, you know, when it comes from eastern Indiana down here [to Kansas]. It was divided." The 1846 Removal unknowingly prepared the Western Miamis for another removal during the late 1860s and early 1870s to northeastern Oklahoma, near present-day-Miami, Oklahoma. A Western Miami elder once described this final removal: "They . . . shipped 'em like cattle. From Kansas up here just like cattle in cattle cars. It was terrible."[52] Other Indian communities removed to this region included the Shawnee, Seneca-Cayuga, Quapaw, Peoria, Ottawa, Wyandotte, and Modoc tribes; all remain in the area today.

Although the Eastern Miamis remained on their ancestral homelands, they also grieved over their separation from kin. Maconaquah never recovered fully from the grief she felt when the Miamis left Peru. Their lives changed as cultural clashes became clearer, and they "felt increasingly isolated." The late Eastern Miami elder Lora Siders once commented, "We were nothing. We were not citizens. . . . We were not foreigners. . . . We were not considered Indians. We were just out there in a vacuum."[53] Travel between Indiana and Kansas, and eventually between Indiana and Oklahoma, became commonplace for years to come, serving as an important way to sustain Miami identity—a practice that continues today.

Resentment over removal and its residual problems remain unforgotten by the Western and Eastern Miamis, but at various times these differences have been set aside. In 1889, the Western Miamis filed suit for the Eastern Miamis, where the latter were charging the government with violating the terms of a treaty ratified in 1854. From the late nineteenth century and throughout the twentieth century, both Miami groups united again in further litigation against the government. While the Western Miamis have always maintained their status as a federally recognized tribe, the Eastern Miamis lost their status as "Indians" in 1897, in an unfounded administrative decision by Assistant Attorney General Willis Van Devanter. Van Devanter claimed their status had been terminated in earlier legislation, and they could not therefore be dually recognized as citizens and tribal members. Interestingly, though, once he became an associate justice for the United States Supreme Court, he contradicted his earlier position in two different rulings in 1915 and 1930, stating an Indian could be both a citizen and a tribal member.[54] The Eastern Miamis have since attempted to regain federal recognition and were last denied recognition in 1990. They are currently petitioning for state recognition in Indiana.

The Miamis persistently reorganized ethnically, in that several cultural and linguistic practices shifted in the milieu of politics and American expansionism. However, over the past few years, both communities have participated together at powwows and in various administrative actions. Perhaps the most significant is the language reclamation project, which began in 1995 under the direction of Daryl Baldwin. Language revitalization programs have since led to the creation of their first dictionary, language compact discs, interactive computer programming, and the establishment of annual language classes and camps. Ongoing language/cultural projects include rigorous mapping and lunar calendar projects, a cookbook, storybooks, an active ethnobotany program, and continuous translation work of French Jesuit documents. Most importantly, there are at least three families and many others who speak Miami, a feat particularly remarkable since their last fluent speaker passed away in 1963, and no audio or video recordings were ever made of the Miami language. Appropriately, Baldwin's efforts have received national acclaim.[55]

Although unsuccessful in thwarting removal altogether, the Miamis established the terms for their survival during the Removal Era. Just as the federal government sought control of the Miamis through removal, resistance by the Miamis shaped the removal process as well. Given the pressures they were under, Miami leadership was successful in maintaining a Miami presence in both the Lower Great Lakes and in the West. Both Eastern and Western Miamis remain a persistent people who are steadfastly committed to maintaining a distinctive Miami identity in their respective ancestral and historical landscapes. Although their statuses remain different, through individual and collaborative efforts they have come together when needed—a quality that no doubt sustained them during the Removal Era. No removal story was identical, and it is the details and nuances of tribal histories, like the Miamis', that demonstrate how perseverance in very difficult times enabled Native resilience before, during, and beyond removal. These same qualities have ensured a continued dynamic Miami identity that has thrived up to the present day.

NOTES

1. Joseph Manzo, "Emigrant Indian Objections to Kansas Residence," *Kansas History* 4 (1981): 247; Suzette McCord-Rogers, "To Have and Have Not: The Vanishing Lands of Native America," *Kansas Heritage* (1996): 5; Francis Paul Prucha, "Indian Removal and the Great American Desert," *Indiana Magazine of History* [hereafter *IMH*] 59, no. 4 (1963): 299–322.

2. Kate Berry and Melissa Rinehart, "A Legacy of Forced Migration: The Removal of the Miami Tribe in 1846," *International Journal of Population Geography* 9 (2003): 94.

3. Referred to as "ethnic survival" by Joane Nagel and C. Matthew Snipp, "Ethnic Reorganization: American Indian Social, Economic, Political, and Cultural Strategies for Survival," *Ethnic and Racial Studies* 16, no. 2 (1993).

4. Charles Callender, "Miami," in *Handbook of North American Indians*, vol. 15, *Northeast*, ed. Bruce G. Trigger (Washington, DC: Smithsonian Institution, 1978), 681; Stewart Rafert, *The Miami Indians of Indiana: A Persistent People, 1654–1994* (Indianapolis: Indiana Historical Society, 1996), 16; *Miami Origin Story*, collected by Jacob Dunn from Gabriel Godfroy, unpublished manuscript, Jacob Piatt Dunn Manuscript Collection, Indiana State Library, Indianapolis, from a redaction by David J. Costa; Daryl Baldwin, *Nahi Meehtohseeniwinki—To Live in a Good Way*, unpublished manuscript, Miami Tribal Office of Cultural Preservation, Miami, OK, 8.

5. Henry Hay, *Journal from Detroit to the Miami River, Fort Wayne in 1790*, ed. Milo Milton Quaife (1790; Fort Wayne: Allen County Public Library, 1955); Dani Tippmann, personal communication, April 13, 2005; Baldwin, *Nahi Meehtohseeniwinki*, 8–9; W. Vernon Kinietz, *The Indians of the Western Great Lakes, 1615–1760* (Ann Arbor: University of Michigan Museum of Anthropology, Occasional Contributions 10, 1965), 211–12; Bacqueville de la Potherie, "History of the Savage Peoples Who Are Allies of New France, 1753," in *The Indian Tribes of the Upper Mississippi Valley and Region of the*

Great Lakes, ed. Emma Blair (Cleveland: Arthur H. Clark, 1911–1912), 332; Baldwin, *Nahi Meehtohseeniwinki*, 8.

6. Leon Gordon II, "The Red Man's Retreat from Northern Indiana," *IMH* 46, no. 1 (1950): 58; Gregory Evans Dowd, "Michigan Murder Mysteries: Death and Rumor in the Age of Indian Removal," in *Enduring Nations: Native Americans in the Midwest*, ed. R. David Edmunds (Urbana: University of Illinois Press, 2008), 126.

7. Dorothy Riker, "Documents: Two Accounts of the Upper Wabash County, 1819–1820. Journal of Henry P. Benton," *IMH* 37, no. 4 (1941): 387; Bert Anson, *The Miami Indians* (Norman: University of Oklahoma Press, 1970), 196; Ella Lonn, "Ripples of the Blackhawk War in Northern Indiana," *IMH* 20, no. 3 (1924): 288–307; Darwin Kelley, "Securing the Land: John Tipton and the Miami Indians," *Old Fort News* 25, no. 1 (1962): 6.

8. Indiana State Legislature, "Memorial of the Legislature of Indiana, Praying that the title of the Miami Indians, to large tracts of land in the state, may be extinguished," 21st Cong., 1st sess., December 24, 1829; *Senate Doc. No. 194*, General Assembly of the State of Indiana, "Resolution of the General Assembly of Indiana in Relation to the Right of Preemption to the 'Miami Reserve' in that State," 25th Cong., 2nd sess., serial set 316, February 13, 1838; *H.R. Doc. No. 129*, General Assembly of the State of Indiana, "Memorial and Joint Resolution of the General Assembly of Indiana in regard to the Pottawatamie and Miami Indians in this State," 23rd Cong., 2nd sess., serial set 273, February 4, 1835; Hugh McCulloch, *Men and Measures of Half a Century: Sketches and Comments* (New York: Charles Scribner & Sons, 1888), 103.

9. Rafert, *The Miami Indians of Indiana*, 65; Waldo Mitchell, "Indiana's Growth, 1812–1820," *IMH* 10, no. 3 (1914): 317; Anson, *The Miami Indians*, 191.

10. Articles 4 and 5 in Treaty of 1803, Treaties of 1834, 1838, and 1840, in Charles Kappler, *Indian Affairs: Laws and Treaties* (1904), http://digital.library.okstate.edu/kappler [hereafter *IALT*]; Berry and Rinehart, "A Legacy of Forced Migration," 98.

11. Kappler, Articles 1 and 2, Treaty of 1826, *IALT*; Charles Poinsatte, *Fort Wayne during the Canal Era, 1828–1855: A Study of a Western Community in the Middle Period of American History* (Indianapolis: Indiana Historical Bureau, 1969), 17–18; George Mather, *Frontier Faith: The Story of the Pioneer Congregations of Fort Wayne, Indiana, 1820–1860* (Fort Wayne, IN: Allen County–Fort Wayne Historical Society, 1992), 26, 29–31; Berry and Rinehart, "A Legacy of Forced Migration," 98.

12. Henry Hoover, *Journal of the Proceedings at the Treaty Held with the Miami Indians*, September 10, 1832, Henry Hoover Collection, William Henry

Smith Memorial Library (Indianapolis: Indiana Historical Society), 14, 15, and 17; Kappler, Articles 1 and 2, Treaty of 1834, *IALT*; Sen. Exec. Journal, "Presidential Transmission of the 1834 Treaty to the Committee on Indian Affairs and the Senate of the United States," Related correspondence included with report, October 4, 1837, 25th Cong., 1st sess.

13. *Sen. Exec. Journal*, "Presidential Transmission," 1837.

14. Ibid.; Bureau of Indian Affairs, *Summary under the Criteria and Evidence for Proposed Finding against Federal Acknowledgement of the Miami Nation of Indians of the State of Indiana, Inc.*, July 12, 1990.

15. *Sen. Exec. Journal*, "Report from Joel Roberts Poinsett of the War Dept., to President Andrew Jackson," December 14, 1838, 25th Cong., 3rd sess., 165; *Sen. Exec. Journal*, "Submitted Treaty Articles as Negotiated with the Miami Tribe of Indians in Indiana by Samuel Milroy and Allen Hamilton in 1840," Related correspondence included with report, January 18, 1841, 26th Cong., 2nd sess.; Kappler, Articles 1, 4, and 10, *IALT*.

16. Kappler, Article 6, *IALT*; Poinsatte, *Fort Wayne during the Canal Era*, 5; Phyllis Gernhardt, "'Justice and Public Policy': Indian Trade, Treaties, and Removal from Northern Indiana, 1826–1846," in *Boundaries Between Us: Natives and Newcomers along the Frontiers of the Old Northwest Territory, 1750–1850*, ed. Daniel Barr (Kent, OH: Kent State University Press, 2006), 187; Logan Esarey, *A History of Indiana* (New York: Harcourt, Brace and Co., 1922), 125; *Sen. Exec. Journal*, "Presidential Transmission," 1837.

17. *Sen. Doc. No. 164*, "Report from the Secretary of War in compliance with a resolution of the Senate, the report of the Commissioner to investigate claims against the Miami Indians for the year 1839," February 10, 1840, 26th Cong., 1st sess., serial set 357, 5.

18. Kelley, "Securing the Land," 6; *H.R. Doc. No. 43*, "Estimate Treaty with the Miami Indians. Letter from the Secretary of War Transmitting an Estimate of Funds Required to Carry into Effect the Treaty with the Miami Indians," August 3, 1841, 27th Cong., 1st sess., serial set 392.

19. *Sen. Exec. Journal*, "Submitted Treaty Articles," 1841.

20. Ibid.

21. Kappler, Articles 1, 2, and 8, *IALT*; President James Polk, True copy of the Original Executive Report to William Medill, Commissioner of Indian Affairs. Confirmation of the old Miami claims, March 5, 1846, box 5.11, Allen County–Fort Wayne Historical Society, Fort Wayne, IN.

22. Abstract of Title, Will of John [Jean] Baptiste Richardville, Lot 25, Winterset, sec. 1, Dreibelbiss Title Co., Inc., Fort Wayne; LaBlonde Richardville and Susan Richardville Deed of Trust, ibid.; Abstract of Title, Will of

LaBlonde-Maria Louisa Richardville; *Sen. Exec. Journal,* "Submitted Treaty Articles," 1841, 6 and 11.

23. Bradley Birzer, "Jean Baptiste Richardville: Miami Métis," in *Enduring Nations: Native Americans in the Midwest,* ed. R. David Edmunds (Urbana: University of Illinois Press, 2008), 98–99; John Forsythe, Correspondence to John Tipton, January 26, 1829, John Tipton Papers, 1828–1838, vol. 2, Indiana Historical Collections, Indiana Historical Society, Indianapolis, 134; Asa Johnson, Correspondence to Milton Badger, November 1, 1839, *Indiana Letters: Abstracts from Missionaries on the Indiana Frontier to the American Home Missionary Society, 1824–1893* [hereafter *AMIF*], ed. L. C. Rudolph, W. W. Wimberly, Thomas Clayton, and June Conger (Ann Arbor, MI: University Microfilms International, 1979).

24. Correspondence to Francis Godfroy, October 8, 1829, Francis Godfroy Papers, 1824–1847, Indiana State Library, Indianapolis; Anson, *The Miami Indians,* 189; Jean Baptiste Richardville quoted in McCulloch, *Men and Measures,* 110.

25. Asa Johnson, Correspondence to Charles Hall, May 10, 1847, *AMIF*; Berry and Rinehart, "A Legacy of Forced Migration," 101; Charles Camp, "Temperance Movements and Legislation in Indiana," *IMH* 16, no. 1 (1920): 9; Mather, *Frontier Faith,* 15; James Chute, Correspondence to Absalom Peters, June 13, 1832, *AMIF.*

26. Thomas Dowling, Correspondence to John Dowling, June 5, 1844, Donald J. Berthrong Collection, University of Oklahoma, Norman, M745, box 31, folder 162; Correspondence to Thomas Hartley Crawford, Commissioner of Indian Affairs, October 17, 1844; Nellie Robertson, John Hays as quoted in "John Hays and the Fort Wayne Indian Agency," *IMH* 39, no. 3 (1943): 231; Allen Hamilton, Correspondence to Thomas Hartley Crawford, Commissioner of Indian Affairs, May 24, 1843, Donald J. Berthrong Collection, University of Oklahoma, Norman, M745, box 31, folder 161. This is interesting as Hamilton was a merchant himself who repeatedly befriended key Miami leaders for his own financial gain.

27. James Chute, Correspondence to Absalom Peters, December 12, 1831, *AMIF*; Anson, *The Miami Indians,* 193; Lois Shepherd Headings, "This Distinguished and Extraordinary Man: Chief Jean Baptiste Richardville," *Old Fort News* 61, nos. 1–2, (1998): 11; Poinsatte, *Fort Wayne during the Canal Era,* 16, 18.

28. James Chute, Correspondence to Absalom Peters, June 13, 1832; Martin Post, Correspondence to Absalom Peters, August 30, 1831, *AMIF*; Asa Johnson, Correspondence to Milton Badger, May 19, 1845; James Chute, Correspondence to Absalom Peters, September 12, 1832, *AMIF.*

29. Kappler, Article 14, *IALT*; *H.R. Doc. No. 620*, "Correspondence from William Medill to Daniel Moreau Barringer, Chairman of Committee on Indian Affairs, May 17, 1848," 30th Cong., 1st sess., serial set 526; Berry and Rinehart, "A Legacy of Forced Migration," 107.

30. This is ironic given that the primary goal of Miami leadership at the time was to gain some sort of legal status for remaining tribal members in Indiana, and not just recognition as a mixed group of Indian descendants.

31. *Sen. Doc. No. 122*, "Senate Report with Petition to Congress for Frances Slocum's Exemption to Removal," January 17, 1845, 28th Cong., 2nd sess., serial set 456; *H.R. Doc. No. 620*.

32. *H.R. Journal*, "A petition of Shapendoshia and nine other Miami Indians with David Foster and 100 white men that Indians be permitted to remain in the country instead of removing west of the Mississippi River," vol. 1, House of Rep., January 27, 1846; "A memorial of 291 citizens of the State of Indiana praying that certain members of the Miami Tribe of Indians be permitted to remain on their reserved lands," vol. 41, House of Rep., July 27, 1846; *H.R. Doc. 43*.

33. Mather, *Frontier Faith*, 17; 'M,' "An Appeal for the Miamies," *Fort Wayne Times*, February 5, 1846, 1. This poem laments Miami removal in a paternalistic manner, acknowledging on one hand how the Miami were forcibly removed from their ancestral lands, but that they were still but a "helpless brood . . . With minds untrained, Passions unchained, With liquor swill'd, by hell distill'd, By White men—hold! To God, belongs, The arm of vengeance for their wrongs." According to this anonymous author, the Miamis were now further from the reach of Christian salvation, but their souls were yet salvageable.

34. Thomas Dowling, Correspondence to Allen Hamilton, May 27, 1844, Donald J. Berthrong Collection, University of Oklahoma, Norman, M745, box 31, folder 162; Thomas Dowling, Correspondence to John Dowling, April 11 and April 24, 1844, John Dowling Papers, Indiana Historical Society, Indianapolis.

35. Thomas Dowling, Correspondence to Allen Hamilton, July 30, 1844, Donald J. Berthrong Collection, University of Oklahoma, Norman, M745, box 31, folder 162; William G. Ewing, Signed copy of Petition to the Senate, January 26, 1846, Ewing Papers, Indiana State Library, Indianapolis.

36. William G. Ewing, Report to Commissioner of Indian Affairs, November 24, 1846, Letters Received by the Office of Indian Affairs, 1824–1881, record group 75, microcopy 234, reel 418; Manzo, "Emigrant Indian Objections," 252.

37. George Wood, "The Miami Delegation," *Fort Wayne Sentinel*, July 9, 1842, 1; Anson, *The Miami Indians*, 258–59.

38. Charles Blanchard, ed., *History of the Catholic Church in Indiana* (Logansport, IN: A.W. Bowen & Co., 1898).

39. Alexis Coquillard and Samuel Edsall, "Report of the Acting Contractors for the Emigration of the Miami Indians," November 4, 1848, Letters received by the Office of Indian Affairs, record group 75, microcopy 234, reel 418; Paul Strack quoted from *Three Rivers in Time*, video, written, produced, and directed by D. Neary, Three Rivers in Time, Inc., Fort Wayne, IN, 1994; Floyd Leonard and Joseph Leonard, "The Miami Nation: Nineteenth and Twentieth Centuries," *Native Americans and Early Settlers: The Meeting of Cultures, 1780's–1980's* (Celina, OH: Mercer County Historical Society, 1989), 7; Colerick quoted in Bert Griswold, *The Pictorial History of Fort Wayne, Indiana* (Chicago: Robert O. Law Co., 1917), 378.

40. Rose Carver, interview by J. W. Tyner, September 9, 1968, Special Collections, University of Oklahoma, Norman; Forest Olds, ethnographic interview by Peggy Dycus, May 17, 1969, Miami Tribal Library, Miami, OK.

41. Dawson quoted in Griswold, *Pictorial History*, 379.

42. Joseph Sinclair, Correspondence to William Medill, Commissioner of Indian Affairs, October 21 and November 1, 1846, Miami Tribe Library, Miami, OK.

43. Ibid.; Francis La Fontaine, Correspondence to unknown recipient, November 1, 1846, Allen County–Fort Wayne Historical Society, Fort Wayne, IN; Alexis Coquillard, Correspondence on the second Miami emigration to William Medill, Commissioner of Indian Affairs, May 18, 1847, Letters received by the Office of Indian Affairs, 1824–1881, record group 75, microcopy 234, reel 418, 39.

44. Alfred Vaughan, Emigration census taken at Osage sub-Agency to Thomas Harvey, November 12, 1846, Letters received by the Office of Indian Affairs, 1824–1881, record group 75, microcopy 234, reel 416; Col. William Comparet, Notarized report to the Miami sub-Agent, Osage sub-Agency to Joseph Sinclair, November 5, 1846, Letters received by the Office of Indian Affairs, 1824–1881, record group 75, microcopy 234, reel 418; Anonymous trader quoted in McCulloch, *Men and Measures*, 110; Anonymous author, "Indians," reprinted from the *St. Louis Republican* in the *Fort Wayne Sentinel*, November 7, 1846, Newspaper Collection, Allen County–Fort Wayne Historical Society, Fort Wayne.

45. McCulloch, *Men and Measures*, 110.

46. Toh-pe-ah, Con-cum-sey, Peh-she-wah, Me-za-quah, Pe-mah-is-to-mah, Anthony Rivarre, Cah-quaw-re-ah, O-zan-diah, Quah-kah-wah, Cor-ah-she-peh-nah, Seek, Wahpee-mung-quah, Mon-go-zah, Wah-tep-piah, Neh-pee-mon-zah, Lun-kee-cum-cum-wah, Rah-rah-mung-quah, Wah-cah-con-nan,

Wah-wiani-tah, Ni-con-zah, Wah-bah-peh-senan, Poh-kong-quah, Bandeah, Correspondence to President James Polk, November 26, 1846, Signed and Sealed in Council at the Miami Land Osage River Agency, Miami Tribe Library, Miami, OK.

47. Anson, *The Miami Indians*, 230; *H.R. Doc. 620*, 1848.

48. *H.R. Doc. 620*, 1848.

49. Joseph Sinclair, Correspondence to William Medill, Commissioner of Indian Affairs, October 14, 1846, Miami Tribe Library, Miami, OK; Alexis Coquillard, Correspondence, 1847.

50. Kappler, Article 2, Treaty of 1826, *IALT*.

51. Susan Sleeper-Smith, "Resistance to Removal: The 'White Indian,' Frances Slocum," in *Enduring Nations*, 109, 118.

52. Leonard and Leonard, "The Miami Nation," 7; Rosa Boington Beck, interview by Peggy Dycus, May 15, 1969, Miami Tribe Library, Miami, OK; Carver, interview, 1968.

53. Ross Lockridge, "History on the Mississinewa," *IMH* 30, no. 1 (1934): 55; Berry and Rinehart, "A Legacy of Forced Migration," 108; Lora Siders quoted from *Eagle Gone*, video, produced and narrated by W. Watson and T. Doran, Change Now Productions, Fort Wayne, IN.

54. Rafert, *The Miami Indians of Indiana*, 174; Bureau of Indian Affairs, *Summary*, 1990.

55. Melissa Rinehart, "Miami Indian Language Shift and Recovery," PhD dissertation (Michigan State University, 2006); Daryl Baldwin and David Costa, *Myaamia neehi peewaalia kaloosioni mahsinaakani: A Miami-Peoria Dictionary*, 1st ed. (Miami, OK: Miami Nation, 2005); Catherine Johnson, *Myaamiaki Piloohsaki Amahsinaakanemawe Iilaataweenki: A Miami Children's Language Curriculum* (Oxford, OH: Myaamia Project, 2003); Miami Tribe of Oklahoma, *Myaamia Iilaataweenki*, Audio Lesson 1, produced in collaboration with the Myaamia Project at Miami University and the Office of Cultural Preservation of the Miami Tribe of Oklahoma, 2002; Miami Nation of Indiana, *Myaamia Iilaataweenki*, interactive CD, version 2 (Peru, IN: Miami Nation of Indiana, 1999); Myaamia Project, "The Myaamia Project at Miami University: Research and Development," http://www.myaamiaproject .org/research.html, 2009; *Myaamiaki Eemamwiciki—Miami. Awakening*, video, produced by Upstream Productions, 41 min., 2008; Jeffrey Bartholet, "In an unprecedented wave of destruction, half of the world's languages will likely die off. Should we care?" *Newsweek International*, June 19, 2000; The Linguists, Public Broadcasting Station, "Reviving the Myaamia Language (Miami Language)," at http://www.pbs.org/thelinguists/For-Educators/Video -Extras.html#Reviving.

The Politics of Indian Removal on the Wyandot Reserve, 1817–1843

JAMES BUSS

In October 1831, James Gardiner, the United States Indian agent assigned to negotiate a removal treaty with the Wyandots of Ohio, accompanied William Walker Jr. and an expedition of Wyandot leaders to Cincinnati and watched them depart on a steamboat heading west. The Indian agent had met tribal leaders over the previous months at the "Grand Reserve"—a 150,000-acre reservation in the central part of the state that Gardiner desperately wanted to place in the hands of white settlers—and negotiated the skeletal works of a treaty. Although he was confident that a final agreement could be reached, the Wyandots demanded a concession. They wished that a delegation of Indians be permitted to visit their new home in the West before signing the document. Gardiner acquiesced and informed secretary of war Lewis Cass that the tribe had selected William Walker Jr.—whom he described as a "white man" and merchant—to lead the party. Before they left, the Indian agent entrusted Walker with a note for $1,000 to pay for expenses incurred during the travels.[1]

By the beginning of the next year, early rumors reached Gardiner that Walker and the exploring party were *highly pleased with the country assigned them.*" On January 4, 1832, Gardiner boasted to Secretary Cass, "I flatter myself that I shall be able in four or five weeks, to present you with a definitive treaty with this sagacious, intelligent and *crafty* tribe of Indians." He explained that Walker, whom he trusted as delegation leader, and the expedition were expected to arrive shortly. Although he admitted that Walker may have been "*one of the nation,*" Gardiner declared that "a more suitable person" could not be found. Despite the fact that Walker was one-quarter

Wyandot, Gardiner clearly identified him as white rather than Indian, going as far as describing the exploring party as consisting of "four of their men [Wyandots], and their white friend [Walker]." That same day, he informed Elbert Herring in the Office of Indian Affairs that "when notified of their arrival," he would immediately travel to the reservation and conclude the treaty for "final cessions of all the Wyandot lands in Ohio."[2]

Gardiner's excitement soon turned to despair and frustration. Within twenty-four hours of reporting that a treaty was imminent, Gardiner discovered that the Wyandot exploring party had already returned to their reservation and begun deliberating without him. Additionally, new sources in southern Ohio, who had spoken with the expedition on their trip back to the reserve, told him that the Wyandots were ready to abandon the idea of removal altogether. Despite telling people in St. Louis that they were pleased with the lands in the West, William Walker informed officials in Dayton, Ohio, that the Wyandots "were determined *not to cede*" their reservation.[3]

In an interesting twist, Gardiner quickly blamed the expedition's leader for his failures in finalizing the treaty. The agent protested to superiors and explained that Walker refused to take the delegation to the designated lands, and, in fact, he believed that they "*never saw the country* . . . and spent but one night in the woods." He claimed that Walker stood at the center of a ruse "matured at Upper Sandusky" the previous summer and designed to filch "from the Government the money for such a tour, and then making *just such a Report*." A day after claiming Walker suitable, and white enough, for the job, Gardiner changed his story. He told Lewis Cass that he had "discovered much discontent" among the Wyandots with the "persons chosen as Delegates." He directed his attack at William Walker, accusing him of distributing letters to important Ohio politicians that "spoke in contemptuous and sarcastic terms of the '*Indian Paradise*.'" Gardiner insisted that "all the emigrating tribes had been '*most shamefully imposed upon*.'" He also claimed that Walker, despite previous promises, failed to alert him first of the delegation's findings. "Whites [Methodist missionaries] and partly whites [now speaking of Walker]," Gardiner believed, had concocted the entire charade, because they were "the only gainers by [the Wyandots'] continued residence in Ohio."[4] The entire situation must have been embarrassing for a man who previously declared his trust in the suitable "white man," only to discover that the mixed-raced delegate turned the exploring party and the Wyandots against him. The Wyandots would remain in Ohio for another decade before moving west.

William Walker's thwarting of removal efforts through the role of the exploring party was more than the story of a mixed-race Wyandot taking advantage of a gullible American agent. His ability to shape Wyandot strategies aimed at stopping removal reflected the influence of outside voices from before the War of 1812, and changes in tribal leadership that followed it. Although divisions between Wyandot leaders carried over from the years before the war into the decades that followed, the three years of violence and bloodshed had upset the organization of tribal governance and created opportunities for cultural go-betweens, like Walker, who could broker agreements between whites and Wyandots, to capture positions of power within the nation. Walker's understanding of Wyandot and American diplomacy derived from his experience as a member of the Wyandot Nation and lessons learned from his white and Wyandot parents, who emerged before the War of 1812 as influential voices among the Wyandot community. In important ways, Walker represented both the continuation of Wyandot strategies that predated the war and new approaches that resulted from postwar reconfigurations of the Wyandot Nation.

Historians in the past few decades have done much to remind us that Native peoples were active agents in the history of North America, but this has not been typically true for the treatment of the period between the end of the War of 1812 and the "Removal Era" of the 1830s and 1840s.[5] Even Richard White's seminal work *The Middle Ground: Indians, Empires, and Republics in the Great Lakes Region, 1650–1815* ends with a foreboding message for Native peoples in the Great Lakes in the postwar period. "The middle ground itself withered and died," he concluded. "The Americans arrived and dictated."[6] Great Lakes historians often follow this direction and skip ahead to Removal, glossing over the years between the War of 1812 and the 1830s. But, such selective hindsight overlooks the role of Native peoples in shaping their relationships with Americans in those years. It also underplays the connections between pre- and postwar years by ignoring centuries of contact between Native peoples and Euro-Americans, which influenced Wyandot strategies during the Removal Era. More recent studies of individual indigenous communities in the former Old Northwest have begun to shatter the former notion that Native peoples simply and quietly moved west in the wake of American advancement.[7] The story of the Wyandots in Ohio is but one of many stories where Native communities employed ingenious strategies of persistence and survival, and demonstrated a keen awareness of the changing worlds around them.

The Grand Reserve, which Gardiner wanted and Walker fought to protect, was not the ancestral homeland of the Wyandots. For nearly three centuries, the Wyandots had been a people on the move; their migration, from the eastern Great Lakes across Canada and then to Ohio, had fractured the tribe both politically and geographically. Before the War of 1812, Wyandot communities dotted the landscape from Detroit to modern-day central Ohio. In those years, most Wyandot leaders viewed Americans as the least likely of allies. As late as the 1790s, Wyandot leaders had almost unanimously resisted an American presence in the Lower Great Lakes. In 1794, Principal Chief Tarhe helped lead Wyandot warriors in defending the region from American intruders during the Battle of Fallen Timbers. After this victory, however, Tarhe's attitude toward Americans changed, as shifting imperial hands in the Lower Great Lakes made opposition to American queries for an alliance more difficult. The following summer, at negotiations for the Treaty of Greenville, Chief Tarhe spoke on behalf of the Wyandots, Delawares, and Shawnees, informing American general Anthony Wayne that the tribes would agree to ally themselves with the Americans. He believed that the United States would act as a father to the gathered tribes, granting them protection from harm and respecting tribal boundaries. On one hand, he instructed other Indian leaders to "be obedient" to their new father, while on the other hand, he warned Wayne that he should "take care" of all his "little ones" and be careful not to "shew [*sic*] favor to one, to the injury of any."[8]

Poor conditions among the Wyandot villages may have convinced Wyandot leaders, like Tarhe, that they needed help beyond what government agents were willing to promise or able to provide. Shortly after signing the treaty, Tarhe led a campaign to accommodate other Americans, as he openly welcomed Quaker missionaries into his Wyandot community and, when that failed, asked Presbyterians to open a mission. In 1798, Quaker missionaries visited the Wyandot "national council" and witnessed the failure of government agents in "taking care" of their Wyandot children following the treaty. When they arrived in Wyandot country, the missionaries witnessed the deleterious effect of alcohol on the Wyandot Nation. Drunken and mostly naked Indians greeted them with outstretched arms, bearing open bottles of whiskey and rum. Indians who had gathered "about the chief's house . . . were fighting, and nearly all were engaged in some excess or violence." The missionaries were especially startled by instances where "two, and sometimes three, were mounted on a single horse, riding at full speed, and apparently without any object, in every direction—the one behind carrying a bottle of rum, and the one before, endeavouring to guide the horse." When the missionaries approached the Wyandot families for food, they found that among the more than two hundred Wyandot families living in central Ohio, none could provide them with "a single morsel of meat."[9] Still, individual clan leaders did not always agree about whom the Wyandot should trust and allow into their villages.

The Wyandot Nation had once consisted of at least twelve clans, but Quaker missionaries recognized only seven when they visited the Wyandot "national council" in 1798. There, they discovered a fractured system of governance, where matters "merely regard[ing] a town or family" were "settled by the chief and principal men of the town," while larger matters that concerned the entire Wyandot Nation were "deliberated on and determined in a national council, composed of the different tribes, attended by the head warriors and chiefs of the towns."[10] Subsequent missionaries recognized additional clan affiliations (perhaps ten or eleven), but by the end of the War of 1812, only seven clans were represented at tribal councils.[11] Differing clan and village affiliations produced a variety of opinions about how the Wyandot Nation should handle outsiders, including missionaries.

Additionally, centuries of interaction with Europeans and decades of warfare between Englishmen and Americans had significantly changed the composition of the Wyandot nation, leading to the scattered and diverse Wyandot villages that dotted the Lower Great Lakes' landscape by the nineteenth century. Sexual relationships between French traders and Wyandot women had produced a growing number of mixed-race children, and warfare with Americans, coupled with the inclusion of white captives in the nation, meant that a sizable number of outsiders had been integrated within the tribe. Moreover, marriages between the individuals described above led to a generation of younger Wyandot members who had tenuous biological, but deep kinship and clan-affiliated, ties to the community itself. By the War of 1812, an impressive number of Wyandots on the Grand Reserve could trace their ancestry to an entangled web of French, Wyandot, Delaware, English, German, and American parents and grandparents.[12]

Some Wyandot leaders openly refused aid from American missionaries and agents, creating divisions among Wyandot leaders that eventually led to conflict and violence. In 1806, younger tribal members, seeking to separate themselves from leaders who openly welcomed American missionaries and agents, like Tarhe, invited the Shawnee prophet Tenskawatawa to conduct a witch-hunt among their villages. As principal chief, Tarhe was forced to defend four Wyandot women accused of witchcraft, ultimately saving them from execution, but the event created deeper divisions between pro-American and anti-American Wyandot factions. In 1810, a cohort of Wyandot leaders led by War Chief Roundhead, defied Tarhe and delivered the calumet to Tenskawatawa at Prophetstown, announcing their allegiance to the "Shawnee Prophet" and his British allies. Tarhe responded by replacing

Roundhead as war chief, but the move merely led to more tension among Wyandot communities. This time, Wyandots living near Lower Sandusky executed two Wyandot women accused of witchcraft, while Roundhead's followers near Columbus, Ohio, executed Wyandot chief Leatherlips for refusing to join the Prophet's cause.[13]

Other Wyandot chiefs, like Tarhe and Between-the-Logs, welcomed indigenous visionaries from the East. In 1806, and again in 1808, several Wyandot communities welcomed the Seneca prophet Handsome Lake to their villages. He preached a revivalist message of returning to indigenous spiritual and cultural customs, and also promoted the acceptance of white agriculture, education, and living conditions as a means of securing Wyandot autonomy. In the years that followed, Tarhe, Between-the-Logs, and others joined Native leaders such as Blackhoof and his Shawnee faction in welcoming white missionaries and government agents onto their lands in central and north-central Ohio. In exchange for goods and guidance, these leaders pledged neutrality in conflicts between the British and Americans in the West.[14]

A few Wyandot villages near Detroit, who tried to remain neutral during the war, were unable to dodge feuding British and American armies. British officials forced William Walker Sr. and his family to move from Brownstown (south of Detroit) to Canada. As they left, the British burned their home and confiscated their possessions. While some of the Wyandots living near Detroit joined the Prophet, others, like Walker, declared themselves captives of the enemy. William Walker Jr. may have been present and accompanied his father to Canada; he was eleven or twelve years old at the time and only recently had returned to Brownstown with his brothers after attending a Christian mission school near Lower Sandusky.[15]

The aftermath of the War of 1812 colored the Wyandot experience in the Lower Great Lakes, as Wyandot leaders faced the daunting task of trying to maintain tribal autonomy amid increasing pressures of Americans to assimilate or perish. At a second treaty council held at Greenville near the end of the war, Brownstown chief Ronioness, who had previously fought alongside the British, agreed to join the Americans. Tarhe followed by presenting American General William Henry Harrison with two British medals presented to him years earlier to mark an alliance between the British and the Wyandots. He struck the medals with a large knife, symbolizing an end to his allegiance with Britain.[16] Tarhe's actions and the political realities of the postwar West forced a sizable number of Wyandots to accept or reconfirm an alliance with the Americans. Again, individual Wyandot leaders disagreed about what that alliance would look like.

Amid that backdrop, John Stewart (a mulatto and self-trained Methodist preacher) arrived at the doorstep of William Walker Sr., newly appointed United States Indian subagent and interpreter for the Wyandot villages around Upper Sandusky. Stewart hoped to covert the Wyandots to Christianity. Walker suspected that Stewart was a runaway slave, so he initially refused to interpret his message to the Wyandots, instead directing him to the door of Jonathon Pointer (a former slave and captive of the Wyandots who had joined the nation). Pointer tried to dissuade Stewart from preaching, arguing that "many great and learned white men had been there before him, and used all their power, but could accomplish nothing." Nonetheless, he agreed to interpret. White traders, who "wanted to continue profiting from liquor trade to the Wyandot," tried to convince tribal members that "as he was a colored man, the whites would not have him preach for *them*, although they considered him good enough to teach *Indians*; and that it was a degradation to the nation to have a colored man for their preacher." For their part, members of the Wyandot Nation who were open to conversion appeared to worry little about Stewart's race.[17]

Wyandot leaders, who had followed the Shawnee Prophet before the war, were especially unwilling to open the Wyandot Nation to the influence of missionaries, but they were not alone. Catholic converts were also reluctant to grant access to Methodist missionaries. Jesuit priests had been working to convert the Wyandots for over a century, most recently when communities of Wyandots had resided near Detroit. Although French priests had largely abandoned them in the previous decades, Stewart found Catholic Wyandots some of the hardest to convert.[18] They refused to cease prayers to the Virgin Mother, abandon their rosaries, and forgo participation in syncretic Catholic and indigenous ceremonies that he attributed to hard-to-break pagan practices.[19] Stewart's arrival exposed tensions between leaders who had long debated the level of access that outsiders should be granted among Wyandot villages.

In 1816, the year that Stewart arrived at the home of William Walker, the Wyandots experienced two losses: the deaths of Chief Roundhead and Principal Chief Tarhe. The deaths signaled a shift in tribal governance, as it opened opportunities for the voices of younger leaders to emerge. Still, these younger voices continued to reflect older, often conflicting ideas about the relationship between the Wyandot Nation and Americans. Over the course of the following few years, the reaction of Wyandot leaders to American agents and missionaries often resonated with the influence of older leaders (a few of whom still participated in tribal governance) and indigenous prophets from before the War of 1812.

Stewart, along with Jonathon Pointer as his interpreter, spent most of 1816 and early 1817 preaching to a growing congregation of Wyandot followers. In early 1817 he temporarily left the Wyandots to visit family in Tennessee, and when he returned, he found renewed opposition to conversion. Two prominent chiefs, Two-Logs and Mononcue, argued in his absence that the Great Spirit would abandon the Wyandots if they "forsook him" by following Stewart.[20] Wyandot Nation member John Hicks contended, "We are willing to receive good advice from you, but we are not willing to have the customs and institutions which have been kept sacred by our Fathers, thus assailed and abused."[21] Still, Mononcue confided in Hicks: "I have some notion of giving up some of my Indian customs; but I can not agree to quit painting my face. This would be wrong, as it would jeopardy [*sic*] my health." Throughout the summer of 1817, Wyandot leaders appeared to reject Stewart's message, as they hosted dances, partook in feasts, raced horses, and participated in games of chance.[22]

Moreover, in his absence, white traders regained influence among the Wyandots and renewed the sale of alcohol, resulting in one prominent Wyandot young man being "killed in a drunken frolic."[23] Decades of trade with Americans before the war, and a military alliance with them during it, had allowed Indian traders to gain incredible influence among the Wyandot community. In Stewart's absence, white traders again tried to convince Wyandot leaders that Stewart could not help them, as he was a black man, marginalized by the white American community.[24] Despite the influence of (and perhaps as a reaction to) white traders, some Wyandot followers welcomed Stewart back. William Walker Sr., Mononcue, Between-the-Logs, and John Hicks eventually changed their minds and embraced Stewart's message. They may have viewed missionaries, and the expectation of more missionaries to come, as a more promising alternative to alcohol-peddling traders. Walker and his wife, Catherine Rankin, played a pivotal role in encouraging Wyandot leaders to welcome Stewart back. William Walker Sr., who initially was hesitant to introduce Stewart to the Wyandot Nation, now told them "that he believed Steward [*sic*] was a good man, and if licensed and encouraged would be a blessing to the nation."[25]

In order to combat intrusions onto Wyandot lands and consolidate tribal power in Ohio, the Wyandots adopted additional strategies. In the autumn of 1817, Wyandot leaders (along with other tribes) met with American officials at the rapids of the Maumee River (near modern-day Toledo, Ohio). Together they agreed to cede title to more than three million acres in northwest Ohio in exchange for an annuity of $4,000, a twelve-square-mile reserve (the Grand Reserve), and a nearby one-square-mile tract that included a cranberry bog. Wyandot leaders sought to consolidate power and landholdings at the Grand Reserve—centered at the pro-American villages during the late war—in an attempt to maintain tribal autonomy and prevent further cessions. Although they could not grant men like William Walker Sr. land, as they refused to recognize him as a member of the Wyandot Nation, American officials granted an individual plot to Catherine Rankin on the edge of the reserve for the Walkers to live on.[26] The consolidation of lands established boundaries that could then be regulated by the tribal council, who would determine who would be granted access to the larger community. Additionally, American officials agreed to appoint a government agent to the Wyandot reserve, to oversee the construction of a sawmill and gristmill, and to employ a blacksmith for the tribe.[27]

Government promises were not fulfilled quickly and may have further convinced Wyandot leaders to gamble on missionary assurances for aid, supplies, and an alternative to the destructive practices of Indian traders. Following the Treaty of 1817 and another in 1818, American officials failed to appoint a government agent to supervise the improvements guaranteed in the treaties. Nearby Indian agent John Johnston attempted to coordinate the building of a mill and blacksmith shop, but failing health and distance between his location in Piqua and the Grand Reserve retarded progress.[28] Construction of buildings occurred slowly, if at all. Indian agent John Shaw, appointed to the Grand Reserve, did not arrive until the end of 1820. And when he did, he listened to Wyandot tribal leaders complain of whites who trespassed on Indian lands and stole their animals; Shaw also found that whiskey was flowing onto the reservation. On one hand, the early converts may have questioned their decision to welcome outsiders onto the reservation. But on the other hand, they needed Indian agents and white missionaries if they were to be successful in reaching their greater goal of economic and political autonomy.[29]

The group of early converts, including Walker Sr., Between-the-Logs, Mononcue, and John Hicks, viewed their conversion and the role of missionaries on the Grand Reserve as part of a larger strategy of acculturation that, they hoped, would temper pressures by Americans to relinquish more of their lands, and curb the negative influence of traders.[30] Scholars have often highlighted the eagerness of Methodists in expanding their influence in the region, but few have sought to understand why Wyandot leaders welcomed Stewart back after rejecting him.[31] In doing so, the Wyandot leaders who were open to the idea of a mission on the Grand Reserve may have reflected a strategy from an earlier time.

When he visited them in 1806, the Seneca prophet Handsome Lake had warned the Wyandot of impending doom. "Judgments [were] coming on the nations," he told them, "unless they reform."[32] He outlined what this reform should look like; it centered on a "social gospel" that included temperance, social unity, "good feelings toward whites," preservation of a tribal land base, an acculturation policy that emphasized education, and domestic morality. Between-the-Logs, who advocated for the Methodist mission, had embraced Handsome Lake's message in the prewar years and even traveled from Sandusky to New York to invite the Seneca prophet back to Ohio.[33] Handsome Lake's earlier message of openness toward Anglo education and temperance resonated in the newer call for a mission among the Wyandots.

By 1818, Mononcue, Between-the-Logs, and John Hicks vigorously defended Stewart against the attacks of other Wyandot chiefs.[34] Mononcue and Between-the-Logs had been particularly drawn to the Methodist call for temperance. After witnessing the devastating consequence of alcohol introduced by Indian traders who had denounced Stewart, Mononcue concluded that he could "compare whiskey to nothing but the devil; for it brings with it all kinds of evil."[35] Between-the-Logs connected the Methodist missionary's message of redemption to his personal struggle with alcohol; years earlier he had murdered his wife while intoxicated.[36] He used his personal travails to entice other Wyandots to convert to Methodism and join the mission.[37] By 1818, Between-the-Logs became convinced that Stewart offered a road toward salvation, and more importantly, redemption from his personal demons.

John Hicks's conversion offers insights into other reasons why Wyandot leaders might have followed Stewart. The son of German parents, Hicks had been taken captive at a young age and adopted by the Wyandots. With no biological connections to the Wyandot Nation, and two teenage children who had already adopted Anglo names, Hicks may have seen the presence of the Methodist missionary as an opportunity for his sons, Francis and John Jr., to gain an Anglo education. Less than a year after denouncing Stewart, but only a few months after affixing his names to the second of two cession treaties, John Hicks joined Between-the-Logs, Mononcue, Stewart, and William Walker Sr. in attending the Methodist Quarterly Meeting in nearby Urbana, Ohio. They asked that Stewart be licensed to open a mission on the Grand Reserve; Methodist officials responded by agreeing to expand the size and scope of its missionary efforts.[38]

In February 1819, help arrived on the Grand Reserve by way of additional missionaries. Methodist leaders sent Reverend Moses Henkle to aid Stewart. The Wyandot congregation grew slowly over the first year, but

Henkle and Stewart already were outlining their plans for expanding the mission. They told their new converts that they needed to construct a meeting house "to worship in, and let no foolish feasting & dancing be done in it." The Methodist leaders saw an extirpation of Wyandot rituals as central to their purpose, but Wyandot converts asked for something else; they wanted a school and teachers. The Methodists delayed sending a teacher, however, claiming that they had "no good Master ready" and did not want "a bad man to teach" the children of the Wyandots. Still, the role of education clearly remained on the minds of those Wyandots who were willing to welcome Stewart and Henkle on the condition that they provide suitable educational opportunities for Wyandot children.[39] Help came soon enough.

Reverend James Finley arrived at the reserve in 1821, and his arrival marked a significant turning point for the Methodist mission and the relationship of the Wyandot Nation with the United States government. Finley had watched the mission's progress since 1819, when he took over as head of the Methodist district that oversaw the area where the Grand Reserve was located. After witnessing the failures of both government agents and previous missionaries to erect buildings and open a school, he decided to move to the reserve to play a more direct role in shaping the mission.

Within six years of John Stewart's arrival, and a year after Finley appeared at the reserve, the Methodist mission had expanded to include a mission house, mills, a blacksmith shop, and a small schoolhouse. One of Finley's first decisions involved assigning the young William Walker Jr. to teach at the school. The new minister recognized Walker as a person "who belonged to the nation, and could speak the language."[40] William Walker Jr. followed the examples of his father and mother by promoting Methodism and the aims of the mission. Moreover, his ties to the Methodist church initiated a long friendship with Reverend Finley, especially after 1823, when William Walker Sr. died. William and his brother Isaac became trusted confidants of Finley, as they emerged as important cultural mediators between the mission and federal agents.[41]

Wyandot aims for economic and political autonomy were reflected in Methodist goals for the mission. Methodist missionary Charles Elliott (who replaced Finley for one year in 1822) believed that Wyandot children should be taught to "become industrious farmers, good citizens, intelligent men, tender parents, affectionate husbands, and obedient children." The same year, Finley echoed Elliot's sentiments in an article he penned for *Methodist Magazine.* "I want to grasp all the children," he wrote, "and learn the girls to knit, spin, weave and the art of housewifery; and the boys agriculture; and all of them to read the Holy Scripture."[42] Throughout the

1820s, white settlers pushed in from all sides of the Grand Reserve, but, unlike most white settlers, Methodist missionaries who carried Bibles also brought much-needed cash, supplies, and educational opportunities for the Wyandots. Money led to improvements, improvements led to greater sustainability, and with sustainability came the promise of autonomy. For some Wyandot leaders, the missionaries offered an avenue toward persistence and survival in the region.

Initially, American officials agreed and hoped that missionaries would succeed in converting Native peoples into Christians and Americans; but by the late 1820s, impatient government agents believed that mission schools fell short of turning the Wyandots into acceptable American citizens— something the Wyandots probably never wanted or expected.[43] Years before Andrew Jackson signed the Indian Removal Act, politicians and land-hungry white settlers pushed for the dispossession of Ohio's Native populations. Despite pressure from government agents, Methodist missionaries at the Wyandot reservation tried to ward off removal, in constant fear that they might forgo the progress already made in "civilizing" and converting the Indians. During his early years at the mission, Finley served as both superintendent to the missionary and subagent for Indian affairs. But eventually, religious and government interests clashed, and as early as 1825, Finley complained that the greatest threat to his work was removal. "This moving plan about Indians," he wrote a friend, "has retarded our work much."[44] The Michigan territorial governor and superintendent of Indian Affairs in charge of the Wyandots, Lewis Cass, tried to calm Finley. "The law providing for holding treaties with the Indians, with a view to their removal west . .,. has not passed," Cass told him. "And should it pass, there is nothing compulsory on the Indians. . . . A very few years longer of improvement would place the Wyandots in a situation, for which no one would wish them removed."[45] Secretary of war Thomas McKenney likewise assured Finley that "no steps will be taken to *compel* the Indians to emigrate." But, he warned that the "future happiness and prosperity" of the Wyandots depended on them "having a country of their own" in the West, and instructed Finley to "suspend any extensive improvements" at the mission.[46]

The message of government officials—proceed as normal, but anticipate removal—weighed on the young minister. As mission superintendent, Finley resisted removal as detrimental to his campaign of "civilizing" the Indians. As government agent, he was instructed to consider the interests of both Christian and non-Christian Wyandots—the non-Christian members of the nation increasingly pushing for removal. Eventually, the contradictions of holding both offices led to his dismissal from the government post. In 1825, William Walker Jr.'s brother Isaac (a government-appointed interpreter) complained that the positions stretched Finley too far. Cass responded by appointing his own brother, Charles, to act as subagent.[47]

Finley plodded ahead, voicing his concerns to leaders of the Methodist church and to William Walker Jr. Shortly after the mission undertook the policy of placing Indian children in white homes, Finley wrote a friend: "Enemies have raised up against us supposing that the Methodist and Mission Establishment will prevent the Wyandots from selling their land." Finley's concerns revealed the ways that outsiders linked the missions to the resistance against Indian Removal. In the eyes of pro-removal advocates, Finley, the mission, and men like Walker were part of a larger problem whereby religious authorities chose Indian converts over the advancement of white progress.[48] In the years immediately preceding removal, as white authorities and a growing portion of the American public became increasingly skeptical that religious missionary work could "save" the Indian, a group of Wyandot leaders became increasingly convinced that the missionaries were their only hope of continued autonomy in Ohio.

William Walker Jr. viewed the mission's work as synonymous with the physical and economic improvement of the Grand Reserve, with hopes that economic progress might prevent further American pressures to remove. Yet, he grew increasingly skeptical that this was possible by merely displaying outward signs of improvement; it required a special political tact. His skepticism had been shaped by his knowledge of earlier divisions within the Wyandot community, his parents' role in welcoming and promoting the missionaries at the Grand Reserve, and his personal friendship with Reverend Finley. They each provided him additional insights into the future direction of American Indian policy and how the Wyandots might want to negotiate the highly corrosive world of Indian Removal politics.

Reverend James Finley cited Walker as a success story for the Methodist missionaries. Finley argued that the Wyandots' "approximation to the Whites is Much more than that of any other People of the Forrests they are very Much Mixed with the americans . . . . Many of the Principal families that compose this tribe are the forewith [*sic*] one half or one quarter white and have numerous white relatives living in the state." He believed that Walker represented a portion of the Wyandot Nation who, regardless of race, should be considered American citizens. The reverend concluded that "the approximation of the Wyandot to their white neighbors was 'perhaps the Reason' they were so rapidly mixing." He had "no doubt" that they would "continue to mix until . . . swallowed up" by the white population. After which, they would become full citizens.[49]

William Walker Jr.'s decisions in the Removal Era reflected the increased influence of mixed-race members of the Wyandot Nation, and the political restructuring within the nation that allowed this to happen. Changes within Wyandot tribal governance aided leaders, like Walker, who endorsed the aims of the mission and rejected calls for removal. The Wyandots living at the Grand Reserve represented a mere fraction of the nation that had initially migrated to the Lower Great Lakes, and by the late 1820s, at least two of the clans were so much reduced that they failed to send a chief to the tribal council. As early as the 1790s, tribal leaders had to cope with the devastating consequences of war with the Americans, as the loss of a significant number of warriors from the Deer clan (from which principal chiefs were selected) warranted a tribal-council decision to choose future leaders from the Porcupine clan. Numerous marriages between female members of the Wyandot community and Euro-Americans, coupled with the loss of warriors and older chiefs, had elevated a growing number of mixed-race children, like Walker, to positions of power.[50]

After Chief Deunquot died in 1826, clan leaders hostile to the mission appointed the unconverted leader Warpole to act as interim principal chief. To their surprise, he proclaimed his conversion to Methodism and an alliance with the mission. Clans friendly to the Methodist missionaries delayed the permanent election until they could garner enough support to change the method by which the principal chief and his counselors were chosen. They removed hereditary requirements and, instead, agreed to hold a yearly popular election.[51]

In the early years of the mission, tribal leaders who opposed religious conversion found it difficult to reject outright physical improvements. In 1821, Pagan Chief Deunquot signed a petition authorizing the construction of a mission school at Upper Sandusky; in 1825, Chief Warpole, who initially opposed conversion, signed a petition to have Finley acquire 70,000 bricks to be used in the construction of buildings for the mission; and in 1826, Chief Ronioness, who had fought alongside the British in the War of 1812, signed a certificate complimenting Finley on his work and assigning the Methodist missionary a Wyandot name. But, despite bringing much-needed supplies and improved economic conditions to the Grand Reserve, the presence of the missionaries eventually tore the Wyandot Nation in two. Many Wyandots, including some tribal leaders, aggressively opposed Christian conversion and increasingly viewed the missionaries' goals as synonymous with those of the United States government. Moreover, Wyandot leaders witnessed bickering between American agents and missionaries throughout the 1820s, as Indian agents and subagents battled over the political and economic gains of overseeing the "Grand Reserve." In the minds of some Wyandot leaders, missionaries—including Finley—became (perhaps disingenuously) associated with a growing web of American lies and deceit. The division of the Wyandots also presented a problem for Walker, who attempted to appeal to both Christian and non-Christian Indians in resisting dispossession. By supporting the mission, Walker hoped to ensure economic support from Methodist donors and government coffers, but he also guaranteed that he would draw the ire of those who opposed the religious aims of the missionaries.[52]

Under mounting pressures to remove, the missionaries stressed the need of Wyandot community members to both convert and welcome physical changes on the reserve. Finley and Walker believed that the extirpation of indigenous spiritual practices was necessary in guaranteeing conversion and, hence, making improvements on the reserve. In 1824, when Finley fell ill and had to leave the mission, a group of Wyandots held "a great dance—and a great *Wabanow.*" Walker, who remained at the reserve and reported this all to Finley, could only assume that the leaders used the dance as a move to gain popularity and political stature among the unconverted, thereby supplanting individuals like himself who held positions of power. When he returned, Finley and Charles Elliott, the missionary who temporarily took his place, moved (with Walker's aid) to end indigenous ceremonialism. Walker preached to the unconverted and emphasized the need for them to join the mission, but he also worked to conceal his role in reporting the incident to the missionaries, instructing Finley to "let no person" see the original letter.[53] Walker understood that political and religious divisions were often linked in the minds of Wyandot chiefs, as two distinct groups of political leaders emerged on the Grand Reserve—the "Pagan Party" and the Christian converts. He believed he could promote the physical progress of the mission while concealing his heavy-handed role in the extirpation campaign.

A reexamination of the events that open this article reveals how William Walker used his knowledge of both American and Wyandot diplomacy to employ a coherent strategy for delaying removal: posing as a pro-removal advocate. Gardiner may have been right; Walker never planned on allowing the Wyandots to trade the reserve for lands in the West. Far from embracing the idea of removal, Walker keenly identified impassioned American pleas for the Wyandots to remove as the thinly veiled desires of land-hungry whites and manipulative government agents. The most damning evidence that the exploring party and Walker never intended on moving west can be found in the correspondence between Walker and Finley that preceded the expedition. On May 21, 1831 (months before Gardiner identified Walker as a helpful ally in convincing the Wyandots to remove), an irritated William Walker scrawled an angry letter to his friend James Finley: "Bribes are in tow—corruption will be introduced to the utmost extent," he warned. He told the minister that he believed Gardiner was "characterized by true Jackson tyranny and corruption with all its blasting effects," whose actions revealed "all the skill, chicanery, and adroitness of a well trained diplomat." He mourned that "the long looked for storm, which has been gathering and thickening over our devoted heads, is now commencing its ravages on our nation."[54]

As the treaty negotiations came to an end in October 1831, Walker prodded Wyandot leaders to demand that an exploring party be allowed to examine the lands where they were to move. The strategy of deploying an expedition to appease American agents may have manifested in Walker's mind years earlier. In 1826, Indian agent John Johnston penned a letter to Wyandot leaders at the Grand Reserve informing them that the secretary of war had authorized him to fit exploring parties to examine lands in the West, in the hopes that Ohio's Indians would remove voluntarily.[55] Walker wrote to Finley at the time, mocking Johnston's letter. "Oh ye fugitive sons of the forest," he imagined Johnston saying, "where can ye find an abiding place to rest your wearied limbs and sing the songs of your father in peace! Unhappy people! Never will the white man yield till the Pacific Ocean drinks of your blood."[56] The Wyandots passed at the opportunity, as Finley defended the mission to his superiors and received assurances from men like Cass that progress at the mission might ensure their continued residence in the state. A few months earlier, Cass had written Finley and promised, "If your Indians continue to improve as they have done, and manifest a wish to adopt the opinions and institutions of the whites, no power will compel them to remove."[57]

When Gardiner arrived to negotiate a removal treaty, Walker vowed to Finley that he would defend the Grand Reserve and mission; but he did so clandestinely. Outwardly, he must have presented himself as open to removal, as Gardiner declared confidence in Walker as a suitable person for leading the exploration party, and announced to superiors the inevitability of a finalized removal treaty. But, in private correspondence with Finley, Walker never wavered in his devotion to preserving the mission. Instead, he worried that he would fall victim to an angry American government once his hand in thwarting the removal treaty was revealed. He posited that if he and Finley stood in the way of the federal government's removal efforts, the President would take measures simply to "remove the obstacle"—referring to both him and the mission. Moreover, Walker believed that he was personally "to be sacrificed," since he refused to "be made to subservor [*sic*] to the unhallowed purposes of the '*reign of terror.*'"[58] Certainly, Gardiner was upset with Walker's seemingly changed heart, but many Wyandot leaders—especially converts associated with the mission—later voiced their approval of Walker's efforts through actions of their own.

The changes in political leadership aided the Wyandots in challenging American hegemony and removal efforts throughout the 1830s. As early as 1830, Finley's longtime ally (and Walker's former boss) Lewis Cass came out in support of removal; he believed that the Wyandots could not hold onto their reservation as whites moved in from all sides of the Grand Reserve, a situation that he claimed would bring "destruction upon the Indians." In 1832, Wyandots at the nearby reservation at Big Springs sold their land and joined their brethren at Upper Sandusky. Two years later, pressure mounted as the Ohio state legislature passed a resolution calling for the removal of the Wyandots, and Indian agents returned to the Wyandot reservation to initiate the drafting of another removal treaty.[59] Ohio Governor Robert Lucas traveled to the reserve and authorized another exploring party to travel west and scout lands for their potential removal. Although William Walker did not accompany the expedition westward, he served as interpreter between Lucas and the chiefs, at times interrupting the Wyandot leaders and inserting his own opinion. Lucas discovered that the Wyandot leadership, with Walker's involvement, had passed a law forbidding "any discussion among individuals of the tribe relative to the sale of their lands, under a severe penalty."[60] The law represented the consolidation of power within the hands of chiefs friendly to the aims of the mission and opposed to removal; it also highlights the strategy employed by Walker and his allies of consolidating power on the Grand Reserve and promoting economic improvement, in order to ensure national Wyandot autonomy rather than the previous system of village autonomy. Again, the negotiations resulted in the Wyandots disapproving of the lands in the West, with Walker standing at the center of the anti-removal movement.

In 1836, Christian converts used the new system of popular tribal elections to endorse the political aims of Walker by electing him principal chief. As chief, Walker seemingly switched strategies as he approached government agents with a plan to sell part of the Wyandot land holdings, in spite of the tribal law he endorsed. Robert Lucas, willing to accept any indication that the Wyandots might leave, agreed to purchase sixty sections on the outskirts of the Grand Reserve. Some Indians and whites may have viewed the maneuver as hypocritical, or believed Walker had finally joined the cause of the non-Christian Wyandots, but the sale should not be read as a prelude to removal. Walker sold the land to raise money for additional improvements on the reserve, in hopes of raising desperately needed money to preserve the reserve. In 1834 and 1835, the Wyandot mission had witnessed a series of serious setbacks. Flooding in the previous years had decimated crops in the fields and "destroyed some of the Reserve." The corn crop had been "nearly exhausted" after feeding the hogs, and the supply of oats virtually used up to feed horses and other "stock hogs." Profits from the sale of the five-mile-wide strip of land on the eastern edge of the reserve helped finance the rebuilding of mills, roads, schools, and "other public objects for the improvement" of the reservation.[61] Walker probably hoped that the proceeds could be used to strengthen the mission and ensure its continued existence, but further setbacks and reprehensible government actions thwarted Walker's efforts.

The federal government had discovered that the fracture between the Christian and non-Christian parties of the Wyandots provided an opportunity to remove half the Wyandots from the Grand Reserve, as rumors circulated that the so-called "Pagan Party" wished to leave. In essence, they planned to circumvent Walker and the mission-friendly Wyandots in favor of the Pagan Party. Less than a year after ceding the cranberry bog to the federal government, Walker dejectedly wrote his friend James Finley, who had left the mission years earlier for health reasons, "I could wish, if wishing do any good, . . . give you a flattering account of the condition of the Mission." Throughout the 1830s, the federal government cut finances to the mission, and white supporters, equating the possibility of removal to the futility of the mission, sent fewer and fewer supplies. Moreover, new missionaries held less power than their predecessor, James Finley. Walker glumly noted that the mission, along with its new missionaries, now looked "like a den of robbers and land pirates, haunted by owls, cormorants and satyrs." Walker bemoaned its "most deplorable condition." He reported that since government funding for the mission had dwindled, the Wyandots lived in horrid conditions, with "no bedding, no clothes, and as dirty as Swine."[62] The federal government immediately looked to take advantage of the situation.

Indian commissioners visited the Grand Reserve, persuading whoever would sign a removal treaty to do so. They held no councils. Instead, they either organized meetings with smaller groups of individuals or families, plying some of them with alcohol in return for their signatures, or, according to Walker, left the treaty at the local tavern and allowed "straggling Wyandott" to sign it as they passed through—"signing the treaty was then made the price of a glass of grog!" "They happen to be bloody bent in breaking up the nation," Walker wrote, "but we shall continue inch by inch, and rather than yield, 'perish in the last ditch.'"[63]

In 1838 Congressmen William Hunter and N. H. Swayne were appointed government agents in charge of pushing the Wyandots to remove. Hunter hoped that the approval of Christian Wyandots would expedite the removal process, even while non-Christian Wyandot leaders traveled to Washington in hopes of negotiating their own removal treaty.[64] Treaty talks occurred sporadically over the next year. Hunter, who lost his seat in Congress, nonetheless assumed the position of special Indian commissioner and returned to the reservation to pursue removal. In 1839, the Wyandots, again led by the advice of Walker, asked permission to send an exploring party westward before signing a treaty; the commissioner of Indian Affairs again acquiesced. William Walker did not join this exploration, but his brother Matthew did. After several weeks scouting areas in modern-day Kansas, the Wyandot party asked that more Wyandot leaders be allowed to visit the site they deemed appropriate. This time his other brother, Joel, accompanied six others westward. The exploring party agreed to a removal treaty, but the United States Senate rejected it in 1840. The following year, Indian agent John Johnston returned from retirement to negotiate a new removal treaty with the Wyandots. In 1843, James Finley returned to the mission for a final sermon and reminisced about happier days at the mission. On July 11, 1843, nearly seven hundred Wyandots (including William Walker) left the Grand Reserve.[65]

Reverend James Finley later remembered Walker as a friend who aided him on the Grand Reserve. In 1857, the missionary published a reminiscence of his time at the Grand Reserve, entitled *Life among the Indians*, where he identified Walker as "the teacher" who "sought and found the Lord." His memories of Walker were colored by their work together resisting removal and encouraging conversion. Long after he left the mission, and more than a decade after the Wyandots left Ohio, James Finley recalled, "I plainly saw that there was a storm ahead. I made use of every exertion to prevent it, by keeping up our prayers and class meetings; and was fully and ably sustained by the mission family." He singled out Walker and Robert Armstrong as his allies, and remembered them "as armor-bearers" of the mission.[66] Whether the minister recognized it or not, Walker had benefited from a half century of change among the Wyandots, whereby tribal leaders reorganized the nation in hopes of sustaining their autonomy amid the corrosive world of Indian removal politics; he also represented a history of prophecy by indigenous leaders attempting to predict the "storms" that threatened Wyandot autonomy. For the Wyandots, the end of the War of

1812 had not marked a direct line to removal. Many members of the tribe believed that new strategies, based on old ideas, could lead to an autonomous Wyandot Nation within the state of Ohio. Instead, after 1843, they fought to establish that nation elsewhere, beyond the Mississippi River.

NOTES

Originally published in a slightly different form in James Joseph Buss, *Winning the West with Words: Language and Conquest in the Lower Great Lakes* (Norman: University of Oklahoma Press, 2011), 73–96. Reprinted by permission of the author and the publisher.

1. James Gardiner to Lewis Cass, October 26, 1831, Letters Received by the Office of Indian Affairs, 1824–81, Ohio Agency Emigration, 1831–39, National Archives Microfilm Publications [hereafter NARA], microcopy 234, reel 603; and Gardiner to Lewis Cass, January 4, 1832, ibid.
2. Gardiner to Lewis Cass, January 4, 1832, ibid.; Gardiner to Col. Elbert Herring, January 4, 1832, ibid.; Copy of "The Chiefs of the Wyandotte Tribe Whose Names Are Undersigned," enclosed with Gardiner to Lewis Cass, October 26, 1831, ibid.; and Gardiner to Samuel Hamilton, September 16, 1831, ibid.
3. Gardiner to Lewis Cass, January 5, 1832, ibid. Gardiner, desperate to avert failure, proposed that he forge a removal treaty with part of the tribe "willing to treat." Ultimately, he abandoned the idea.
4. Gardiner to Lewis Cass, January 4, 1832, ibid; and Report of the Wyandot Exploring Delegation, January 28, 1832, ibid. Historians have examined the Wyandots since their dispossession occurred late in the era of Indian Removal (1843), but most scholars simply recognize Walker as a "mixed-blood" chief who opposed removal. Historian John Bowes's recent assessment of Great Lakes Indian removal does more to examine Walker's "importance to both Indian and white communities" than previous works, but he focuses primarily on Walker's rise to power following Wyandot emigration westward. John P. Bowes, *Pioneers and Exiles: Eastern Indians in the Trans-Mississippi West* (New York: Cambridge University Press, 2007), 164, 184. Early histories of Removal include short examinations of the Wyandots; see Grant Foreman, *The Last Trek of the Indians* (Chicago: University of Chicago Press, 1946). Foreman discusses Walker, but at times confuses the son with the father. The *Northwest Ohio Quarterly* recently published an entire issue devoted to the

Wyandots in Ohio, but here too, each article details a different aspect of Wyandot life, Methodist missions, and removal; see *Northwest Ohio Quarterly* 75, no. 2 (2004). Carl Grover Klopfenstein's doctoral dissertation still serves as the authoritative study of the Wyandots in Ohio. While he provides a detailed account of Wyandot removal, Klopfenstein is several generations removed from the current literature on American Indian studies, and his study contains many instances of antiquated and racist assumptions about Native peoples; see "The Removal of the Indians from Ohio, 1820–1843" (PhD dissertation, Case Western University, 1955).

5. Many historians who study American Indian Removal tend to either ignore the entire Great Lakes region or underplay the agency of Native peoples in the period leading up to removal by focusing on the "voluntary removal" of Great Lakes Indians. Moreover, scholars often portray Native communities as mere victims of white land lust as they chronicle the details of the Indian Removal process; see Anthony F. C. Wallace, *The Long, Bitter Trail: Andrew Jackson and the Indians* (New York: Hill and Wang, 1993); David S. Heidler and Jeanne T. Heidler, eds., *Indian Removal* (New York: W.W. Norton, 2007), esp. 30–34; Ronald Satz, *American Indian Policy in the Jacksonian Era* (Norman: University of Oklahoma Press, 2002). Alfred Cave reminds us, "Tecumseh is easily idealized, for he was indeed handsome, heroic, generous, and, after 1813, dead—the white man's ideal Indian." Cave, "The Shawnee Prophet, Tecumseh, and Tippecanoe: A Case Study of Historical Myth-Making," *Journal of the Early Republic* 22, no. 4 (Winter 2002), 671.

6. Richard White, *The Middle Ground: Indians, Empires, and Republics in the Great Lakes Region, 1650–1815* (New York: Cambridge University Press, 1991), 523.

7. The strategies employed by the Wyandots, and divisions that emerged between villages and tribal leaders resemble the experience of the Shawnees in the approximate time and place, particularly in regard to accommodating white agents and Christian missionaries; see Stephen Warren, *The Shawnee and Their Neighbors, 1795–1870* (Urbana: University of Illinois Press, 2005), esp. 43–68.

8. Walter Lowrie, ed., *American State Papers: Documents, Legislative and Executive, of the Congress of the United States, in Relation to Indian Affairs* (Washington, DC: Gales and Seaton, 1832–1834) [hereafter *ASPIA*], 1:575, 580.

9. "Narrative of a Journey to Sandusky, Ohio, to Visit the Wyandot Indians Residing There," *Friends Miscellany* 7, no. 7 (October 1835): 292–95, 321–25, 326. For information on the Presbyterian mission, see Robert E. Smith, "The Clash of Leadership at the Grand Reserve: The Wyandot Subagency and the Methodist Mission, 1820–1824," *Ohio History* 89, no. 2 (Spring 1980), 182; and Charlotte Reeve Conover, ed., *Recollections of 60 Years on the Ohio Frontier: Including Accounts of Notable Ohio Indians,*

Examples of the Shawnee and Wyandot Languages, and Manners and Customs of the Tribes (Dayton, OH: John Henry Patterson, 1915; reprint, Whitefish, MT: Kessinger Publishing, 2010), 59.

10. "Narrative of a Journey to Sandusky, Ohio," 326–27.

11. James B. Finley, *History of the Wyandott Mission* (Cincinnati, OH: J. F. Wright, 1840), 375–77; and J. W. Powell, "Wyandot Government: A Short Study of Tribal Society," An Address before the Subsection of Anthropology, American Association for the Advancement of Science: Boston Meeting, August, 1880 (Salem, MA: Salem Press, 1881).

12. Historian Thelma Marsh spent thirty years conducting an extensive genealogical study of the Wyandot Nation. Her work demonstrates the complex web of marriages, intermarriages, and captivities that helped color the Wyandot Nation by the early nineteenth century: the Armstrong, Walker, Hicks, Zane, Brown, and Vanmetre families could be traced to late eighteenth-century captivity stories, and Henry Jacques and the Williams family to French traders. Methodist missionary James Finley, who served on the Wyandot Reserve in the 1820s, suspected that nearly three-fourths of the Wyandots could trace their lineages to Euro-American ancestors. Finley to Cass, December 15, 1825, Finley Collection (microfilm collection at the Hayes Presidential Library), original copies at Ohio Wesleyan University [hereafter OWU]. Chiefs Council Resolution, May 2, 1825, quoted in James Finley, *Life among the Indians; or, Personal Reminiscences and Historical Incidents Illustrative of Indian Life and Character* (Cincinnati, OH: Curts and Jennings, 1857), 371. Nearly seven hundred note cards containing genealogical information on the Wyandots can be found in the Thelma Marsh Collection, Upper Sandusky County Library, Upper Sandusky, Ohio. A copy of the cards also can be found on microfilm at the Center for Archival Collections, Bowling Green State University Library, Bowling Green, Ohio.

13. Alfred A. Cave, *Prophets of the Great Spirit: Native American Revitalization Movements in Eastern North America* (Lincoln: University of Nebraska Press, 2006), 87, 107; and Cave, "The Failure of the Shawnee Prophet's Witch-Hunt," *Ethnohistory* 42, no. 3 (Summer 1995): 460–62. R. David Edmunds, *The Shawnee Prophet* (Lincoln: University of Nebraska Press, 1985), 46–47.

14. Finley, *History of the Wyandott Mission*, 101–3, 351; M. W. Walsh, "The 'Heathen Party': Methodist Observation of the Ohio Wyandot," *American Indian Quarterly* 16, no. 2 (Spring 1992): 189–202; and Anthony F. C. Wallace, *The Death and Rebirth of the Seneca* (New York: Knopf, 1970), 297–98. For an overview of Handsome Lake's message, see Wallace, 303–37.

15. At least one source indicates that Walker attended a mission school in Worthington, much farther south of Lower Sandusky (near modern Sandusky,

Ohio); see Larry K. Hancks, *The Emigrant Tribes: Wyandot, Delaware, and Shawnee* (Kansas City: n.p., 1998), 65.

16. *ASPIA*, 1:834.

17. Finley, *Life among the Indians*, 239. A similar version, although differently worded, appears in Charles Elliott, *Indian Missionary Reminiscences, Principally of the Wyandot Nation: In Which is Exhibited the Efficacy of the Gospel in Elevating Ignorant and Savage Men* (New York: Mason and Lane, 1837), 17. "When Johnston ascertained his errand, he endeavored to dissuade him from undertaking, telling that many wise and learned men had already, to no purpose, preached to the Indians." On the racist attitudes of white outsiders toward Pointer, see Joseph Mitchell, *The Missionary Pioneer; or a Brief Memoir of the Life, Labours and Death of John Stewart* (New York: J. C. Totten, 1827), 31; and Finley, *Life among the Indians*, 315–16. Methodist missionary James Finley recollected that Stewart had told him that his "parents claimed to be mixed with Indian blood"; see ibid., 234.

18. Finley, *Life among the Indians*, 240–41. Visitors to the Wyandot Grand Reserve in the 1820s recalled older Wyandots who wore silver crosses under their shirts; they also believed that words in the Wyandot language could be traced to Latin roots (evidence of the centuries-long influence of the Jesuits); see Johnston to Caleb Atwater, October 2, 1843, in Charlotte Reave Conover, ed., *Recollections of 60 Years on the Ohio Frontier*, 58.

19. Finley, *Life among the Indians*, 240–41.

20. Finley, *History of the Wyandott Mission*, 257.

21. Mitchell, *The Missionary Pioneer*, 31.

22. Finley, *Life among the Indians*, 245.

23. Ibid., 257.

24. Ibid., 315–16.

25. Elliott, *Indian Missionary Reminiscences*, 24–25.

26. *ASPIA*, 2:131–34. The list of individuals who were granted individual reserves included Elizabeth Whitaker, Robert Armstrong, John Vanmeter, the children of William M'Collock, Sarah Williams, Joseph Williams, Rachel Nugent, Catharine Walker, John Walker, and Cherokee Boy.

27. Senators refused to approve stipulations of the treaty that ceded individual plots of land, so another treaty needed to be negotiated the following September along the St. Mary's River in Ohio. Helen Hornbeck Tanner, ed., *Atlas of Great Lakes Indian History* (Norman: University of Oklahoma Press, 1987), 159; *ASPIA*, 2:166.

28. Smith, "Clash of Leadership on the Grand Reserve," 184.

29. Finley, *Life among the Indians*, 263, 233.

30. Historian Gregory Dowd's work on spiritual resistance in the period immediately preceding 1816 reminds us that Native spiritual movements often
included political and social agendas. Additionally, historian Robert F. Berkhofer Jr. has argued that missionaries did not separate their spiritual mission
from the government-sponsored civilization campaigns that often accompanied missionaries onto Indian lands—neither did Indians. Religion, cultural
practices, politics, and economic interests blended together in a symbiotic
representation of the larger culture. Robert F. Berkhofer Jr., *Salvation and
the Savage: An Analysis of Protestant Missions and American Indian Response,
1787–1862* (Lexington: University of Kentucky Press, 1965).

31. Paul Westrick, "The Race to Assimilate: The Wyandot Indians in White
Ohio," *Northwest Ohio History* 75, no. 2 (2004): 123–48.

32. Wallace, *Death and Rebirth*, 297.

33. Ibid., 277–84, 297–98.

34. Mitchell, *The Missionary Pioneer*, 52–53; and Finley, *Life among the Indians*,
259.

35. Finley, *History of the Wyandott Mission*, 45–46.

36. Ibid., 98.

37. Stewart had not been the first evangelist to draw Between-the-Logs's confidence. In the years before the War of 1812, he had followed the message of
the Shawnee Prophet, seeing it as an opportunity for personal redemption
and a path toward Native revivalism that would rid Great Lakes Indians of the
destructive influence of white traders, including alcohol. But, he felt betrayed
by the failure of the Prophet's spiritual movement in ridding the region of
the harmful influence of white traders, and accused the Prophet of failing to
follow his own preaching. In fact, he admitted that he first opposed Stewart's
attempts at conversion because he thought the black missionary would "be
like the others." Ibid., 102–5.

38. Finley, *Life among the Indians*, 236–39; and Elliott, *Indian Missionary Reminiscences*, 21–25, 30.

39. "To the Chiefs the Speakers . . . ," August 16, 1820, James B. Finley Papers,
Rutherford B. Hayes Presidential Library, Fremont, Ohio [hereafter cited as
Hayes].

40. Finley, *Life among the Indians*, 324. Historian Daniel Richter demonstrates
how the expectations of religious missionaries often shaped their views of the
Native peoples they encountered in the early nineteenth century and made it
impossible for them to accept the realities that they witnessed once they traveled to indigenous communities; see Daniel K. Richter, "'Believing That Many
of the Red People Suffer Much for the Want of Food': Hunting, Agriculture,

and a Quaker Construction of Indian-ness in the Early Republic," *Journal of the Early Republic* 19, no. 4 (Winter 1999): 601–28.

41. William Walker Sr. took credit for helping introduce the Wyandots to the Christian Bible. In the preface to *The Missionary Pioneer*, the author claims that Walker Sr. examined John Stewart's Bible and verified to the head chiefs that it was the word of God. According to the preface, the contents for *The Missionary Pioneer* were "collected and arranged" by Walker himself. Although Walker chronicled little of his thoughts on Methodism, race, or removal in print during the early nineteenth century (most of his life in Ohio is chronicled in late-life reminiscences or a handful of private correspondence), his fingerprints appear throughout the historical record. Walker was everywhere at the Wyandot mission: he served a long career as interpreter for the federal government and the local missionaries; he befriended the head missionary at the reserve and became a close confidant; he served as Lewis Cass's private secretary in the 1810–1820 period; he occupied the office of postmaster for nearly a decade and a half; he taught at the missionary school; he ran the mission store; and he attended both the chief's councils and an occasional Methodist annual conference.

42. Journal entry, November 15, 1822, in Elliott, *Indian Missionary Reminiscences*, 83. Finley's article quoted in Charles C. Cole Jr., *Lion of the Forest: James B. Finley, Frontier Reformer* (Lexington: University Press of Kentucky, 1994), 48.

43. Johnston to Finley, September 10, 1825, OWU; Johnston to Finley, November 5, 1825, ibid; Johnston to Finley, November 30, 1825, ibid. Indian agent John Johnston pushed Finley to remove Indian children from the larger Wyandot community and place them within white homes. He became convinced that unless the Indian scholars were "scattered a *part* of the year in white families," Finley's "labour and expense" would be lost. Johnston led by example; he financed the education of an Indian boy, whom he had named after himself; see Johnston to Finley, December 5, 1825, ibid.; and Cole Jr., *Lion of the Forest*, 51. Gardiner accused Johnston of trying to delay the removal of the Shawnees in 1831; see Gardiner to Cass, December 1, 1831, NARA, roll 603.

44. Finley to Ruter, December 19, 1825, Finley Papers, Cincinnati Historical Society. [Photocopies of these letters also can be found in the James Finley Papers at the Rutherford B. Hayes Presidential Library, Fremont, Ohio.]

45. Lewis Cass to Finley, March 25, 1825, Hayes.

46. McKenney to Finley, September 10, 1825, quoted in Finley, *History of the Wyandott Mission*, 304. Government agents and officials fed confusing and often contradictory information to Finley about Indian Removal.

John Johnston, who later would push for removal, tried to convince the reverend that despite Cass's assurances, Michigan's territorial governor truly believed that removal was the only answer. Johnston informed Finley that Cass planned a council at Wapakoneta "on the subject of removing to the west." Johnston to Finley, May 16, 1825, OWU. Circulating rumors about an impending removal caused the managers of the Mission Society to with-hold money due to "the uncertain state of things." Thomas Jackson to Finley, April 27, 1825, Hayes.

47. Cass to Finley, February 6, 1826, Hayes; Cass to Finley, February 26, 1826, OWU; and Johnston to Finley, November 30, 1825, ibid.

48. Finley to Martin Ruter, December 19, 1825, Cincinnati Historical Society.

49. Finley to Lewis Cass, December 15, 1825, OWU.

50. Finley, *History of the Wyandott Mission*, 375–77; and Powell, "Wyandot Government."

51. Finley, *History of the Wyandott Mission*, 376–78; and Bowes, *Exiles and Pioneers*, 162–64.

52. Finley, *History of the Wyandott Mission*, 110–11; Chiefs Council, May 2, 1825, Hayes; "Chiefs Certificate," January 31, 1826, Hayes.

53. Walker to Finley, May 17, 1824, Hayes. Their friendship may have gone beyond mere formality. Finley believed that he had saved Walker's wife dur-ing a particularly difficult childbirth; see Finley to Martin Ruter, February 15, 1825, Cincinnati Historical Society. Letters from Finley to Walker are scarce, but the tone of letters sent to Walker by the reverend can be understood via Walker's responses; see Walker to Finley, May 21, 1831, Hayes; Walker to Finley, March 15, 1837, OWU.

54. Walker to Finley, May 21, 1831, Hayes.

55. Johnston wrote Finley at the beginning of the year, warning, "The Indians must all leave this country sooner or later this is a position which every reflect-ing man must assent to"; see Johnston to Finley, January 10, 1826, OWU.

56. Walker to Finley, July 15, 1826, OWU.

57. Cass to Finley, March 22, 1826, Hayes. Walker would have been particularly aware of Cass's attitudes on the issue, as he had served as a secretary and aide for Cass around the War of 1812.

58. Chiefs Certificate, January 31, 1826, Hayes; William Walker to Finley, May 21, 1831, Hayes.

59. Satz, *American Indian Policy*, 54; Elizabeth Gaspar Brown, "Lewis Cass and the American Indian," *Michigan History* 37 (September 1953): 286–98; Tan-ner, *Atlas of Great Lakes Indian History*, 136; *General and Local Laws and Joint Resolutions Passed by the General Assembly of Ohio* (Columbus, OH, 1834), 32:434.

60. Journal of the Proceedings, August and September, 1834, and Robert Lucas to Lewis Cass, March 1835, in Dwight Smith, "An Unsuccessful Negotiation for Removal of the Wyandot Indians from Ohio, 1834," *Ohio Archaeological and Historical Quarterly* 58 (1949): 305–31. Also, see Robert Lucas to Lewis Cass, August 19, 1834; John McElvain to Robert Lucas, August 27, 1834, in ibid.

61. The Methodist missionary in charge of overseeing the Wyandot mission reported low yields and depleted stores of grain and livestock in his 1835 report; see Thomas Thompson to the Bishops and Members of the Ohio Annual Conference, August 1835, Hayes. Historian Carl G. Klopfenstein posits a similar argument; see "The Removal of the Wyandots from Ohio," *Ohio Historical Quarterly* 66, no. 2 (April 1957): 124.

62. Walker to Finley, March 15, 1837, OWU.

63. Walker to Finley, August 8, 1837, OWU.

64. Robert E. Smith, "The Wyandot Exploring Expedition of 1839," *Chronicles of Oklahoma* (Fall 1977): 285; Petition of William Walker, March 3, 1838, 25th Cong., 2nd sess., HR Report 632. Hunter to Crawford, November 6, 1838, NARA, roll 601. Hunter completely misread Walker's intentions as he declared to superiors that Walker worked to oust the non-Christian chiefs and stop removal in order to "remain in the enjoyment of a valuable property."

65. Smith, "The Wyandot Exploring Expedition of 1839," 286. Hunter to Crawford, November 28, 1839, NARA, roll 602; and Articles of a Treaty with the Shawnees, December 18, 1839, ibid. For an account of the failed treaty, see Smith, "The Wyandot Exploring Party of 1839," 282–92.

66. Finley, *Life among the Indians*, 325, 405–6.

Bibliography

Aley, Ginette. "Bringing about the Dawn: Agriculture, Internal Improvements, Indian Policy, and Euro-American Hegemony." In *The Center of a Great Empire: The Ohio Country in the Early American Republic*, edited by Andrew R. L. Cayton and Stuart D. Hobbs. Athens: Ohio University Press, 2005.

American State Papers, Indian Affairs. 2 vols. Washington, DC: Gales and Seaton, 1832–61.

Anderson, M. B., ed. *Relation of the Discoveries and Voyages of Cavelier de LaSalle from 1679 to 1681: The Official Narrative.* Chicago: Caxton Club, 1901.

Anson, Bert. *The Miami Indians.* Norman: University of Oklahoma Press, 1970.

Aron, Stephen. "Pigs and Hunters: 'Rights in the Woods' on the Trans-Appalachian Frontier." In *Contact Points: American Frontiers from the Mohawk Valley to the Mississippi, 1750–1830*, edited by Andrew R. L. Cayton and Fredrika J. Teute. Chapel Hill: University of North Carolina Press and the Omohundro Institute of Early American History and Culture, 1998.

Barnhart, John D., and Dorothy L. Riker. *Indiana to 1816: The Colonial Period.* Indianapolis: Indiana Historical Bureau and Indiana Historical Society, 1971.

Baldwin, Daryl, and David Costa. *Myaamia neehi peewaalia kaloosioni mahsinaakani: A Miami-Peoria Dictionary.* 1st ed. Miami, OK: Miami Nation.

Barr, Daniel P., ed. *The Boundaries Between Us: Natives and Newcomers along the Frontiers of the Old Northwest Territory, 1750–1850.* Kent, OH: Kent State University Press, 2006.

Bates, Elisha. *The Doctrines of Friends.* Providence, RI: Knowles & Vose, 1840.

Becker, Rory. "Eating Ethnicity: Examining 18th Century French Colonial Identity through Selective Consumption of Animal Resources in the North American Interior." Master's thesis, Department of Anthropology, Western Michigan University, 2004.

Benn, Carl. *The Iroquois in the War of 1812.* Toronto: University of Toronto Press, 1998.

Bergmann, William H. "A 'Commercial View of This Unfortunate War': Economic Roots of an American National State in the Ohio Valley, 1775–1795." *Early American Studies* (Spring 2008): 137–64.

Berkhofer, Robert F., Jr. *Salvation and the Savage: An Analysis of Protestant Missions and American Indian Response, 1787–1862.* Lexington: University of Kentucky Press, 1965.

Berry, Kate, and Melissa Rinehart. "A Legacy of Forced Migration: The Removal of the Miami Tribe in 1846." *International Journal of Population Geography* 9 (2003): 93–112.

Berthrong, D. J. *An Historical Report on Indian Use and Occupancy of Northern Indiana and Southwestern Michigan.* New York: Garland, 1974.

Bettarel, R. L., and H. G. Smith. *The Moccasin Bluff Site and the Woodland Cultures of Southwestern Michigan.* Ann Arbor: Anthropological Papers, Museum of Anthropology, University of Michigan, 1973.

Bierhorst, John. *Mythology of the Lenape: Guide and Texts.* Tucson: University of Arizona Press, 1995.

Birzer, Bradley. "Jean Baptiste Richardville: Miami Métis." In *Enduring Nations: Native Americans in the Midwest,* edited by R. David Edmunds. Urbana: University of Illinois Press, 2008.

Blanchard, Charles, ed. *History of the Catholic Church in Indiana.* Logansport, IN: A.W. Bowen & Co., 1898.

Bliss, Eugene F., trans. and ed. *Diary of David Zeisberger, a Moravian Missionary among the Indians of Ohio.* Vol. 2. Cincinnati, OH: Robert Clarke & Co., 1885.

Bohaker, Heidi. "'Nindoodemag': The Significance of Algonquian Kinship Networks in the Eastern Great Lakes Region, 1600–1701." *William and Mary Quarterly,* 3rd series, 63, no. 1 (January 2006): 23–52.

Bond, Beverly W., Jr., ed. *The Correspondence of John Cleves Symmes, Founder of the Miami Purchase.* New York: Macmillan, 1926.

Bowes, John P. *Pioneers and Exiles: Eastern Indians in the Trans-Mississippi West.* New York: Cambridge University Press, 2007.

Brain, Jeffrey P. *Tunica Treasure.* Papers of the Peabody Museum of Archaeology and Ethnology, Harvard University, vol. 71. Cambridge, MA: Peabody Museum of Salem and Harvard University, 1979.

Brandão, J. A., and William A. Starna. "The Treaties of 1701: A Triumph of Iroquois Diplomacy." *Ethnohistory* 43, no. 2 (Spring 1996): 209–44.

Brandão, José António, and Michael S. Nassaney. "A Capsule Social and Material History of Fort St. Joseph (1691–1763) and Its Inhabitants." *French Colonial History* 7 (2006): 61–75.

———. "Suffering for Jesus: Penitential Practices at Fort St. Joseph (Niles, MI) during the French Regime." *Catholic Historical Review* 94, no. 3 (2008): 476–99.

Brinton, Daniel G. *The Lenape and Their Legends.* Philadelphia: n.p., 1885.

Bronner, Edwin B. "The Quakers and Non-Violence in Pennsylvania." *Pennsylvania History* 35, no. 1 (1968): 1–22.

———. *William Penn's "Holy Experiment:" The Founding of Pennsylvania, 1681–1701.* Philadelphia: Temple University Press, 1963.

Brooks, Lisa. "Two Paths to Peace: Competing Visions of Native Space in the Old Northwest." In *The Boundaries Between Us: Natives and Newcomers along the Frontiers of the Old Northwest Territory, 1750–1850*, edited by Daniel P. Barr. Kent, OH: Kent State University Press, 2006.

Brose, David S. "The Direct Historical Approach in Michigan Archaeology." *Ethnohistory* 18 (1971): 51–61.

Bross, Kristina, and Hilary E. Wyss, eds. *Early Native Literacies in New England: A Documentary and Critical Anthology.* Amherst: University of Massachusetts Press, 2008.

Brown, Elizabeth Gaspar. "Lewis Cass and the American Indian." *Michigan History* 37 (September 1953): 286–98.

Brown, George, et al. *Dictionary of Canadian Biography.* Toronto: University of Toronto Press, 1966.

Brown, Ian W. "The Calumet Ceremony in the Southeast and Its Archaeological Manifestations." *American Antiquity* 54, no. 2 (1989): 311–31.

Brown, Jennifer. *Strangers in Blood: Fur Trade Company Families in Indian Country.* Norman: University of Oklahoma Press, 1996.

Buell, Rowena, ed. *The Memoirs of Rufus Putnam and Certain Official Papers and Correspondence.* Boston: Houghton, Mifflin and Co., 1903.

Burton, Clarence Monroe, and M. Agnes Burton, eds. *Journal of Pontiac's Conspiracy, 1763.* Translated by R. Clyde Ford. Detroit: Speaker-Hines Printing Company, 1912.

Caffrey, Margaret M. "Complementary Power: Men and Women of the Lenni Lenape." *American Indian Quarterly* 24, no. 1 (Winter 2000): 44–63.

Cahill, Cathleen, and Kerry Wynn, eds. *Frontiers: A Journal of Women's Studies* 29 (2008): 2–3.

Callender, Charles. "Miami." In *Handbook of North American Indians*, vol. 15, *Northeast*, edited by Bruce G. Trigger. Washington, DC: Smithsonian Institution Press, 1978.

Calloway, Colin. *New Worlds for All: Indians, Europeans, and the Remaking of Early America.* Baltimore: Johns Hopkins University Press, 1998.

———. *The Scratch of a Pen: 1763 and the Transformation of North America.* New York: Oxford University Press, 2006.

Camp, Charles. "Temperance Movements and Legislation in Indiana." *Indiana Magazine of History* 16, no. 1 (1920): 9.

Carson, James Taylor. "Ethnogeography and the Native American Past." *Ethnohistory* 49, no. 4 (2002): 769–88.

Cave, Alfred A. "The Failure of the Shawnee Prophet's Witch-Hunt." *Ethnohistory* 42, no. 3 (Summer 1995): 445–75.

———. *Prophets of the Great Spirit: Native American Revitalization Movements in Eastern North America.* Lincoln: University of Nebraska Press, 2006.

———. "The Shawnee Prophet, Tecumseh, and Tippecanoe: A Case Study of Historical Myth-Making." *Journal of the Early Republic* 22, no. 4 (Winter 2002): 637–74.

Cayton, Andrew R. L. *Ohio: The History of a People.* Columbus: Ohio State University Press, 2002.

Cayton, Andrew, and Stuart Hobbs, eds. *The Center of a Great Empire: The Ohio Country in the Early Republic.* Columbus: Ohio State University Press, 2005.

Cayton, Andrew, and Fredrika Teute. *Contact Points: American Frontiers from the Mohawk Valley to the Mississippi, 1750–1830.* Chapel Hill: University of North Carolina Press, 1998.

Charlevoix, Pierre Joseph. *Journal of a Voyage to North America.* London: R. and J. Dodsley, 1761.

Clifton, James A. "Potawatomi." In *Handbook of North American Indians,* vol. 15, *Northeast,* edited by Bruce G. Trigger, 725–42. Washington, DC: Smithsonian Institution Press, 1978.

———. "Potawatomi." In *Peoples of the Three Fires: The Ottawa, Potawatomi, and Ojibway of Michigan,* edited by J. A. Clifton, G. L. Cornell and J. M. McClurken, 39–74. Grand Rapids: Michigan Indian Press, Grand Rapids Inter-Tribal Council, 1986.

———. *The Prairie People: Continuity and Change in Potawatomi Indian Culture, 1665–1965.* Lawrence: Regents Press of Kansas, 1977.

Cole, Charles C., Jr. *Lion of the Forest: James B. Finley, Frontier Reformer.* Lexington: University Press of Kentucky, 1994.

Collections of the State Historical Society of Wisconsin. Madison: State Historical Society of Wisconsin, 1854–1931.

Conover, Charlotte Reave, ed. *Recollections of 60 Years on the Ohio Frontier: Including Accounts of Notable Ohio Indians, Examples of the Shawnee and Wyandot Languages, and Manners and Customs of the Tribes.* Dayton, OH: John Henry Patterson, 1915; reprint, Whitefish, MT: Kessinger Publishing, 2010.

Craig, Neville B., ed. *The Olden Time.* Vol. 2. Pittsburgh, PA: Wright & Charlton, 1874; reprint, New York: Kraus Reprint Co., 1976.

Cremin, William M. "The Berrien Phase of Southwest Michigan: Proto-Potawatomi?" In *Investigating the Archaeological Record of the Great Lakes State: Essays in Honor of Elizabeth Baldwin Garland,* edited by M. B. Holman, J. G. Brashler and

K. E. Parker, 383–413. Kalamazoo: New Issues Press, Western Michigan University, 1996.

―――. "Late Prehistoric Adaptive Strategies on the Northern Periphery of the Carolinian Biotic Province: A Case Study from Southwest Michigan." *Midcontinental Journal of Archaeology* 8, no. 1 (1983): 91–107.

―――. "Researching the 'Void' between History and Prehistory in Southwest Michigan." *Michigan Archaeologist* 38, no. 1–2 (1992): 19–37.

―――. "The Schwerdt Site: A Fifteenth Century Fishing Station on the Lower Kalamazoo River, Southwest Michigan." *Wisconsin Archaeologist* 61, no. 2 (1980): 280–91.

Cremin, William M., ed. *Archaeological Investigations in the Lower Galien River Valley of Southwest Michigan.* Technical Report No. 23. Kalamazoo: Department of Anthropology, Western Michigan University, 1990.

Cremin, William M., and Michael S. Nassaney. "Background Research." In *An Archaeological Reconnaissance Survey to Locate Remains of Fort St. Joseph (20BE23) in Niles, Michigan.* Archaeological Report No. 22, edited by M. S. Nassaney, 7–30. Kalamazoo: Department of Anthropology, Western Michigan University, 1999.

―――. "Sampling Archaeological Sediments for Small-Scale Remains: Recovery, Identification, and Interpretation of Plant Residues from Fort St. Joseph (20BE23)." *Michigan Archaeologist* 49, nos. 3–4 (2003): 73–85.

Cremin, William M., Gregory R. Walz, and Daniel B. Goatley. *A Report of Significant Data Recovered from Features 6 and 48 on Site 20BE410 during Archaeological Investigations Undertaken by Western Michigan University in the Lower Galien River Valley of Southwest Michigan.* Report of Investigations No. 99. Kalamazoo: Department of Anthropology, Western Michigan University, 1991.

Culin, Stewart. *Games of the North American Indians.* Reprint. New York: Dover, 1975. Originally published, *Twenty-Fourth Annual Report of the Bureau of American Ethnology.* Washington, DC: Smithsonian Institution, 1907.

Cutler, William Parker, and Julia Perkins Cutler. *Life, Journals and Correspondence of Rev. Manasseh Cutler, LL.D.* Cincinnati, OH: R. Clarke & Co., 1888.

Delâge, Denys. "French and English Colonial Models in North America." *Le Journal* 18, no. 3 (2002): 4–8.

Dennis, Matthew. *Cultivating a Landscape of Peace.* Ithaca, NY: Cornell University Press, 1993.

Denny, Ebenezer. *Military Journal of Major Ebenezer Denny: An Officer in the Revolutionary and Indian Wars, with an Introductory Memoir.* New York: Arno, 1971.

Dixon, David. *Never Come to Peace Again: Pontiac's Uprising and the Fate of the British Empire in North America.* Norman: University of Oklahoma Press, 2005.

Documentary History of the State of New York, The. Edited by E. B. O'Callaghan. Albany, NY: Weed, Parsons, 1849–1851.

Documents Relative to the Colonial History of the State of New York. Edited by E. B. O'Callaghan and Berthold Fernow. Albany, NY: Weed, 1853–1887.

Doddridge, Joseph, Narcissa Doddridge, John Ritenour, and William T. Lindsey. *Notes on the Settlement and Indian Wars of the Western Parts of Virginia and Pennsylvania from 1763 to 1783.* Pittsburgh, PA, 1912; reprint, Parsons, WV: McClain Printing Co., 1976. http://books.google.com/books?id=FXl5AAAAM AAJ (accessed January 2011).

Dollier de Casson, François, and René Brehan de Galinée. *Exploration of the Great Lakes, 1669–1670.* Translated and edited by J. H. Coyne. Toronto: Ontario Historical Society Papers and Records, 1917.

Dorsey, Bruce. "Friends Becoming Enemies: Philadelphia Benevolence and the Neglected Era of American Quaker History." *Journal of the Early Republic* 18, no. 3 (Autumn 1998): 395–428.

Dowd, Gregory Evans. *A Spirited Resistance: The North American Indian Struggle for Unity, 1745–1815.* Baltimore: Johns Hopkins University Press, 1992.

———. "Michigan Murder Mysteries: Death and Rumor in the Age of Indian Removal." In *Enduring Nations: Native Americans in the Midwest,* edited by R. David Edmunds. Urbana: University of Illinois Press, 2008.

———. *War under Heaven: Pontiac, the Indian Nations, and the British Empire.* Baltimore: Johns Hopkins University Press, 2002.

Dunn, Mary Maples, and Richard S. Dunn, eds. *The Papers of William Penn.* Philadelphia: University of Pennsylvania Press, 1981.

Dunnigan, Brian Leigh. "Portaging Niagara." *Inland Seas* 42, no. 3 (Spring 1986): 181–82.

Eccles, W. J. "The Fur Trade and Eighteenth-Century Imperialism." *William and Mary Quarterly* 40, no. 3 (1983): 341–62.

Edmunds, R. David. "'Evil Men Who Add to Our Difficulties': Shawnees, Quakers, and William Wells, 1807–1808." *American Indian Culture and Research Journal* 14, no. 4 (1990): 1–14.

———. *The Shawnee Prophet.* Lincoln: University of Nebraska Press, 1983.

———, ed. *Enduring Nations: Native Americans in the Midwest.* Urbana: University of Illinois Press, 2008.

Elliott, Charles. *Indian Missionary Reminiscences, Principally of the Wyandot Nation: In Which is Exhibited the Efficacy of the Gospel in Elevating Ignorant and Savage Men.* New York: Mason and Lane, 1837.

Esarey, Logan. *A History of Indiana.* New York: Harcourt, Brace and Co., 1922.

Faribault-Beauregard, Martha. *La population des forts français d'Amérique (XVIIIe siècle).* 2 vols. Montreal: Éditions Bergeron, 1982.

Ferris, Neal. *The Archaeology of Native-Lived Colonialism: Challenging History in the Great Lakes.* Tucson: University of Arizona Press, 2008.

Finley, James B. *History of the Wyandott Mission.* Cincinnati, OH: J. F. Wright, 1840.

———. *Life Among the Indians; or, Personal Reminiscences and Historical Incidents Illustrative of Indian Life and Character.* Cincinnati, OH: Curts and Jennings, 1857.

Ford, Richard I. "The Moccasin Bluff Corn Holes." In *The Moccasin Bluff Site and the Woodland Cultures of Southwestern Michigan,* compiled by R. L. Bettarel and H. G. Smith, 188–93. Anthropological Papers No. 49. Ann Arbor: Museum of Anthropology, University of Michigan, 1973.

Ford, Worthington C., et al., eds. *Journals of the Continental Congress, 1774–1789.* 34 vols. Washington, DC, 1904–37. http://lcweb2.loc.gov/ammem/amlaw/lwjc.html (accessed January 2011).

Foreman, Grant. *The Last Trek of the Indians.* Chicago: University of Chicago Press, 1946.

Fur, Gunlög Maria. "Cultural Confrontation on Two Fronts: Swedes Meet Lenapes and Saamis in the Seventeenth Century." PhD dissertation, University of Oklahoma, 1993.

General and Local Laws and Joint Resolutions Passed by the General Assembly of Ohio. Columbus, OH, 1834.

Gernhardt, Phyllis. "'Justice and Public Policy': Indian Trade, Treaties, and Removal from Northern Indiana, 1826–1846." In *The Boundaries Between Us: Natives and Newcomers along the Frontiers of the Old Northwest Territory, 1750–1850,* edited by Daniel P. Barr, 179–81. Kent, OH: Kent State University Press, 2006.

Gillespie, Michele, and Robert Beachy, eds. *Pious Pursuits: German Moravians in the Atlantic World.* New York: Berghahn Books, 2007.

Giordano, Brock. "Crafting Culture at Fort St. Joseph: An Archaeological Investigation of Labor Organization on the Colonial Frontier." Master's thesis, Department of Anthropology, Western Michigan University, 2005.

Gipson, Lawrence Henry, ed. *The Moravian Indian Mission on White River.* Indianapolis: Indiana Historical Bureau, 1938.

Godbeer, R. "Eroticizing the Middle Ground: Anglo-Indian Sexual Relations along the Eighteenth-Century Frontier." In *Sex, Love, and Race: Crossing Boundaries in North American History,* edited by Martha E. Hodes, 91–111. New York: New York University Press, 1999.

Goddard, Ives. "Delaware." In *Handbook of North American Indians,* vol. 15, *Northeast,* edited by Bruce G. Trigger, 213–39. Washington, DC: Smithsonian Institution, 1978.

Gordon II, Leon. "The Red Man's Retreat from Northern Indiana." *Indiana Magazine of History* 46, no. 1 (1950).

Griffin, Patrick. "Reconsidering the Ideological Origins of Indian Removal: The Case of the Big Bottom 'Massacre.'" In *The Center of a Great Empire: The Ohio Country in the Early American Republic*, edited by Andrew R. L. Cayton and Stuart D. Hobbs, 11–35. Athens: Ohio University Press, 2005.

Gruenwald, Kim M. *River of Enterprise: The Commercial Origins of Regional Identity in the Ohio Valley, 1790–1850*. Bloomington: Indiana University Press, 2002.

Haldimand, Sir Frederick. Unpublished Papers and Correspondence, 1758–84. Microfilm. London: World Microfilm Publications, 1977.

Hamilton, J. Taylor, and Kenneth G. Hamilton. *History of the Moravian Church: The Renewed Unitas Fratrum, 1722–1957*. Bethlehem, PA: Interprovincial Board of Christian Education, Moravian Church in America, 1967.

Hancks, Larry K. *The Emigrant Tribes: Wyandot, Delaware, and Shawnee*. Kansas City, KS: n.p., 1998.

Handbook of North American Indians. Series edited by William C. Sturtevant. Vol. 15, *Northeast*, edited by Bruce G. Trigger. Washington, DC: Smithsonian Institution, 1978.

Harper, Robert W. *John Fenwick and Salem County in the Province of West Jersey: 1609–1700*. Pennsville, NJ: Associated Printers, 1978.

Harris, Richard Colebrook, ed. *Historical Atlas of Canada*. Vol. 1, *From the Beginning to 1800*. Toronto: University of Toronto Press, 1987.

Havard, Gilles. *Empire et métissage: Indiens et Français dans le Pays d'en Haut, 1660–1715*. Sillery and Paris: Septentrion et les Presses de l'Université Paris-Sorbonne, 2003.

———. "Postes français et villages indiens: Un aspect de l'organisation de l'espace colonial français dans le Pays d'En Haut (1660–1715)." *Recherches Amerindiennes au Quebec* 30, no. 2 (2000): 11–22.

Hay, Henry. *Journal from Detroit to the Miami River, Fort Wayne in 1790*. Edited by Milo Milton Quaife. 1790; Fort Wayne: Allen County Public Library, 1955.

Headings, Lois Shepherd. "This Distinguished and Extraordinary Man: Chief Jean Baptiste Richardville," *Old Fort News* 61, nos. 1–2, (1998): 11

Heckewelder, John. *History, Manners, and Customs of the Indian Nations*. Philadelphia: Historical Society of Pennsylvania, 1876.

———. *A Narrative of the Missions of the United Brethren among the Delaware and Mohegan Indians from Its Commencement in the Year 1740 to the Close of the Year 1808*. Philadelphia: McCarty & Davis, 1820.

Heidler, David S., and Jeanne T. Heidler. *Indian Removal: A Norton Casebook*. New York: W.W. Norton, 2007.

Henry, Alexander. *Travels and Adventures in Canada in the Years 1760–1776*. Chicago: R. R. Donnelly and Sons, 1921.

Hinderaker, Eric. *Elusive Empires: Constructing Colonialism in the Ohio Valley, 1673–1800*. Cambridge: Cambridge University Press, 1997.

Hindle, Brooke. "The March of the Paxton Boys." *William and Mary Quarterly* 3, no. 4 (1946): 462–86.

Hodes, Martha, ed. *Sex, Love, and Race: Crossing Boundaries in North American History*. New York: New York University Press, 1999.

Hopkins, Gerard T. *A Mission to the Indians, from the Indian Committee of Baltimore Yearly Meeting, to Fort Wayne, in 1804*. Philadelphia: T. Ellwood Zell, 1862. http://books.google.com/books?id=SB4oAAAAYAAJ (accessed January 2011).

H. R. Document No. 129. General Assembly of the State of Indiana. "Memorial and Joint Resolution of the General Assembly of Indiana in regard to the Pottawatamie and Miami Indians in this State." 23rd Cong., 2nd sess., serial set 273, February 4, 1835.

Hulbert, Archer Butler, and William Nathaniel Schwarze, eds. "David Zeisberger's History of the Northern American Indians." In *Ohio Archaeological and Historical Publications*. Columbus, OH: Fred J. Herr, 1910.

Hunter, Charles E. "The Delaware Nativist Revival of the Mid-Eighteenth Century." *Ethnohistory* 18 (1971): 39–49.

Hurt, R. Douglas. *The Ohio Frontier: Crucible of the Old Northwest, 1720–1830*. Bloomington: Indiana University Press, 1996.

Idle, Dunning. *The Post of the St. Joseph River during the French Regime, 1679–1761*. Niles, MI: Support the Fort, Inc., 2003.

James, James Alton. *The Life of George Rogers Clark*. New York: Greenwood Press, 1928.

James, Sydney V. "The Impact of the American Revolution on the Quakers' Ideas about Their Sect." *William and Mary Quarterly* 19, no. 3 (1962): 360–82.

Jameson, Franklin J., ed. *Narratives of New Netherland, 1609–1664*. New York: Charles Scribner's Sons, 1909.

Jelinek, Arthur. "A Late Historic Burial from Berrien County." *Michigan Archaeologist* 4, no. 3 (1958): 48–51.

Jennings, Francis. *The Ambiguous Iroquois Empire: The Covenant Chain Confederation of Indian Tribes with the English Colonies from Its Beginnings to the Lancaster Treaty of 1744*. New York: W.W. Norton, 1984.

———. "Brother Miquon: Good Lord!" In *The World of William Penn*, edited by Richard S. Dunn and Mary Maples Dunn, 195–214. Philadelphia: University of Pennsylvania Press, 1986.

———. "Miquon's Passing: Indian-European Relations in Colonial Pennsylvania, 1674–1755." PhD dissertation, University of Pennsylvania, 1965.

———. "The Scandalous Indian Policy of William Penn's Sons: Deeds and Documents of the Walking Purchase." *Pennsylvania History* 30, no. 1 (1970): 19–39.

Johnson, Amandus. *The Instruction for Johan Printz, Governor of New Sweden.* Philadelphia: Swedish Colonial Society, 1930.

Johnson, Catherine. *Myaamiaki Piloohsaki Amahsinaakanemawe Iilaataweenki: A Miami Children's Language Curriculum.* Oxford, OH: Myaamia Project, 2003.

Johnson, William. *Papers of Sir William Johnson.* 14 vols. Edited by James Sullivan. Albany: University of the State of New York, 1921–1965.

Jones, Robert Leslie. *History of Agriculture in Ohio to 1880.* Kent, OH: Kent State University Press, 1983.

Jones, Rufus M. *The Later Periods of Quakerism.* London: Macmillan, 1921.

Jones, T. Canby, ed. *"The Power of the Lord Is Over All": The Pastoral Letter of George Fox.* Richmond, IN: Friends United Press, 1989.

Jordan, Kurt A. *The Seneca Restoration, 1715–1754: An Iroquois Local Political Economy.* Gainesville: University Press of Florida, 2008.

Kappler, Charles J., ed. *Indian Affairs: Laws and Treaties.* Washington, DC: Government Printing Office, 1904. http://digital.library.okstate.edu/kappler.

Kelley, Darwin. "Securing the Land: John Tipton and the Miami Indians." *Old Fort News* 25, no. 1 (1962): 6.

Kelsey, Rayner W. *Friends and the Indians, 1655–1917.* Philadelphia: Associated Executive Committee of Friends on Indian Affairs, 1917.

Kent, Donald H. *Pennsylvania and Delaware Treaties: 1629–1737.* Washington, DC: University Publications of America, 1979.

Kiefer, Luke Justin. "Gentlemen, Rogues, and Savages: United States–Native American Relations in the Old Northwest Territory, 1783–1812." Master's thesis, Ohio State University, 1996.

Kinietz, W. V. *The Indians of the Western Great Lakes, 1615–1760.* Ann Arbor: University of Michigan Press, 1972.

Klopfenstein, Carl Grover. "The Removal of the Indians from Ohio, 1820–1843." PhD dissertation, Case Western University, 1955.

———. "The Removal of the Wyandots from Ohio." *Ohio Historical Quarterly* 66, no. 2 (April 1957): 119–36.

Kohn, Rita, and W. Lynwood Montell. *Always a People: Oral Histories of Contemporary Woodland Indians.* Bloomington: Indiana University Press, 1997.

Lacey, John. "Memoirs of Brigadier-General John Lacey of Pennsylvania." *Pennsylvania Magazine of History and Biography* 25, no. 1 (1901): 1–13.

Leder, Lawrence H., ed. *The Livingston Indian Records.* Gettysburg: Pennsylvania Historical Association, 1956.

Lemon, James. *The Best Poor Man's Country: A Geographic Study of Early Southeastern Pennsylvania.* Baltimore: Johns Hopkins University Press, 1972.

Leonard, Floyd, and Joseph Leonard. "The Miami Nation: Nineteenth and Twentieth Centuries." *Native Americans and Early Settlers: The Meeting of Cultures, 1780's–1980's.* Celina, OH: Mercer County Historical Society, 1989.

Letters and Papers of Cadwallader Colden. New York: New York Historical Society, 1918–1937.

Letters Received by the Office of Indian Affairs, 1824–81. Ohio Agency Emigration, 1831–39. National Archives Microfilm Publications, microcopy 234, reel 603.

Lockridge, Ross. "History on the Mississinewa." *Indiana Magazine of History* 30, no. 1 (1934): 55.

Lonn, Ella. "Ripples of the Blackhawk War in Northern Indiana." *Indiana Magazine of History* 20, no. 3 (1924): 288–307.

Loren, Diana DiPaolo. "The Intersection of Colonial Policy and Colonial Practice: Creolization on the Eighteenth-Century Louisiana/Texas Frontier." *Historical Archaeology* 34, no. 3 (2000): 85–98.

Lowrie, Walter, ed. *American State Papers, Documents, Legislative and Executive, of the Congress of the United States, from the First Session of the First to the Second Session of the Seventeenth Congress, Inclusive: Commencing March 4, 1789, and Ending March 3, 1823.* Vol. 9. Washington, DC: Gales and Seaton, 1834.

Lowrie, Walter, and Matthew St. Clair, eds. *American State Papers, Documents, Legislative and Executive of the Congress of the United States (1789–1838), Class 2, Indian Affairs.* 2 vols. Washington, DC: Gales and Seaton, 1832–34.

Malischke, LisaMarie. "The Excavated Bead Collection at Fort St. Joseph (20BE23) and Its Implications for Understanding Adornment, Ideology, Cultural Exchange, and Identity." Master's thesis, Department of Anthropology, Western Michigan University, 2009.

Mancall, Peter C. *Deadly Medicine: Indians and Alcohol in Early America.* Ithaca, NY: Cornell University Press, 1995.

Mann, Rob. "The Silenced Miami: Archaeological and Ethnohistorical Evidence for Miami-British Relations, 1795–1812." *Ethnohistory* 46, no. 3 (Summer 1999): 399–427.

Mansfield, J. B. *The History of Tuscarawas County, Ohio.* Chicago: Warner, Beers & Co., 1884. http://books.google.com/books?id=5DguAAAAYAAJ (accessed January 2011).

Manzo, Joseph. "Emigrant Indian Objections to Kansas Residence." *Kansas History* 4 (1981): 247.

Margry, Pierre. *Découvertes et établissements des français dans l'ouest et dans le sud de l'Amérique septentrionale, 1614–1754.* 6 vols. Paris: D. Jouaust, 1876–1886.

———. *Relations et Mémoires inédits pour servir à l'histoire de la France dans les pays d'outremer.* Paris: Challamel, 1867.

Marietta, Jack D. *The Reformation of American Quakerism, 1748–1783.* Philadelphia: University of Pennsylvania Press, 1984.

Marsh, Dawn G. "Hiding in Plain Sight: Hannah Freeman, A Lenape Woman in Pennsylvania." PhD dissertation, University of California, Riverside, 2004.

Martin, Terrance. "The Archaeozoology of French Colonial Sites in the Illinois Country." In *Dreams of the Americas: Overview of New France Archaeology,* edited by Christian Roy and Hélène Côté, 185–204. Quebec: Archéologiques, Collection Hors Séries 2, 2008.

Mason, Ronald J. *Great Lakes Archaeology.* New York: Academic Press, 1981.

Mason, Ronald J. *Rock Island: Historical Indian Archaeology in the Northern Lake Michigan Basin.* MCJA Special Paper No. 6. Kent, OH: Kent State University Press, 1986.

Mather, George. *Frontier Faith: The Story of the Pioneer Congregations of Fort Wayne, Indiana, 1820–1860.* Fort Wayne: Allen County–Fort Wayne Historical Society, 1992.

McConnell, Michael N. *Army and Empire: British Soldiers on the American Frontier, 1758–1775.* Lincoln: University of Nebraska Press, 2005.

———. *A Country Between: The Upper Ohio Valley and Its Peoples, 1724–1774.* Lincoln: University of Nebraska Press, 1992.

McCord-Rogers, Suzette. "To Have and Have Not: The Vanishing Lands of Native America." *Kansas Heritage* 4 (Summer 1996).

McCulloch, Hugh. *Men and Measures of Half a Century: Sketches and Comments.* New York: Charles Scribner & Sons, 1888.

Meekel, Arthur J. *The Relation of the Quakers to the American Revolution.* Washington, DC: University Press of America, 1979.

Merritt, Jane T. *At the Crossroads: Indians and Empires on a Mid-Atlantic Frontier, 1700–1763.* Chapel Hill: University of North Carolina Press for the Omohundro Institute of Early American History and Culture, 2003.

———. "Cultural Encounters along a Gender Frontier: Mahican, Delaware, and German Women in Eighteenth-Century Pennsylvania." *Pennsylvania History* (2000): 502–31.

———. "The Gender Frontier Revisited: Native American Women in the Age of Revolution." In *Ethnographies and Exchanges: Native Americans, Moravians, and Catholics in Early North America,* edited by A. G. Roeber, 165–74. University Park: Pennsylvania State University Press, 2008.

Metcalf, Alida. *Go-Betweens and the Colonization of Brazil, 1500–1600.* Austin: University of Texas Press, 2005.

Metcalf, Samuel L. *A Collection of Some of the Most Interesting Narratives of Indian Warfare in the West, containing an Account of the Adventures of Daniel Boone, One of the First Settlers of Kentucky, comprehending the most important occurrences relative to its early history—Also, an account of the Manners, and Customs of the Indians, their Traditions and Religious Sentiments, their Police or Civil Government, their Discipline and method of War: To which is added, An Account of the Expeditions of Genl's Harmer, Scott, Wilkinson, St. Clair, & Wayne.* Lexington, KY: William G. Hunt Co., 1821.

Michigan Pioneer and Historical Society. *Collections and Researches.* Lansing, MI: Michigan Pioneer and Historical Society, 1877–1929.

Middleton, Richard. *Pontiac's War: Its Causes, Course, and Consequences.* New York: Routledge, 2007.

Mitchell, Joseph. *The Missionary Pioneer, or A Brief Memoir of the Life, Labours, and Death of John Stewart, (Man of Colour,) Founder, Under God of the Mission Among the Wyandotts at Upper Sandusky, Ohio.* New York: J. C. Totten, 1827.

Mitchell, Waldo. "Indiana's Growth, 1812–1820." *Indiana Magazine of History* 10, no. 3 (1914): 317.

Monaghan, E. Jennifer. *Learning to Read and Write in Colonial America.* Worcester: University of Massachusetts Press, 2005.

Moogk, Peter N. *La Nouvelle France: The Making of French Canada—A Cultural History.* East Lansing: Michigan State University Press, 2000.

Moore, John M., ed. *Friends in the Delaware Valley: Philadelphia Yearly Meeting, 1681–1981.* Haverford, PA: Friends Historical Association, 1981.

Myers, Robert C., and Joseph L. Peyser. "Four Flags over Fort St. Joseph." *Michigan History* 75, no. 5 (1991): 11–21.

Nagel, Joane, and C. Matthew Snipp. "Ethnic Reorganization: American Indian Social, Economic, Political, and Cultural Strategies for Survival." *Ethnic and Racial Studies* 16, no. 2 (1993).

"Narrative of a Journey to Sandusky, Ohio, to Visit the Wyandot Indians Residing There." *Friends Miscellany* 7, no. 7 (October 1835): 292–326.

Nash, Gary B. "The Hidden History of Mestizo America." In *Sex, Love, and Race: Crossing Boundaries in North American History*, edited by Martha Hodes, 10–32. New York: New York University Press, 1999.

———. *Quakers and Politics: Pennsylvania, 1681–1726.* Princeton, NJ: Princeton University Press, 1968.

Nassaney, Michael S. *An Archaeological Reconnaissance Survey to Locate Remains of Fort St. Joseph (20BE23) in Niles, Michigan.* Archaeological Report No. 22. Kalamazoo: Department of Anthropology, Western Michigan University, 1999.

———. "Commemorating French Heritage at Fort St. Joseph, an Eighteenth-Century Mission, Garrison, and Trading Post Complex in Niles, Michigan." In *Dreams of the Americas: Overview of New France Archaeology*, edited by Christian

Roy and Hélène Côté, 96–111. Quebec: Archéologiques, Collection Hors Séries 2, 2008.

———. "Identity Formation at a French Colonial Outpost in the North American Interior." *International Journal of Historical Archaeology* 12, no. 4 (2008): 297–318.

———. "Native American Gender Relations and Material Culture in Seventeenth-Century Southeastern New England." *Journal of Social Archaeology* 4, no. 3 (2004): 334–67.

———. "Transcending Colonial Borders through the Archaeology of Fort St. Joseph." Paper presented at the 42nd Annual Conference on Underwater and Historical Archaeology, Toronto, 2009.

Nassaney, Michael S., and J. A. Brandão. "The Materiality of Individuality at Eighteenth-Century Fort St. Joseph: A Mission-Garrison-Trading Post Complex on the Edge of Empire." In *The Materiality of Individuality*, edited by Carolyn L. White, 19–36. New York: Springer Press, 2009.

Nassaney, Michael S., Jose A. Brandão, William M. Cremin, and Brock A. Giordano. "Archaeological Evidence of Economic Activities at an 18th Century Frontier Outpost in the Western Great Lakes." *Historical Archaeology* 41, no. 4 (2007): 1–17.

Nassaney, Michael S., and William M. Cremin. "Realizing the Potential of the Contact Period in Southwest Michigan through the Fort St. Joseph Archaeological Project." *Wisconsin Archaeologist* 83, no. 2 (2002): 123–34.

Nassaney, Michael S., William M. Cremin, R. Kurtzweil, and Jose A. Brandão. "The Search for Fort St. Joseph (1691–1781) in Niles, Michigan." *Midcontinental Journal of Archaeology* 28, no. 2 (2003): 1–38.

Nassaney, Michael S., William M. Cremin, and Daniel Lynch. "The Archaeological Identification of Colonial Fort St. Joseph, Michigan." *Journal of Field Archaeology* 29, nos. 3–4 (2002–2004): 309–21.

Nassaney, Michael S., and Eric S. Johnson. "The Contributions of Material Objects to Ethnohistory in Native North America." In *Interpretations of Native North American Life: Material Contributions to Ethnohistory*, edited by M. Nassaney and E. Johnson, 1–30. Gainesville: University Press of Florida, 2000.

Nassaney, Michael S., Daniel Osborne, and Stacy Bell. *Salvage Excavations near the Junction of French and St. Joseph Streets, Niles, Michigan*. Report of Investigations No. 108. Kalamazoo: Department of Anthropology, Western Michigan University, 2000.

Nester, William R. *"Haughty Conquerors": Amherst and the Great Indian Uprising of 1763*. Westport, CT: Praeger, 2000.

Nichols, Roger L. *The American Indian*. 6th ed. Norman: University of Oklahoma Press, 2008.

O'Donnell III, James H. *Ohio's First Peoples.* Athens: Ohio University Press, 2004.

O'Gorman, Jodie A. "The Myth of Moccasin Bluff: Rethinking the Potawatomi Pattern." *Ethnohistory* 54, no. 3 (2007): 373–406.

Olmstead, Earl P. *Blackcoats among the Delaware: David Zeisberger on the Ohio Frontier.* Kent, OH: Kent State University Press, 1991.

———. *David Zeisberger: A Life among the Indians.* Kent, OH: Kent State University Press, 1997.

Paré, George, and M. M. Quaife. "The St. Joseph Baptismal Register." *Mississippi Valley Historical Review* 13 (September 1926–1927): 201–39.

Parkman, Francis. *The Conspiracy of Pontiac and the Indian War after the Conquest of Canada.* 2 vols. Lincoln: University of Nebraska Press, 1994.

Parmenter, William. "Pontiac's War: Forging New Links in the Anglo-Iroquois Covenant Chain, 1758–1766." *Ethnohistory* 44, no. 4 (Autumn 1997): 617–54.

Parrish, John. "Extracts from the Journal of John Parrish, 1773." *Pennsylvania Magazine of History and Biography* 26, no. 4 (1892).

Peckham, Howard H. *Pontiac and the Indian Uprising.* Detroit: Wayne State University Press, 1994.

Peyser, Joseph L., trans. and ed. *The Fort St. Joseph Manuscripts: Chronological Inventory and Translations.* Ms. on file, Niles Public Library, Niles, Michigan, 1978.

———, trans. and ed. *Letters from New France: The Upper Country, 1686–1783.* Urbana-Champaign: University of Illinois Press, 1992.

Poinsatte, Charles. *Fort Wayne during the Canal Era, 1828–1855: A Study of a Western Community in the Middle Period of American History.* Indianapolis: Indiana Historical Bureau, 1969.

Porherie, Bacqueville de la. "History of the Savage Peoples Who Are Allies of New France, 1753." In *The Indian Tribes of the Upper Mississippi Valley and Region of the Great Lakes,* edited by Emma Blair. Cleveland: Arthur H. Clark, 1911–1912.

Pouchot, Pierre. *Memoir upon the Late War in North America between the French and the English, 1755–60.* Edited and translated by Franklin B. Hough. Roxbury, MA: W. E. Woodward, 1866.

Powell, J. W. "Wyandot Government: A Short Study of Tribal Society." An Address before the Subsection of Anthropology, American Association for the Advancement of Science: Boston Meeting, August, 1880. Salem, MA: Salem Press, 1881.

Prucha, Francis Paul. "Indian Removal and the Great American Desert." *Indiana Magazine of History* 59, no. 4 (1963): 299–322.

Quimby, George I. *Indian Culture and European Trade Goods.* Madison: University of Wisconsin Press, 1966.

Rafert, Stewart. *The Miami Indians of Indiana: A Persistent People, 1654–1994.* Indianapolis: Indiana Historical Society, 1996.

Records, Spencer. "Spencer Records' Memoir of the Ohio Valley Frontier, 1766–1795." Edited by Donald F. Carmony. *Indiana Magazine of History* 55, no. 4 (December 1959): 323–77.

Records of the Moravian Mission among the Indians of North America. Archives of the Moravian Church, Bethlehem, PA. New Haven, CT: Research Publications, 1970. Microfilm copy.

Religious Society of Friends. *Faith and Practice.* Philadelphia: Philadelphia Yearly Meeting of the Religious Society of Friends, 1984.

Richter, Daniel K. "'Believing That Many of the Red People Suffer Much for the Want of Food': Hunting, Agriculture, and a Quaker Construction of Indianness in the Early Republic." *Journal of the Early Republic* 19, no. 4 (Winter 1999): 601–28.

———. *The Ordeal of the Longhouse: The Peoples of the Iroquois League in the Era of European Colonization.* Chapel Hill: University of North Carolina Press, 1992.

Richter, Daniel K., and James H. Merrell, eds. *Beyond the Covenant Chain: The Iroquois and Their Neighbors in Indian North America, 1600–1800.* Syracuse, NY: Syracuse University Press, 1987.

Riker, Dorothy. "Documents: Two Accounts of the Upper Wabash County, 1819–1820. Journal of Henry P. Benton." *Indiana Magazine of History* 37, no. 4 (1941): 387.

Rinehart, Melissa. "Miami Indian Language Shift and Recovery." PhD dissertation, Michigan State University, 2006.

Sabbathy-Judd, Linda, ed. *Moravians in Upper Canada: The Diary of the Indian Mission of Fairfield on the Thames, 1792–1813.* Toronto: The Champlain Society, 1999.

Satz, Ronald N. *American Indian Policy in the Jacksonian Era.* Norman: University of Oklahoma Press, 2002.

Scamyhorn, Richard, and John Steinle. *Stockades in the Wilderness: The Frontier Settlements of Southwestern Ohio, 1788–1795.* Dayton, OH: Landfall Press, 1986.

Schutt, Amy C. "Female Relationships and Intercultural Bonds in Moravian Indian Missions." In *Friends and Enemies in Penn's Woods: Indians, Colonies, and the Racial Construction of Pennsylvania*, edited by William A. Pencak and Daniel K. Richter. University Park: Pennsylvania State University, 2004.

———. *Peoples of the River Valleys: The Odyssey of the Delaware Indians.* Philadelphia: University of Pennsylvania Press, 2007.

———. "'What will become of our young people?' Goals for Indian Children in Moravian Missions." *History of Education Quarterly* 38 (Fall 1998): 268–86.

Scott, Stuart D. *An Archaeological Survey of Artpark and the Lower Landing, Lewiston, New York.* Lewiston, NY: Edwin Mellen Press, 1993.

Scull, G. D., ed. "The Journals of Captain John Montresor." In *Collections of the New York Historical Society for the Year 1881*. New York Historical Society, 1882.

Select Comm. on Indian Land Cessions in the United States, 1784 to 1894. In J. W. Powell, *Eighteenth Annual Report of the Bureau of American Ethnology to the Secretary of the Smithsonian Institution, 1896–1897*, pt. 2. Printed as *H.R. Doc. No. 736*, 56th Cong., 1st sess., 666–67.

Senate Document No. 122. "Senate Report with Petition to Congress for Frances Slocum's Exemption to Removal." 28th Cong., 2nd sess., serial set 456, January 17, 1845.

Senate Document No. 164. "Report from the Secretary of War in compliance with a resolution of the Senate, the report of the Commissioner to investigate claims against the Miami Indians for the year 1839." 26th Cong., 1st sess., serial set 357, February 10, 1840.

Senate Document No. 194. General Assembly of the State of Indiana. "Resolution of the General Assembly of Indiana in Relation to the Right of Preemption to the 'Miami Reserve' in that State." 25th Cong., 2nd sess., serial set 316, February 13, 1838.

Senate Executive Journal. "Presidential Transmission of the 1834 Treaty to the Committee on Indian Affairs and the Senate of the United States." Related correspondence included with report. 25th Cong., 1st sess., October 4, 1837.

———. "Report from Joel Roberts Poinsett of the War Dept., to President Andrew Jackson, 14 Dec., 1838." 25th Cong., 3rd sess., 165.

———. "Submitted Treaty Articles as Negotiated with the Miami Tribe of Indians in Indiana by Samuel Milroy and Allen Hamilton in 1840." Related correspondence included with report. 26th Cong., 2nd sess., January 18, 1841.

Severance, Frank H. *An Old Frontier of France: The Niagara Region and Adjacent Lakes under French Control*. New York: Dodd, Mead and Co., 1917.

Sheehan, Bernard W. *Seeds of Extinction: Jeffersonian Philanthropy and the American Indian*. Chapel Hill: University of North Carolina Press and Institute of Early American History and Culture, 1973.

Silliman, Stephen W. "Culture Contact or Colonialism? Challenges in the Archaeology of Native North America." *American Antiquity* 70, no. 1 (2005): 55–74.

Skaggs, David Curtis, and Larry Nelson. *The Sixty Years' War for the Great Lakes: 1754–1814*. East Lansing: Michigan State University Press, 2010.

Sleeper-Smith, Susan. *Indian Women and French Men: Rethinking Cultural Encounter in the Western Great Lakes*. Amherst: University of Massachusetts Press, 2001.

Smaby, Beverly P. "'No one should lust for power . . . women least of all': Dismantling Female Leadership among Eighteenth-Century Moravians." In *Pious Pursuits: German Moravians in the Atlantic World*. New York: Berghahn Books, 2007.

Smith, Dwight. "An Unsuccessful Negotiation for Removal of the Wyandot Indians from Ohio, 1834." *Ohio Archaeological and Historical Quarterly* 58 (1949): 305–31.

Smith, Paul H., ed. *Letters of Delegates to Congress, 1774–1789*. 25 vols. Washington, DC: Library of Congress, 1976–2000. http://lccn.loc.gov/76002592 (accessed January 2011).

Smith, Robert E. "The Clash of Leadership at the Grand Reserve: The Wyandot Subagency and the Methodist Mission, 1820–1824." *Ohio History* 89, no. 2 (Spring 1980): 181–205.

———. "The Wyandot Exploring Expedition of 1839." *Chronicles of Oklahoma* (Fall 1977): 282–92.

Smith, William Henry, ed. *The St. Clair Papers: The Life and Public Service of Arthur St. Clair: Soldier of the Revolutionary War, President of the Continental Congress, and Governor of the North-Western Territory*. 2 vols. New York: Da Capo Press, 1971.

Spencer, O. M. *The Indian Captivity of O.M. Spencer*. Edited by Milo Milton Quaife. Chicago: Lakeside Press, 1917; reprint, New York: Dover Publications, 1995.

Sugrue, Thomas. "The Peopling and Depeopling of Early Pennsylvania: Indians and Colonists, 1680–1720." *Pennsylvania Magazine of History and Biography* 116 (1992): 3–31.

Sword, Wiley. *President Washington's Indian War: The Struggle for the Old Northwest, 1790–1795*. Norman: University of Oklahoma Press, 1985.

Tanner, Helen Hornbeck, ed. *Atlas of Great Lakes Indian History*. Norman: University of Oklahoma Press, 1987.

Tantaquidgeon, Gladys. *Folk Medicine of the Delaware and Related Algonkian Indians*. Harrisburg: Pennsylvania Historical and Museum Commission, 2001.

Temple, W. C. "Indian Villages of the Illinois Country: Historic Tribes." In *Scientific Papers*, vol. 2, pt. 2. Springfield: Illinois State Museum, 1958.

Thomas Gage Papers, American Series. William L. Clements Library, University of Michigan, Ann Arbor.

Thornbrough, Gayle, ed. *Outpost on the Wabash, 1787–1791: Letters of Brigadier General Josiah Harmar and Major John Francis Hamtramck*. Indianapolis: Indiana Historical Society, 1957.

Thwaites, Ruben Gold. *The Jesuit Relations*. Cleveland: Burrows Brothers Company, 1899.

Tiro, Karim. "'We Wish to Do You Good': The Quaker Mission to the Oneida Nation, 1790–1840." *Journal of the Early Republic* 26 (Fall 2006): 353–76.

Tolles, Frederick B. *Meeting House and Counting House*. Chapel Hill: University of North Carolina Press, 1948.

Tolzmann, Don Henrich, ed. *The First Description of Cincinnati and Other Ohio Settlements: The Travel Report of Johann Heckewelder (1792)*. Introduction by H. A. Rattermann. New York: University Press of America, 1988.

Transactions of the Royal Society of Canada (Ottawa), 3rd series, 22 (1928).

Trigger, Bruce G. *The Children of Aataentsic: A History of the Huron People to 1660*. 2 vols. Montreal: McGill-Queen's University Press, 1976.

———, ed. *Handbook of North American Indians*. Vol. 15, *Northeast*. Washington, DC: Smithsonian Institution, 1978.

Trouillot, Michel-Rolph. *Silencing the Past: Power and the Production of History*. Boston: Beacon Press, 1995.

Turgeon, Laurier, Denys Delâge, and Réal Ouellet, eds. *Cultural Transfer, America and Europe: 500 Years of Interculturation*. Quebec: Les Presses de l'Université Laval, 1996.

Van Kirk, Sylvia. *Many Tender Ties: Women in Fur Trade Society, 1679–1870*. Norman: University of Oklahoma Press, 1983.

Vaughan, Alden T., ed. *Early American Indian Documents: Treaties and Laws, 1606–1789*. Vol. 1, *Pennsylvania and Delaware Treaties: 1629–1737*. Washington, DC: University Publications of America, 1979.

Volo, James M., and Dorothy Denneen Volo. *Daily Life on the Old Colonial Frontier*. Westport, CT: Greenwood Press, 2002.

Wallace, Anthony F. C. *The Death and Rebirth of the Seneca*. New York: Knopf, 1970.

———. *King of the Delawares: Teedyuscung*. Philadelphia: University of Pennsylvania Press, 1949.

———. *The Long, Bitter Trail: Andrew Jackson and the Indians*. New York: Hill and Wang, 1993.

Walsh, M. W. "The 'Heathen Party': Methodist Observation of the Ohio Wyandot." *American Indian Quarterly* 16, no. 2 (Spring 1992): 189–202.

Warren, Stephen. "The Ohio Shawnees' Struggle against Removal, 1814–30." In *Enduring Nations: Native Americans in the Midwest*, edited by R. David Edmunds, 72–93. Urbana: University of Illinois Press, 2008.

———. *The Shawnee and Their Neighbors, 1795–1870*. Urbana: University of Illinois Press, 2005.

Washburn, Wilcomb E. "Seventeenth-Century Indian Wars." In *Handbook of North American Indians*, vol. 15, *Northeast*, edited by Bruce G. Trigger. Washington DC: Smithsonian Institution, 1978.

Webster, J. C. "Life of John Montresor." *Transactions of the Royal Society of Canada*, 3rd series, 22 (May 1928): 14–18.

Weeks, Stephen. *Southern Quakers and Slavery*. New York: Bergman, 1968.

Wehr, Paul W. "The Treaty of Fort Finney, 1786: Prelude to the Indian Wars." Master's thesis, Miami University, 1958.

Wellenreuther, Herman, and Carola Wessel, eds. *The Moravian Mission Diaries of David Zeisberger, 1772–1781.* University Park: Pennsylvania State University Press, 2005.

Weslager, C. A. *The Delaware Indian Westward Migration.* Wallingford, PA: Middle Atlantic Press, 1978.

———. *The Delaware Indians.* New Brunswick, NJ: Rutgers University Press, 1991.

———. *The English on the Delaware: 1610–1682.* New Brunswick, NJ: Rutgers University Press, 1967.

———. *New Sweden on the Delaware.* Wilmington, DE: Middle Atlantic Press, 1988.

———. *Red Men on the Brandywine.* Wilmington, DE: Hambleton, 1953.

Westrick, Paul. "The Race to Assimilate: The Wyandot Indians in White Ohio." *Northwest Ohio History* 75, no. 2 (2004): 123–48.

Wheeler, Rachel. *To Live upon Hope: Mohicans and Missionaries in the Eighteenth-Century Northeast.* Ithaca, NY: Cornell University Press, 2008.

White, Marian E. *Iroquois Culture History in the Niagara Frontier Area of New York State.* Ann Arbor: University of Michigan, 1961.

———. "Late Woodland Archaeology in the Niagara Frontier of New York and Ontario." In *The Late Prehistory of the Lake Erie Drainage Basin: A 1972 Symposium Revised,* edited by David S. Brose. Cleveland: Cleveland Museum of Natural History, 1976.

White, Richard. *The Middle Ground: Indians, Empires, and Republics in the Great Lakes Region, 1650–1815.* Cambridge: Cambridge University Press, 1991.

Whittlesey, Charles. *Historical, Topographical, and Geological Notices of Hamilton County, Ohio.* Cincinnati, OH: Cincinnati Historical Society. n.d.

Williams, Frazer E., ed. *Journal of Capt. Daniel Bradley: An Epic of the Ohio Frontier.* Greenville, OH: Frank H. Jobes and Son, 1935.

Contributors

Charles Beatty-Medina is associate professor of history at the University of Toledo. His areas of specialization include the history of Native and African peoples of the early Atlantic world and colonial Latin America. He holds a PhD in history from Brown University.

James Buss is associate professor and chair of the Department of History at Oklahoma City University. He is the author of *Winning the West with Words: Language and Conquest in the Lower Great Lakes* (2011). His research explores the intersections of language, race, and memory in the history of the Great Lakes.

William M. Cremin is professor emeritus of anthropology at Western Michigan University. He was instrumental in establishing Western Michigan University's annual archaeological field program and has spent much of his career conducting research on the Oneota-related Berrien phase of southwest Michigan. Cremin spent three seasons with Michael Nassaney and the field school excavating the site of Fort St. Joseph.

Daniel Ingram is assistant professor of history at Ball State University. He is the author of *Indians and British Outposts in Eighteenth-Century America* (2012) and is working currently on a study of George Rogers Clark in historical memory.

LisaMarie Malischke earned her M A in anthropology and a graduate certificate in ethnohistory in 2009 from Western Michigan University. She is currently a doctoral student at the University of Alabama where she is researching colonial French and Native interactions in French Louisiana and the Lower Mississippi Valley.

Dawn Marsh is assistant professor at Purdue University specializing in Native American and indigenous history. She earned her PhD from the University of California, Riverside. Her book-length manuscript centers on the experiences of a Lenape woman who continued to live in William Penn's "peaceable kingdom" long after her people were dispossessed of their homelands in Pennsylvania.

Sarah E. Miller is assistant professor of history at the University of South Carolina at Salkehatchie. Her research interests include Native Americans and the early American republic. She has published several articles about Ohio Indians and is currently studying Native Americans of the southeastern United States.

Michael S. Nassaney is professor of anthropology at Western Michigan University and principal investigator of the Fort St. Joseph Archaeological Project, an interdisciplinary program in community service learning that examines the history and archaeology of the fur trade and colonialism in the St. Joseph River Valley.

Greg O'Brien is associate professor at the University of North Carolina at Greensboro. His research interests include the American Indians of the Southeast and American environmental history. His publications include *Pre-Removal Choctaw History: Exploring New Paths* (2008) and *The Timeline of Native Americans: The Ultimate Guide to North America's Indigenous Peoples* (2008).

Melissa Rinehart is visiting assistant professor of anthropology at Miami University at Middletown. She earned her PhD in cultural anthropology with a focus on Native American studies at Michigan State University. She has published on the Miami removal, Miami language shift and revitalization efforts, and Native American representation and resistance at the Chicago World's Fair.

Amy C. Schutt is assistant professor of history at the State University of New York College at Cortland. In addition to Native American history, her research interests include the history of children and youth in early America. She is the author of *Peoples of the River Valleys: The Odyssey of the Delaware Indians* (2007). Schutt holds a PhD in history from Indiana University.

Index